Mometrix

TEST PREPARATION

MCA

Success Strategies High School Science

I0894303

DEAR FUTURE EXAM SUCCESS STORY

First of all, **THANK YOU** for purchasing Mometrix study materials!

Second, congratulations! You are one of the few determined test-takers who are committed to doing whatever it takes to excel on your exam. **You have come to the right place.** We developed these study materials with one goal in mind: to deliver you the information you need in a format that's concise and easy to use.

In addition to optimizing your guide for the content of the test, we've outlined our recommended steps for breaking down the preparation process into small, attainable goals so you can make sure you stay on track.

We've also analyzed the entire test-taking process, identifying the most common pitfalls and showing how you can overcome them and be ready for any curveball the test throws you.

Standardized testing is one of the biggest obstacles on your road to success, which only increases the importance of doing well in the high-pressure, high-stakes environment of test day. Your results on this test could have a significant impact on your future, and this guide provides the information and practical advice to help you achieve your full potential on test day.

Your success is our success

We would love to hear from you! If you would like to share the story of your exam success or if you have any questions or comments in regard to our products, please contact us at **800-673-8175** or **support@mometrix.com**.

Thanks again for your business and we wish you continued success!

Sincerely,
The Mometrix Test Preparation Team

Written and edited by the Mometrix Test Preparation Team
Printed in the United States of America

TABLE OF CONTENTS

Introduction

Thank you for purchasing this resource! You have made the choice to prepare yourself for a test that could have a huge impact on your future, and this guide is designed to help you be fully ready for test day. Obviously, it's important to have a solid understanding of the test material, but you also need to be prepared for the unique environment and stressors of the test, so that you can perform to the best of your abilities.

For this purpose, the first section that appears in this guide is the **Success Strategies**. We've devoted countless hours to meticulously researching what works and what doesn't, and we've boiled down our findings to the most impactful steps you can take to improve your performance on the test. We start at the beginning with study planning and move through the preparation process, all the way to the testing strategies that will help you get the most out of what you know when you're finally sitting in front of the test.

We recommend that you start preparing for your test as far in advance as possible. However, if you've bought this guide as a last-minute study resource and only have a few days before your test, we recommend that you skip over the first two Success Strategies since they address a long-term study plan.

If you struggle with **test anxiety**, we strongly encourage you to check out our recommendations for how you can overcome it. Test anxiety is a formidable foe, but it can be beaten, and we want to make sure you have the tools you need to defeat it.

Strategy #1 – Plan Big, Study Small

There's a lot riding on your performance. If you want to ace this test, you're going to need to keep your skills sharp and the material fresh in your mind. You need a plan that lets you review everything you need to know while still fitting in your schedule. We'll break this strategy down into three categories.

Information Organization

Start with the information you already have: the official test outline. From this, you can make a complete list of all the concepts you need to cover before the test. Organize these concepts into groups that can be studied together, and create a list of any related vocabulary you need to learn so you can brush up on any difficult terms. You'll want to keep this vocabulary list handy once you actually start studying since you may need to add to it along the way.

Time Management

Once you have your set of study concepts, decide how to spread them out over the time you have left before the test. Break your study plan into small, clear goals so you have a manageable task for each day and know exactly what you're doing. Then just focus on one small step at a time. When you manage your time this way, you don't need to spend hours at a time studying. Studying a small block of content for a short period each day helps you retain information better and avoid stressing over how much you have left to do. You can relax knowing that you have a plan to cover everything in time. In order for this strategy to be effective though, you have to start studying early and stick to your schedule. Avoid the exhaustion and futility that comes from last-minute cramming!

Study Environment

The environment you study in has a big impact on your learning. Studying in a coffee shop, while probably more enjoyable, is not likely to be as fruitful as studying in a quiet room. It's important to keep distractions to a minimum. You're only planning to study for a short block of time, so make the most of it. Don't pause to check your phone or get up to find a snack. It's also important to **avoid multitasking**. Research has consistently shown that multitasking will make your studying dramatically less effective. Your study area should also be comfortable and well-lit so you don't have the distraction of straining your eyes or sitting on an uncomfortable chair.

The time of day you study is also important. You want to be rested and alert. Don't wait until just before bedtime. Study when you'll be most likely to comprehend and remember. Even better, if you know what time of day your test will be, set that time aside for study. That way your brain will be used to working on that subject at that specific time and you'll have a better chance of recalling information.

Finally, it can be helpful to team up with others who are studying for the same test. Your actual studying should be done in as isolated an environment as possible, but the work of organizing the information and setting up the study plan can be divided up. In between study sessions, you can discuss with your teammates the concepts that you're all studying and quiz each other on the details. Just be sure that your teammates are as serious about the test as you are. If you find that your study time is being replaced with social time, you might need to find a new team.

Strategy #2 – Make Your Studying Count

You're devoting a lot of time and effort to preparing for this test, so you want to be absolutely certain it will pay off. This means doing more than just reading the content and hoping you can remember it on test day. It's important to make every minute of study count. There are two main areas you can focus on to make your studying count.

Retention

It doesn't matter how much time you study if you can't remember the material. You need to make sure you are retaining the concepts. To check your retention of the information you're learning, try recalling it at later times with minimal prompting. Try carrying around flashcards and glance at one or two from time to time or ask a friend who's also studying for the test to quiz you.

To enhance your retention, look for ways to put the information into practice so that you can apply it rather than simply recalling it. If you're using the information in practical ways, it will be much easier to remember. Similarly, it helps to solidify a concept in your mind if you're not only reading it to yourself but also explaining it to someone else. Ask a friend to let you teach them about a concept you're a little shaky on (or speak aloud to an imaginary audience if necessary). As you try to summarize, define, give examples, and answer your friend's questions, you'll understand the concepts better and they will stay with you longer. Finally, step back for a big picture view and ask yourself how each piece of information fits with the whole subject. When you link the different concepts together and see them working together as a whole, it's easier to remember the individual components.

Finally, practice showing your work on any multi-step problems, even if you're just studying. Writing out each step you take to solve a problem will help solidify the process in your mind, and you'll be more likely to remember it during the test.

Modality

Modality simply refers to the means or method by which you study. Choosing a study modality that fits your own individual learning style is crucial. No two people learn best in exactly the same way, so it's important to know your strengths and use them to your advantage.

For example, if you learn best by visualization, focus on visualizing a concept in your mind and draw an image or a diagram. Try color-coding your notes, illustrating them, or creating symbols that will trigger your mind to recall a learned concept. If you learn best by hearing or discussing information, find a study partner who learns the same way or read aloud to yourself. Think about how to put the information in your own words. Imagine that you are giving a lecture on the topic and record yourself so you can listen to it later.

For any learning style, flashcards can be helpful. Organize the information so you can take advantage of spare moments to review. Underline key words or phrases. Use different colors for different categories. Mnemonic devices (such as creating a short list in which every item starts with the same letter) can also help with retention. Find what works best for you and use it to store the information in your mind most effectively and easily.

Strategy #3 – Practice the Right Way

Your success on test day depends not only on how many hours you put into preparing, but also on whether you prepared the right way. It's good to check along the way to see if your studying is paying off. One of the most effective ways to do this is by taking practice tests to evaluate your progress. Practice tests are useful because they show exactly where you need to improve. Every time you take a practice test, pay special attention to these three groups of questions:

- The questions you got wrong
- The questions you had to guess on, even if you guessed right
- The questions you found difficult or slow to work through

This will show you exactly what your weak areas are, and where you need to devote more study time. Ask yourself why each of these questions gave you trouble. Was it because you didn't understand the material? Was it because you didn't remember the vocabulary? Do you need more repetitions on this type of question to build speed and confidence? Dig into those questions and figure out how you can strengthen your weak areas as you go back to review the material.

Additionally, many practice tests have a section explaining the answer choices. It can be tempting to read the explanation and think that you now have a good understanding of the concept. However, an explanation likely only covers part of the question's broader context. Even if the explanation makes perfect sense, **go back and investigate** every concept related to the question until you're positive you have a thorough understanding.

As you go along, keep in mind that the practice test is just that: practice. Memorizing these questions and answers will not be very helpful on the actual test because it is unlikely to have any of the same exact questions. If you only know the right answers to the sample questions, you won't be prepared for the real thing. **Study the concepts** until you understand them fully, and then you'll be able to answer any question that shows up on the test.

It's important to wait on the practice tests until you're ready. If you take a test on your first day of study, you may be overwhelmed by the amount of material covered and how much you need to learn. Work up to it gradually.

On test day, you'll need to be prepared for answering questions, managing your time, and using the test-taking strategies you've learned. It's a lot to balance, like a mental marathon that will have a big impact on your future. Like training for a marathon, you'll need to start slowly and work your way up. When test day arrives, you'll be ready.

Start with the strategies you've read in the first two Success Strategies—plan your course and study in the way that works best for you. If you have time, consider using multiple study resources to get different approaches to the same concepts. It can be helpful to see difficult concepts from more than one angle. Then find a good source for practice tests. Many times, the test website will suggest potential study resources or provide sample tests.

Practice Test Strategy

If you're able to find at least three practice tests, we recommend this strategy:

UNTIMED AND OPEN-BOOK PRACTICE

Take the first test with no time constraints and with your notes and study guide handy. Take your time and focus on applying the strategies you've learned.

TIMED AND OPEN-BOOK PRACTICE

Take the second practice test open-book as well, but set a timer and practice pacing yourself to finish in time.

TIMED AND CLOSED-BOOK PRACTICE

Take any other practice tests as if it were test day. Set a timer and put away your study materials. Sit at a table or desk in a quiet room, imagine yourself at the testing center, and answer questions as quickly and accurately as possible.

Keep repeating timed and closed-book tests on a regular basis until you run out of practice tests or it's time for the actual test. Your mind will be ready for the schedule and stress of test day, and you'll be able to focus on recalling the material you've learned.

Strategy #4 – Pace Yourself

Once you're fully prepared for the material on the test, your biggest challenge on test day will be managing your time. Just knowing that the clock is ticking can make you panic even if you have plenty of time left. Work on pacing yourself so you can build confidence against the time constraints of the exam. Pacing is a difficult skill to master, especially in a high-pressure environment, so **practice is vital**.

Set time expectations for your pace based on how much time is available. For example, if a section has 60 questions and the time limit is 30 minutes, you know you have to average 30 seconds or less per question in order to answer them all. Although 30 seconds is the hard limit, set 25 seconds per question as your goal, so you reserve extra time to spend on harder questions. When you budget extra time for the harder questions, you no longer have any reason to stress when those questions take longer to answer.

Don't let this time expectation distract you from working through the test at a calm, steady pace, but keep it in mind so you don't spend too much time on any one question. Recognize that taking extra time on one question you don't understand may keep you from answering two that you do understand later in the test. If your time limit for a question is up and you're still not sure of the answer, mark it and move on, and come back to it later if the time and the test format allow. If the testing format doesn't allow you to return to earlier questions, just make an educated guess; then put it out of your mind and move on.

On the easier questions, be careful not to rush. It may seem wise to hurry through them so you have more time for the challenging ones, but it's not worth missing one if you know the concept and just didn't take the time to read the question fully. Work efficiently but make sure you understand the question and have looked at all of the answer choices, since more than one may seem right at first.

Even if you're paying attention to the time, you may find yourself a little behind at some point. You should speed up to get back on track, but do so wisely. Don't panic; just take a few seconds less on each question until you're caught up. Don't guess without thinking, but do look through the answer choices and eliminate any you know are wrong. If you can get down to two choices, it is often worthwhile to guess from those. Once you've chosen an answer, move on and don't dwell on any that you skipped or had to hurry through. If a question was taking too long, chances are it was one of the harder ones, so you weren't as likely to get it right anyway.

On the other hand, if you find yourself getting ahead of schedule, it may be beneficial to slow down a little. The more quickly you work, the more likely you are to make a careless mistake that will affect your score. You've budgeted time for each question, so don't be afraid to spend that time. Practice an efficient but careful pace to get the most out of the time you have.

Test-Taking Strategies

This section contains a list of test-taking strategies that you may find helpful as you work through the test. By taking what you know and applying logical thought, you can maximize your chances of answering any question correctly!

It is very important to realize that every question is different and every person is different: no single strategy will work on every question, and no single strategy will work for every person. That's why we've included all of them here, so you can try them out and determine which ones work best for different types of questions and which ones work best for you.

Question Strategies

⊘ Read Carefully

Read the question and the answer choices carefully. Don't miss the question because you misread the terms. You have plenty of time to read each question thoroughly and make sure you understand what is being asked. Yet a happy medium must be attained, so don't waste too much time. You must read carefully and efficiently.

⊘ Contextual Clues

Look for contextual clues. If the question includes a word you are not familiar with, look at the immediate context for some indication of what the word might mean. Contextual clues can often give you all the information you need to decipher the meaning of an unfamiliar word. Even if you can't determine the meaning, you may be able to narrow down the possibilities enough to make a solid guess at the answer to the question.

⊘ Prefixes

If you're having trouble with a word in the question or answer choices, try dissecting it. Take advantage of every clue that the word might include. Prefixes can be a huge help. Usually, they allow you to determine a basic meaning. *Pre-* means before, *post-* means after, *pro-* is positive, *de-* is negative. From prefixes, you can get an idea of the general meaning of the word and try to put it into context.

⊘ Hedge Words

Watch out for critical hedge words, such as *likely, may, can, often, almost, mostly, usually, generally, rarely,* and *sometimes.* Question writers insert these hedge phrases to cover every possibility. Often an answer choice will be wrong simply because it leaves no room for exception. Be on guard for answer choices that have definitive words such as *exactly* and *always.*

⊘ Switchback Words

Stay alert for *switchbacks.* These are the words and phrases frequently used to alert you to shifts in thought. The most common switchback words are *but, although,* and *however.* Others include *nevertheless, on the other hand, even though, while, in spite of, despite,* and *regardless of.* Switchback words are important to catch because they can change the direction of the question or an answer choice.

⊘ FACE VALUE

When in doubt, use common sense. Accept the situation in the problem at face value. Don't read too much into it. These problems will not require you to make wild assumptions. If you have to go beyond creativity and warp time or space in order to have an answer choice fit the question, then you should move on and consider the other answer choices. These are normal problems rooted in reality. The applicable relationship or explanation may not be readily apparent, but it is there for you to figure out. Use your common sense to interpret anything that isn't clear.

Answer Choice Strategies

⊘ ANSWER SELECTION

The most thorough way to pick an answer choice is to identify and eliminate wrong answers until only one is left, then confirm it is the correct answer. Sometimes an answer choice may immediately seem right, but be careful. The test writers will usually put more than one reasonable answer choice on each question, so take a second to read all of them and make sure that the other choices are not equally obvious. As long as you have time left, it is better to read every answer choice than to pick the first one that looks right without checking the others.

⊘ ANSWER CHOICE FAMILIES

An answer choice family consists of two (in rare cases, three) answer choices that are very similar in construction and cannot all be true at the same time. If you see two answer choices that are direct opposites or parallels, one of them is usually the correct answer. For instance, if one answer choice says that quantity *x* increases and another either says that quantity *x* decreases (opposite) or says that quantity *y* increases (parallel), then those answer choices would fall into the same family. An answer choice that doesn't match the construction of the answer choice family is more likely to be incorrect. Most questions will not have answer choice families, but when they do appear, you should be prepared to recognize them.

⊘ ELIMINATE ANSWERS

Eliminate answer choices as soon as you realize they are wrong, but make sure you consider all possibilities. If you are eliminating answer choices and realize that the last one you are left with is also wrong, don't panic. Start over and consider each choice again. There may be something you missed the first time that you will realize on the second pass.

⊘ AVOID FACT TRAPS

Don't be distracted by an answer choice that is factually true but doesn't answer the question. You are looking for the choice that answers the question. Stay focused on what the question is asking for so you don't accidentally pick an answer that is true but incorrect. Always go back to the question and make sure the answer choice you've selected actually answers the question and is not merely a true statement.

⊘ EXTREME STATEMENTS

In general, you should avoid answers that put forth extreme actions as standard practice or proclaim controversial ideas as established fact. An answer choice that states the "process should be used in certain situations, if..." is much more likely to be correct than one that states the "process should be discontinued completely." The first is a calm rational statement and doesn't even make a definitive, uncompromising stance, using a hedge word *if* to provide wiggle room, whereas the second choice is far more extreme.

☑ BENCHMARK

As you read through the answer choices and you come across one that seems to answer the question well, mentally select that answer choice. This is not your final answer, but it's the one that will help you evaluate the other answer choices. The one that you selected is your benchmark or standard for judging each of the other answer choices. Every other answer choice must be compared to your benchmark. That choice is correct until proven otherwise by another answer choice beating it. If you find a better answer, then that one becomes your new benchmark. Once you've decided that no other choice answers the question as well as your benchmark, you have your final answer.

☑ PREDICT THE ANSWER

Before you even start looking at the answer choices, it is often best to try to predict the answer. When you come up with the answer on your own, it is easier to avoid distractions and traps because you will know exactly what to look for. The right answer choice is unlikely to be word-for-word what you came up with, but it should be a close match. Even if you are confident that you have the right answer, you should still take the time to read each option before moving on.

General Strategies

☑ TOUGH QUESTIONS

If you are stumped on a problem or it appears too hard or too difficult, don't waste time. Move on! Remember though, if you can quickly check for obviously incorrect answer choices, your chances of guessing correctly are greatly improved. Before you completely give up, at least try to knock out a couple of possible answers. Eliminate what you can and then guess at the remaining answer choices before moving on.

☑ CHECK YOUR WORK

Since you will probably not know every term listed and the answer to every question, it is important that you get credit for the ones that you do know. Don't miss any questions through careless mistakes. If at all possible, try to take a second to look back over your answer selection and make sure you've selected the correct answer choice and haven't made a costly careless mistake (such as marking an answer choice that you didn't mean to mark). This quick double check should more than pay for itself in caught mistakes for the time it costs.

☑ PACE YOURSELF

It's easy to be overwhelmed when you're looking at a page full of questions; your mind is confused and full of random thoughts, and the clock is ticking down faster than you would like. Calm down and maintain the pace that you have set for yourself. Especially as you get down to the last few minutes of the test, don't let the small numbers on the clock make you panic. As long as you are on track by monitoring your pace, you are guaranteed to have time for each question.

☑ DON'T RUSH

It is very easy to make errors when you are in a hurry. Maintaining a fast pace in answering questions is pointless if it makes you miss questions that you would have gotten right otherwise. Test writers like to include distracting information and wrong answers that seem right. Taking a little extra time to avoid careless mistakes can make all the difference in your test score. Find a pace that allows you to be confident in the answers that you select.

⊘ KEEP MOVING

Panicking will not help you pass the test, so do your best to stay calm and keep moving. Taking deep breaths and going through the answer elimination steps you practiced can help to break through a stress barrier and keep your pace.

Final Notes

The combination of a solid foundation of content knowledge and the confidence that comes from practicing your plan for applying that knowledge is the key to maximizing your performance on test day. As your foundation of content knowledge is built up and strengthened, you'll find that the strategies included in this chapter become more and more effective in helping you quickly sift through the distractions and traps of the test to isolate the correct answer.

Now that you're preparing to move forward into the test content chapters of this book, be sure to keep your goal in mind. As you read, think about how you will be able to apply this information on the test. If you've already seen sample questions for the test and you have an idea of the question format and style, try to come up with questions of your own that you can answer based on what you're reading. This will give you valuable practice applying your knowledge in the same ways you can expect to on test day.

Good luck and good studying!

Earth and Space Sciences

Rocks and Minerals

Geology is the study of the planet Earth as it pertains to the composition, structure, and origin of its rocks. **Minerals** are naturally occurring, inorganic solids with a definite chemical composition and an orderly internal crystal structure. A **polymorph** is two minerals with the same chemical composition, but a different crystal structure. **Rocks** are aggregates of one or more minerals, and may also contain mineraloids (minerals lacking a crystalline structure) and organic remains. The three types of rocks are sedimentary, igneous, and metamorphic. Rocks are classified based on both their formation and mineral content. Minerals, on the other hand, are classified by their chemical composition. The study of rocks, known as **petrology**, examines their composition, texture, structure, occurrence, mode of formation, and history. **Mineralogy** is the study of minerals.

Sedimentary rocks are formed by the process of lithification, which involves compaction, the expulsion of liquids from pores, and the cementation of the pre-existing rock. Pressure and temperature are responsible for this process. Sedimentary rocks are often formed in layers in the presence of water and may contain organic remains, such as fossils. Sedimentary rocks can be organized into three groups: detrital, biogenic, and chemical. When studying sedimentary rock, scientists use the word *texture* to refer the size, shape, and grains of sedimentary rock. Texture can be used to determine how a particular sedimentary rock was created. Composition refers to the types of minerals present in the rock. The origin of sedimentary rock depends on the type of water that was involved in its creation. Marine deposits, for example, likely involved ocean environments, while continental deposits likely involved dry land and lakes.

Igneous Rock

Igneous rock is formed from magma, molten material originating from beneath the Earth's surface. Depending upon where the magma cools, the resulting igneous rock can be classified as intrusive, plutonic, hypabyssal, extrusive, or volcanic. Magma that solidifies at a great depth is intrusive, cools slowly, and forms rock with a coarse grain, such as granite. Magma that solidifies at or near the surface is extrusive, cools quickly, and usually forms rock with a fine grain, such as basalt. Magma that actually flows out of the Earth's surface is called **lava**. Some extrusive rock cools so quickly that crystals do not have time to form. These rocks have a glassy appearance, such as obsidian. Hypabyssal rock is igneous rock that is formed at medium depths.

Metamorphic Rock

Metamorphic rock is rock which has been changed by great heat and pressure. This results in a variety of outcomes, including deformation, compaction, destruction of the characteristics of the original rock, bending and folding. Some levels of heat and pressure can even cause the formation of new minerals because of chemical reactions and changes in the size and shape of the mineral grain. For example, the igneous rock ferromagnesian can be changed into schist and gneiss. The sedimentary rock carbonaceous can be changed into marble. The texture of metamorphic rocks can be classified as foliated and unfoliated. Foliation, or layering, occurs when rock is compressed along one axis during recrystallization. This can be seen in schist and shale. Unfoliated rock does not include this banding. Rocks that are compressed equally from all sides or lack specific minerals will be unfoliated. Marble is an example of an unfoliated rock.

Earth's Structure

The Earth is ellipsoid, not perfectly spherical. This means the diameter is different through the poles and at the equator. Through the poles, the Earth is about 12,715 km in diameter. The approximate center of the Earth is at a depth of 6,378 km. The Earth is divided into a crust, mantle, and core. The core consists of a solid inner portion. Moving outward, the molten outer core occupies the space from about a depth of 5,150 km to a depth of 2,890 km. The mantle consists of a lower and upper layer. The lower layer includes the D' (D prime) and D" (D double-prime) layers. The solid portion of the upper mantle and crust together form the lithosphere, or rocky sphere. Below this, but still within the mantle, is the asthenosphere, or weak sphere. These layers are distinguishable because the lithosphere is relatively rigid, while the asthenosphere resembles a thick liquid.

Plate Tectonic Theory

The theory of plate tectonics states that the lithosphere, the solid portion of the mantle and Earth's crust, consists of major and minor plates. These plates are on top of and move with the viscous upper mantle, which is heated because of the convection cycle that occurs in the interior of the Earth. There are different estimates as to the exact number of major and minor plates. The number of major plates is believed to be between 9 and 15, and it is thought that there may be as many as 40 minor plates. The United States is atop the North American plate. The Pacific Ocean is atop the Pacific plate. The point at which these two plates slide horizontally along the San Andreas Fault is an example of a transform plate boundary. The other two types of boundaries are divergent (plates that are spreading apart and forming new crust) and convergent (the process of subduction causes one plate to go under another). The movement of plates is what causes other features of the Earth's crust, such as mountains, volcanoes, and earthquakes.

Volcanic Activities and Plate Tectonics

Volcanoes can occur along any type of tectonic plate boundary. At a divergent boundary, as plates move apart, magma rises to the surface, cools, and forms a ridge, like the mid-Atlantic ridge. Convergent boundaries, where one plate slides under another, are often areas with a lot of volcanic activity. The subduction process creates magma. When it rises to the surface, volcanoes can be created. Volcanoes can also be created in the middle of a plate over hot spots, locations where narrow plumes of magma rise through the mantle in a fixed place over a long period of time. The Hawaiian Islands and Midway Island are examples of how hot spots can create not only volcanoes, but entire islands. As the plate shifts, the island moves and magma can continue to rise through the mantle and produce another island. Volcanoes can be active, dormant, or extinct. Active volcanoes are those that are erupting or about to erupt. Dormant volcanoes are those that might erupt in the future and still have internal volcanic activity. Extinct volcanoes are those that will not erupt.

The three types of volcanoes are shield, cinder cone, and composite. A shield volcano is created by a long-term, relatively gentle eruption. This type of volcanic mountain is created by each progressive lava flow that occurs over time. A cinder cone volcano is created by explosive eruptions. Lava is spewed out of a vent into the air. As it falls to the ground, the lava cools into cinders and ash, which build up around the volcano in a cone shape. A composite volcano is a combination of the other two types of volcanoes. In this type, there are layers of lava flows and layers of ash and cinder.

Hydrologic Cycle

The hydrologic, or water, cycle refers to water movement on, above, and in the Earth. Water can be in any one of its three states during different phases of the cycle. The three states of water are liquid water, frozen ice, and water vapor. Processes involved in the hydrologic cycle include precipitation, canopy interception, snow melt, runoff, infiltration, subsurface flow, evaporation, sublimation, advection, condensation, and transpiration. Precipitation is when condensed water vapor falls to Earth as rain, fog drip, and various forms of snow, hail, and sleet. Canopy interception is when precipitation lands on plant foliage instead of falling to the ground and evaporating. Snow melt is runoff produced by melting snow. Infiltration occurs when water flows from the surface into the ground. Subsurface flow refers to water that flows underground. Evaporation is when water in a liquid state changes to a gas. Sublimation is when water in a solid state (such as snow or ice) changes to water vapor without going through a liquid phase. Advection is the movement of water through the atmosphere. Condensation is when water vapor changes to liquid water. Transpiration is when water vapor is released from plants into the air.

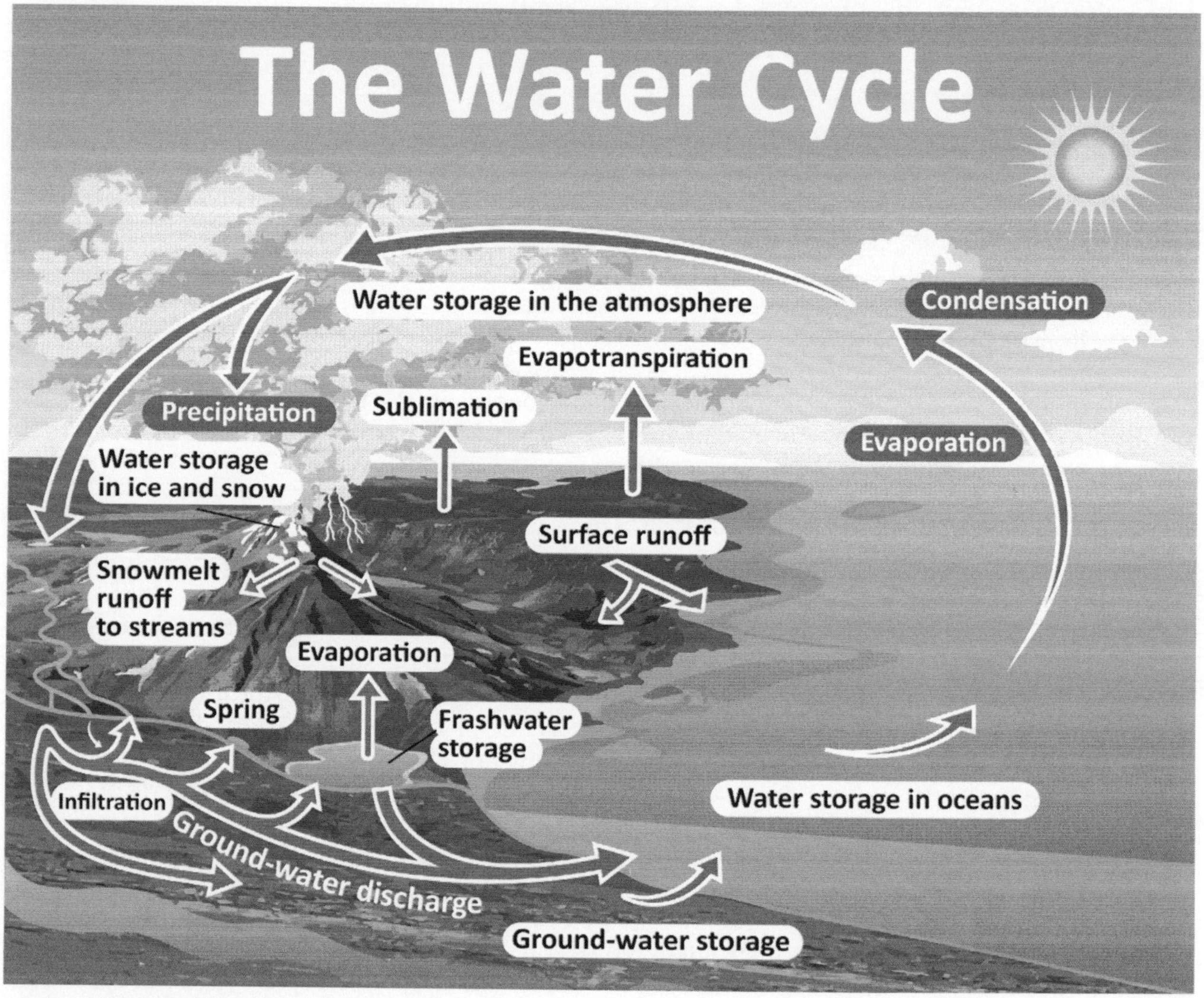

EARTH'S ATMOSPHERE

The atmosphere consists of 78% nitrogen, 21% oxygen, and 1% argon. It also includes traces of water vapor, carbon dioxide and other gases, dust particles, and chemicals from Earth. The atmosphere becomes thinner the farther it is from the Earth's surface, gradually fading into space. It becomes difficult to breathe at about 3 km above sea level. The lowest layer of the atmosphere is called the troposphere. Its thickness varies at the poles and the equator, varying from about 7 to 17 km. This is where most weather occurs. The stratosphere is next and continues to an elevation of about 51 km. The mesosphere extends from the stratosphere to an elevation of about 81 km. It is the coldest layer and is where meteors tend to ablate, or break down. The next layer is the thermosphere. It is where the International Space Station orbits. The exosphere is the outermost layer, extends to 10,000 km, and mainly consists of hydrogen and helium. Beyond the five main layers are the ionosphere, homosphere, heterosphere, and magnetosphere.

Other Layers Above the Surface of the Earth

The ozone layer, although contained within the stratosphere, is determined by ozone (O_3) concentrations. It absorbs the majority of ultraviolet light from the Sun. The ionosphere is part of both the exosphere and the thermosphere. It is characterized by the fact that it is a plasma, a partially ionized gas in which free electrons and positive ions are attracted to each other, but are too energetic to remain fixed as a molecule. It starts at about 50 km above Earth's surface and goes to 1,000 km. It affects radio wave transmission and auroras. The ionosphere pushes against the inner edge of the Earth's magnetosphere, which is the highly magnetized, non-spherical region around the Earth. The homosphere encompasses the troposphere, stratosphere, and mesosphere. Gases in the homosphere are considered well mixed. In the heterosphere, the distance that particles can move without colliding is large. As a result, gases are stratified according to their molecular weights. Heavier gases such as oxygen and nitrogen occur near the bottom of the heterosphere, while hydrogen, the lightest element, is found at the top.

Earth's Chemical Composition

The Earth's core consists of hot iron and forms of nickel. The mantle consists of different materials, including iron, magnesium, and calcium. The crust covers the mantle, consists of a thin layer of much lighter rocks, and is further subdivided into continental and oceanic portions. The continental portion consists mainly of silicates, such as granite. The oceanic portion consists of heavier, volcanic rocks, such as basalt. The upper 10 miles of the lithosphere layer (the crust and part of the mantle) is made up of 95% igneous rock (or its metamorphic equivalent), 4% shale, 0.75% sandstone, and 0.25% limestone. There are over 4,000 known minerals, but only about 20 make up some 95% of all rocks. There are, however, more than 3,000 individual kinds of minerals in the Earth's crust. Silicates are the largest group of minerals.

Orogeny

Orogeny refers to the formation of mountains, particularly the processes of folding and faulting caused by plate tectonics. Folding is when layers of sedimentary rock are pressed together by continental plate movements. Sections of rock that are folded upward are called anticlines. Sections of rock that are folded downward are called synclines. Examples of folded mountains are the Alps and the Himalayans. Fault-block mountains are created when tectonic plate movement produces tension that results in displacement. Mountains in the Southwest United States are examples of fault-blocking mountains. Mountains can also be caused by volcanic activity and erosion.

Earthquakes

Most earthquakes are caused by tectonic plate movement. They occur along fractures called faults or fault zones. Friction in the faults prevents smooth movement. Tension builds up over time, and the release of that tension results in earthquakes. Faults are grouped based on the type of slippage that occurs. The types of faults are dip-slip, strike-slip, and oblique-slip. A dip-slip fault involves vertical movement along the fault plane. In a normal dip-slip fault, the wall that is above the fault plane moves down. In a reverse dip-slip fault, the wall above the fault plane moves up. A strike-slip fault involves horizontal movement along the fault plane. Oblique-slip faults involve both vertical and horizontal movement. The Richter magnitude scale measures how much seismic energy was released by an earthquake.

EROSION

Erosion is the wearing away of rock materials from the Earth's surface. Erosion can be classified as natural geologic erosion and erosion due to human activity. Natural geologic erosion occurs due to weathering and gravity. Factors involved in natural geologic erosion are typically long term forces. Human activity such as development, farming, and deforestation occurs over shorter periods of time. Soil, which supports plant growth, is the topmost layer of organic material. One type of erosion is sheet erosion, which is the gradual and somewhat uniform removal of surface soil. Rills are small rivulets that cut into soil. Gullies are rills that have become enlarged due to extended water run-off. Sandblows are caused by wind blowing away particles. Negative effects of erosion include sedimentation in rivers, which can pollute water and damage ecosystems. Erosion can also result in the removal of topsoil, which destroys crops and prevents plants from growing. This reduces food production and alters ecosystems.

MECHANICAL AND CHEMICAL WEATHERING

There are two basic types of weathering: mechanical and chemical. Weathering is a very prominent process on the Earth's surface. Materials weather at different rates, which are known as differential weathering. Mechanical and chemical weathering is interdependent. For example, chemical weathering can loosen the bonds between molecules and allow mechanical weathering to take place. Mechanical weathering can expose the surfaces of land masses and allow chemical weathering to take place. Impact, abrasion, frost wedging, root wedging, salt wedging, and uploading are types of mechanical weathering. Types of chemical weathering are dissolution, hydration, hydrolysis, oxidation, biological, and carbonation. The primary type of chemical weathering is caused by water dissolving a mineral. The more acidic water is, the more effective it is at weathering. Carbonic and sulfuric acids can enter rain when they are present in the atmosphere. This lowers the pH value of rain, making it more acidic. Normal rain water has a pH value of 5.5. Acid rain has a pH value of 4 or less.

DEPOSITION

Deposition, or sedimentation, is the geological process in which previously eroded material is transported or added to a land form or land mass. Erosion and sedimentation are complementary geological processes. Running water causes a substantial amount of deposition of transported materials in both fresh water and coastal areas. Examples include gravity transporting material down the slope of a mountain and depositing it at the base of the slope. Another example is when sandstorms deposit particles in other locations. When glaciers melt and retreat, it can result in the deposition of sediments. Evaporation is also considered to cause deposition since dissolved materials are left behind when water evaporates. Deposition can include the buildup of organic materials. For example, chalk is partially made up of the small calcium carbonate skeletons of marine plankton, which helps create more calcium carbonate from chemical processes.

UNIFORMITARIANISM, CATASTROPHISM, AND SUPERPOSITION

Also known as gradualism, uniformitarianism is the belief among modern geologists that the forces, processes, and laws that we see today have existed throughout geologic time. It involves the belief that the present is the key to the past, and that relatively slow processes have shaped the geological features of Earth. Catastrophism is the belief that the Earth was shaped by sudden, short-term catastrophic events. In geology, and in the field of stratigraphy in particular, the law of superposition is that underground layers closer to the surface were deposited more recently.

Stratigraphy and Subfields

Stratigraphy is a branch of geology that involves the study of rock layers and layering. Sedimentary rocks are the primary focus of stratigraphy. Subfields include lithostratigraphy, which is the study of the vertical layering of rock types, and biostratigraphy, which is the study of fossil evidence in rock layers. Magnetostratigraphy is the study of changes in detrital remnant magnetism (DRM), which is used to measure the polarity of Earth's magnetic field at the time a stratum was deposited. Chronostratigraphy focuses on the relative dating of rock strata based on the time of rock formation. Unconformity refers to missing layers of rock.

Relative and Absolute Time

A numerical, or "absolute," age is a specific number of years, such as 150 million years ago. A "relative" age refers to a time range, such as the Mesozoic era. It is used to determine whether one rock formation is older or younger than another formation. Radioactive dating is a form of absolute dating and stratigraphy is a form of relative dating. Radioactive dating techniques have provided the most information about the absolute age of rocks and other geological features. Together, geochronologists have created a geologic time scale. Biostratigraphy uses plant and animal fossils within rock to determine its relative age.

Fossils

Fossils are preservations of plant and animal remains or traces that date back to about 10,000 years ago. The fossil record is composed of fossils and where they are found in rock strata. Fossils are formed under a very specific set of conditions. The fossil must not be damaged by predators and scavengers after death, and the fossil must not decompose. Usually, this happens when the organism is quickly covered with sediment. This sediment builds up and molecules in the organism's body are replaced by minerals. Fossils come in an array of sizes, from single-celled organisms to large dinosaurs.

Fossils provide a wealth of information about the past, particularly about the flora and fauna that once occupied the Earth, but also about the geologic history of the Earth itself and how Earth and its inhabitants came to be. Some fossilized remains in the geohistorical record exemplify ongoing processes in the Earth's environment, such as weathering, glaciation, and volcanism. These have all led to evolutionary changes in plants and animals. Other fossils support the theory that catastrophic events caused drastic changes in the Earth and its living creatures. One example of this type of theory is that a meteor struck the Earth and caused dinosaurs to become extinct. Both types of fossils provide scientists with a way to hypothesize whether these types of events will happen again.

Geologic Time Scale

Geologists use the geologic time scale when discussing Earth's chronology and the formation of rocks and minerals. Age is calculated in millions of years before the present time. Units of time are often delineated by geologic or paleontologic events. Smaller units of time such as eras are distinguished by the abundance and/or extinction of certain plant and animal life. For example, the extinction of the dinosaurs marks the end of the Mesozoic era and the beginning of the Cenozoic, the present, era. We are in the Holocene epoch. The supereon encompasses the greatest amount of time. It is composed of eons. Eons are divided into eras, eras into periods, and periods into epochs. Layers of rock also correspond to periods of time in geochronology. Current theory holds that the Earth was formed 4.5 billion years ago.

Development of Geologic Time Scale

The first known observations of stratigraphy were made by Aristotle, who lived before the time of Christ. He observed seashells in ancient rock formations and on the beach, and concluded that the fossilized seashells were similar to current seashells. Avicenna, a Persian scholar from the 11th century, also made early advances in the development of stratigraphy with the concept of superposition. Nicolas Steno, a Danish scientist from the 17th century, expounded upon this with the belief that layers of rock are piled on top of each other. In the 18th century, Abraham Werner categorized rocks from four different periods: the Primary, Secondary, Tertiary, and Quaternary periods. This fell out of use when the belief emerged that rock layers containing the same fossils had been deposited at the same time, and were therefore from the same age. British geologists created the names for many of the time divisions in use today. For example, the Devonian period was named after the county of Devon, and the Permian period was named after Perm, Russia.

Formation of the Earth

Earth's early development began after a supernova exploded. This led to the formation of the Sun out of hydrogen gas and interstellar dust. These same elements swirled around the newly-formed Sun and formed the planets, including Earth. Scientists theorize that about 4.5 billion years ago, Earth was a chunk of rock surrounded by a cloud of gas. It is believed it lacked water and the type of atmosphere that exists today. Heat from radioactive materials in the rock and pressure in the Earth's interior melted the interior. This caused the heavier materials, such as iron, to sink. Lighter silicate-type rocks rose to the Earth's surface. These rocks formed the Earth's earliest crust. Other chemicals also rose to the Earth's surface, helping to form the water and atmosphere. There is one material that has been dated by scientists and found to be 4.4 billion years old. The material is zircon, which consists of zirconium, silicon, and oxygen. Zircon is a mineral that has a high resistance to weathering.

Paleozoic Era

The Paleozoic era began about 542 Ma and lasted until 251 Ma. It is further divided into six periods. The Paleozoic era began after the supercontinent Pannotia started to break up and at the end of a global ice age. By the end of the era, the supercontinent Pangaea had formed. The beginning of the Paleozoic era is marked by Cambrian Explosion, a time when there were abundant life forms according to the fossil record. The end of the era is marked by one of the major extinction events, the Permian extinction, during which almost 90 percent of the species living at the time became extinct. Many plant and animal forms appeared on the land and in the sea during this era. It is also when large land plants first appeared in the fossil record. There are many invertebrates found in the fossil record of the Paleozoic era, and fish, amphibians, and reptiles also first appeared in the fossil record during this era. There were also large swamps and forests, some of which were formed into coal deposits that exist today.

Mesozoic Era

The Mesozoic era is known as the Age of the Dinosaurs. It is also the era during which the dinosaurs became extinct. The fossil record also shows the appearance of mammals and birds. Trees that existed included gymnosperms, which have uncovered seeds and are mostly cone bearing, and angiosperms, which have covered seeds and are flowering plants. The angiosperm group is currently the dominant plant group. It was also during this era that the supercontinent Pangaea divided into the continental pieces that exist today. During the Cretaceous period, sea levels rose until one-third of the Earth's present land mass was underwater, and then receded. This period created huge marine deposits and chalk. The extinction of the dinosaurs happened about 65 Ma, and was believed to have been triggered by the impact of an asteroid.

Cenozoic Era

The Cenozoic era began about 65.5 Ma and continues to the present. It is marked by the Cretaceous-Tertiary extinction event (extinction of the dinosaurs as well as many invertebrates and plants). The Cenozoic era is further divided into the Paleogene, Neogene, and Quaternary periods. During the Cenozoic era, Pangaea continued to drift, and the plates eventually moved into their present positions. The Pleistocene Ice Age, also known as Quaternary glaciation or the current ice age began about 2.58 Ma and includes the glaciation occurring today. Mammals continued to evolve and other plants and animals came into existence during this era. The fossil record includes the ancestors of the horse, rhinoceros, and camel. It also includes the first dogs and cats and the first humanlike creatures. The first humans appeared less than 200,000 years ago.

The Ocean

The ocean is the salty body of water that encompasses the Earth. It has a mass of 1.4×10^{24} grams. Geographically, the ocean is divided into three large oceans: the Pacific Ocean, the Atlantic Ocean, and the Indian Ocean. There are also other divisions, such as gulfs, bays, and various types of seas, including Mediterranean and marginal seas. Ocean distances can be measured by latitude, longitude, degrees, meters, miles, and nautical miles. The ocean accounts for 70.8% of the surface of the Earth, amounting to 361,254,000 km^2. The ocean's depth is greatest at Challenger Deep in the Mariana Trench. The ocean floor here is 10,924 meters below sea level. The depths of the ocean are mapped by echo sounders and satellite altimeter systems. Echo sounders emit a sound pulse from the surface and record the time it takes to return. Satellite altimeters provide better maps of the ocean floor.

Ocean Floor

The ocean floor has features that are also on land (e.g., mountains, ridges, plains, and canyons). The oceanic crust is a thin, dense layer that is about 10 km thick. The greatest volume of water is in the basins. Smaller volumes are in the low-lying areas of the continents. These low-lying areas are known as the continental shelves.

The **continental slope** connects the shelf to the ocean floor of the basin. The **continental rise** is a sloping area between the slope and the basin. A **seamount** is an undersea volcanic peak that rises to a height of at least 1,000 meters. A **guyot** is a seamount with a flat top. A **mid-ocean ridge** is an undersea mountain chain. **Sills** are low parts of ridges that separate ocean basins or other seas. **Trenches** are long, narrow troughs.

Ocean Currents

Surface currents are caused by winds. Subsurface currents, which occur deep beneath the ocean's surface, are caused by land masses and the Earth's rotation. The density of ocean water can also affect currents. Sea water with a higher salinity is denser than sea water with a lower salinity. Water from denser areas flows to areas with water that is less dense. Currents are classified by temperature. Colder polar sea water flows south towards warmer water, forming cold currents. Warm water currents swirl around the basins and equator. In turn, heat lost and gained by the ocean creates winds. Ocean currents play a significant role in transferring this heat toward the poles, which aids in the development of many types of weather phenomena.

Gyres and the Coriolis Effect

Gyres are surface ocean currents that form large circular patterns. In the Northern Hemisphere, they flow clockwise. In the Southern Hemisphere, they flow counterclockwise. These directions are caused by the Coriolis effect. The Coriolis effect occurs due to the fact that the Earth is a rotating object. In the Northern Hemisphere, currents appear to be curving to the right. In the Southern

Hemisphere, currents appear to be curving to the left. This is because the Earth is rotating. Gyres tend to flow in the opposite direction near the Earth's poles. In the portion of the Pacific Ocean north of the equator, the major currents are North Pacific, California, North Equatorial, and Kuroshio. In the South Pacific, they are South Equatorial, East Australia, South Pacific, and Peru. In the North Atlantic, they are the North Atlantic Drift, Canary, North Equatorial, and Gulf Stream. In the South Atlantic, they are South Equatorial, Brazil, South Atlantic, and Benguela.

OCEAN WAVES

Most waves in the ocean are formed by winds. The stronger the winds are, the larger the waves will be. The highest point of a wave is the crest. The lowest point of a wave is the trough. The wavelength is measured from crest to crest. The wave height is measured from the trailing trough to the peak of the crest. The wave frequency refers to the number of wave crests passing a designated point each second. A wave period is the time it takes for a wave crest to reach the point of the wave crest of the previous wave. The energy in the wave runs into the shallow sea floor. This causes the wave to become steeper and then fall over, or break.

TIDES

The gravitational pull of the Sun and Moon causes the oceans to rise and fall each day, creating high and low tides. Most areas have two high tides and two low tides per day. Because the Moon is closer to the Earth than the Sun, its gravitational pull is much greater. The water on the side of the Earth that is closest to the Moon and the water on the opposite side experience high tide. The two low tides occur on the other sides. This changes as the Moon revolves around the Earth. Tidal range is the measurement of the height difference between low and high tide. Tidal range also changes with the location of the Sun and Moon throughout the year, creating spring and neap tides. When all these bodies are aligned, the combined gravitational pull is greater and the tidal range is also greater. This is what creates the spring tide. The neap tide is when the tidal range is at its lowest, which occurs when the Sun and Moon are not at right angles.

CARBON CYCLE OF THE OCEAN

The carbon and nutrient cycles of the ocean are processes that are due in part to the deep currents, mixing, and upwelling that occur in the ocean. Carbon dioxide (CO_2) from the atmosphere is dissolved into the ocean at higher latitudes and distributed to the denser deep water. Where upwelling occurs, CO_2 is brought back to the surface and emitted into the tropical air. Phytoplankton are typically single-celled organisms that are nourished by the Sun. They are photosynthetic autotrophs, meaning they convert water, carbon dioxide, and solar energy into food. They drift with the currents, produce oxygen as a byproduct, and serve as a food source. Zooplankton feed on phytoplankton. Zooplankton are heterotrophic organisms, meaning they do not synthesize their own food. Zooplankton can be single-celled creatures or much larger organisms, such as jellyfish, mollusks, and crustaceans.

CHEMICAL COMPOSITION OF SEAWATER

Salinity is a measure of the amount of dissolved salts in ocean water. It is defined in terms of conductivity. Salinity is influenced by the geologic formations in the area, with igneous formations leading to lower salinity and sedimentary formations leading to higher salinity. Dryer areas with greater rates of evaporation also have higher salt concentrations. Areas where fresh water mixes with ocean water have lower salt concentrations. Hydrogen and oxygen make up about 96.5% of sea water. The major constituents of the dissolved solids of sea water at an atomic level are chlorine (55.3%), sodium (30.8%), magnesium (3.7%), sulfur (2.6%), calcium (1.2%), and potassium (1.1%). The salinity of ocean water is fairly constant, ranging from 34.60 to 34.80 parts per thousand, which is 200 parts per million. Measuring variation on this small of a scale requires instruments that are accurate to about one part per million.

Shoreline and Coastal Processes

The area where land meets the sea is called the shoreline. This marks the average position of the ocean. Longshore currents create longshore drift or transport (also called beach drift). This is when ocean waves move toward a beach at an angle, which moves water along the coast. Sediment is eroded from some areas and deposited in others. In this way, it is moved along the beach. Rip currents are strong, fast currents that occur when part of longshore current moves away from the beach. Hard, man-made structures built perpendicular to the beach tend to trap sand on the up-current side. Erosion occurs on the down-current side. Features formed by the sediment deposited by waves include spits, bay-mouth bars, tombolos, barrier islands, and buildups. Sand is composed of weather-resistant, granular materials like quartz and orthoclase. In some locations, it is composed of rock and basalt.

Beaches

Weathering erodes the parent material of beaches, rock and soil, into sand, which is typically quartz. Other parts of the soil such as clay and silt are deposited in areas of the continental shelf. The larger sand particles get deposited in the form of a beach. This includes a near shore, which is underwater, a fore shore, the area typically considered the beach, and a back shore. The offshore starts about 5 meters from the shoreline and extends to about 20 meters. The beach also includes wet and dry parts and a fore dune and rear dune. Waves typically move sand from the sea to the beach, and gravity and wave action move it back again. Wind gradually pushes sand particles uphill in a jumping motion called saltation. Sand stays deposited in the form of dunes and the dunes appear as if they roll backward. Storms can both erode a beach and provide additional deposition.

Tilt of the Earth and Seasons

The tilt of the Earth on its axis is 23.5°. This tilt causes the seasons and affects the amount of Sun the area receives, which influence temperature. When the Northern or Southern Hemispheres are tilted toward the Sun, the hemisphere tilted toward the sun experiences summer and the other hemisphere experiences winter. This reverses as the Earth revolves around the Sun. Fall and spring occur between the two extremes. The equator gets the same amount of sunlight every day of the year, about 12 hours, and doesn't experience seasons. Both poles have days during the winter when they are tilted away from the Sun and receive no daylight. The opposite effect occurs during the summer. There are 24 hours of daylight and no night. The summer solstice, the day with the most amount of sunlight, occurs on June 21st in the Northern Hemisphere and on December 21st in the Southern Hemisphere. The winter solstice, the day with the least amount of sunlight, occurs on December 21st in the Northern Hemisphere and on June 21st in the Southern Hemisphere.

TROPOSPHERIC CIRCULATION

Most weather takes place in the troposphere. Air circulates in the atmosphere by convection and in various types of "cells." Air near the equator is warmed by the Sun and rises. Cool air rushes under it, and the higher, warmer air flows toward Earth's poles. At the poles, it cools and descends to the surface. It is now under the hot air, and flows back to the equator. Air currents coupled with ocean currents move heat around the planet, creating winds, weather, and climate. Winds can change direction with the seasons. For example, in Southeast Asia and India, summer monsoons are caused by air being heated by the Sun. This air rises, draws moisture from the ocean, and causes daily rains. In winter, the air cools, sinks, pushes the moist air away, and creates dry weather.

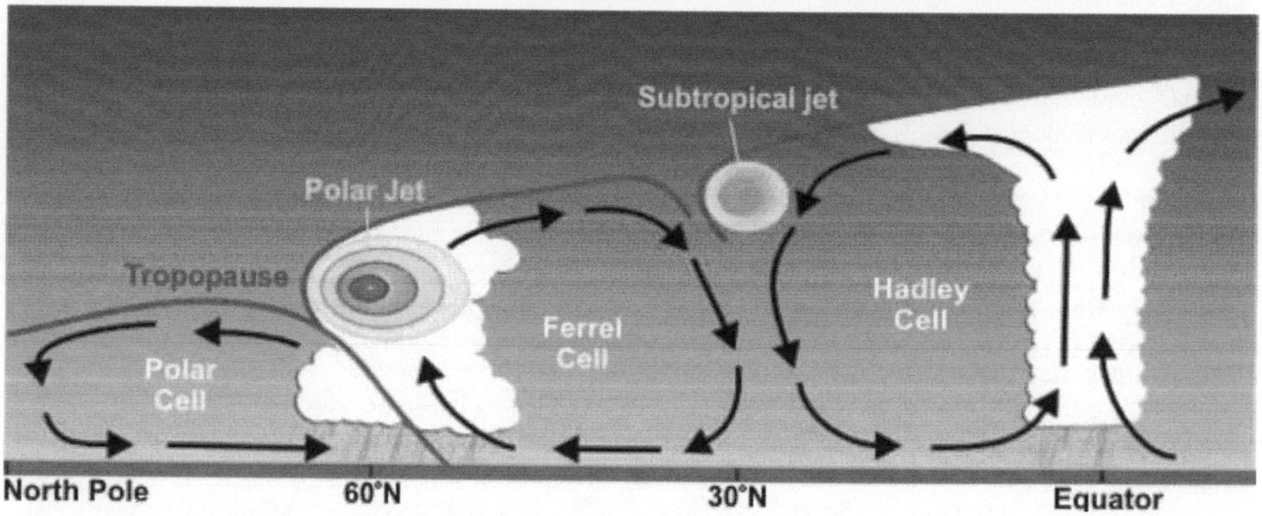

WEATHER, CLIMATE, AND METEOROLOGY

Meteorology is the study of the atmosphere, particularly as it pertains to forecasting the weather and understanding its processes. Weather is the condition of the atmosphere at any given moment. Most weather occurs in the troposphere and includes changing events such as clouds, storms, and temperature, as well as more extreme events such as tornadoes, hurricanes, and blizzards. Climate refers to the average weather for a particular area over time, typically at least 30 years. Latitude is an indicator of climate. Changes in climate occur over long time periods.

COMMON WEATHER PHENOMENA AND METEOROLOGICAL MEASURING EQUIPMENT

Common atmospheric conditions that are frequently measured are temperature, precipitation, wind, and humidity. These weather conditions are often measured at permanently fixed weather stations so weather data can be collected and compared over time and by region. Measurements may also be taken by ships, buoys, and underwater instruments. Measurements may also be taken under special circumstances. The measurements taken include temperature, barometric pressure, humidity, wind speed, wind direction, and precipitation. Usually, the following instruments are used: A thermometer is used for measuring temperature; a barometer is used for measuring barometric/air pressure; a hygrometer is used for measuring humidity; an anemometer is used for measuring wind speed; a weather vane is used for measuring wind direction; and a rain gauge is used for measuring precipitation.

CLOUDS

Clouds form when air cools and warm air is forced to give up some of its water vapor because it can no longer hold it. This vapor condenses and forms tiny droplets of water or ice crystals called clouds. Particles, or aerosols, are needed for water vapor to form water droplets. These are called condensation nuclei. Clouds are created by surface heating, mountains and terrain, rising air masses, and weather fronts. Clouds precipitate, returning the water they contain to Earth. Clouds can also create atmospheric optics. They can scatter light, creating colorful phenomena such as rainbows, colorful sunsets, and the green flash phenomenon.

High, Middle, and Low Cloud Types

Most clouds can be classified according to the altitude of their base above Earth's surface. High clouds occur at altitudes between 5,000 and 13,000 meters. Middle clouds occur at altitudes between 2,000 and 7,000 meters. Low clouds occur from the Earth's surface to altitudes of 2,000 meters. Types of high clouds include cirrus (Ci), thin wispy mare's tails that consist of ice; cirrocumulus (Cc), small, pillow-like puffs that often appear in rows; and cirrostratus (Cs), thin, sheetlike clouds that often cover the entire sky. Types of middle clouds include altocumulus (Ac), gray-white clouds that consist of liquid water; and altostratus (As), grayish or blue-gray clouds that span the sky. Types of low clouds include stratus (St), gray and fog-like clouds consisting of water droplets that take up the whole sky; stratocumulus (Sc), low-lying, lumpy gray clouds; and nimbostratus (Ns), dark gray clouds with uneven bases that indicate rain or snow. Two types of clouds, cumulus (Cu) and cumulonimbus (Cb), are capable of great vertical growth. They can start at a wide range of altitudes, from the Earth's surface to altitudes of 13,000 meters.

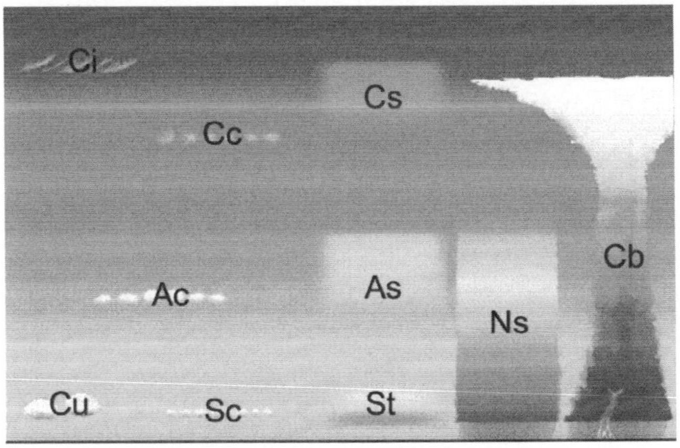

Latitude, Longitude, and Equator

For the purposes of tracking time and location, the Earth is divided into sections with imaginary lines. The lines that run vertically around the globe through the poles are lines of longitude, sometimes called meridians. The Prime Meridian is the longitudinal reference point of 0. Longitude is measured in 15-degree increments toward the east or west. Degrees are further divided into 60 minutes, and each minute is divided into 60 seconds. Lines of latitude run horizontally around the Earth parallel to the equator, which is the 0 reference point for latitude and the widest point of the Earth. Latitude is the distance north or south from the equator and is also measured in degrees, minutes, and seconds.

Latitudinal Variation and Corresponding Ecosystems

Latitude is a measurement of the distance from the equator. The distance from the equator indicates how much solar radiation a particular area receives. The equator receives more sunlight, while polar areas receive less. The Earth tilts slightly on its rotational axis. This tilt determines the seasons and affects weather. There are eight biomes or ecosystems with particular climates that are associated with latitude. Those in the high latitudes, which get the least sunlight, are tundra and taiga. Those in the mid latitudes are grassland, temperate forest, and chaparral. Those in latitudes closest to the equator, desert and tropical rainforest, are the warmest. The eighth biome is the ocean, which is unique because it consists of water and spans the entire globe. Insolation refers to incoming solar radiation, which is at its peak at noon. Diurnal variations refer to the daily changes in insolation.

Tropic of Cancer, Tropic of Capricorn, and Antarctic and Arctic Circles

The Tropic of Cancer is located at 23.5 degrees north. The Sun is directly overhead at noon on June 21st in the Tropic of Cancer, which marks the beginning of summer in the Northern Hemisphere. The Tropic of Capricorn is located at 23.5 degrees south. The Sun is directly overhead at noon on December 21st in the Tropic of Capricorn, which marks the beginning of winter in the Northern Hemisphere. The Arctic Circle is located at 66.5 degrees north, and marks the start of when the Sun is not visible above the horizon. This occurs on December 21st, the same day the Sun is directly over the Tropic of Capricorn. The Antarctic Circle is located at 66.5 degrees south, and marks the start of when the Sun is not visible above the horizon. This occurs on June 21st, which marks the beginning of winter in the Southern Hemisphere and is when the Sun is directly over the Tropic of Cancer.

Winds and Global Wind Belts

Winds are the result of air moving by convection. Masses of warm air rise, and cold air sweeps into their place. The warm air also moves, cools, and sinks. The term "prevailing wind" refers to the wind that usually blows in an area in a single direction. Dominant winds are the winds with the highest speeds. Belts or bands that run latitudinally and blow in a specific direction are associated with convection cells. Hadley cells are formed directly north and south of the equator. The Farrell cells occur at about 30° to 60°. The jet stream runs between the Farrell cells and the polar cells. At the higher and lower latitudes, the direction is easterly. At mid latitudes, the direction is westerly. From the North Pole to the south, the surface winds are Polar High Easterlies, Subpolar Low Westerlies, Subtropical High or Horse Latitudes, North-East Trade winds, Equatorial Low or Doldrums, South-East Trades, Subtropical High or Horse Latitudes, Subpolar Low Easterlies, and Polar High.

Local Atmospheric Variations

Terrain affects several local atmospheric conditions, including temperature, wind speed, and wind direction. When there are land forms, heating of the ground can be greater than the heating of the surrounding air than it would be at the same altitude above sea level. This creates a thermal low in the region and amplifies any existing thermal lows. It also changes the wind circulation. Terrain such as hills and valleys increase friction between the air and the land, which disturbs the air flow. This physical block deflects the wind, and the resulting air flow is called a barrier jet. Just as the heating of the land and air affect sea and land breezes along the coast, rugged terrain affects the wind circulation between mountains and valleys.

Relative Humidity, Absolute Humidity, and Dew Point Temperature

Humidity refers to water vapor contained in the air. The amount of moisture contained in air depends upon its temperature. The higher the air temperature, the more moisture it can hold. These higher levels of moisture are associated with higher humidity. Absolute humidity refers to the total amount of moisture air is capable of holding at a certain temperature. Relative humidity is the ratio of water vapor in the air compared to the amount the air is capable of holding at its current temperature. As temperature decreases, absolute humidity stays the same and relative humidity increases. A hygrometer is a device used to measure humidity. The dew point is the temperature at which water vapor condenses into water at a particular humidity.

Precipitation

After clouds reach the dew point, precipitation occurs. Precipitation can take the form of a liquid or a solid. It is known by many names, including rain, snow, ice, dew, and frost. Liquid forms of precipitation include rain and drizzle. Rain or drizzle that freezes on contact is known as freezing rain or freezing drizzle. Solid or frozen forms of precipitation include snow, ice needles or diamond dust, sleet or ice pellets, hail, and graupel or snow pellets. Virga is a form of precipitation that evaporates before reaching the ground. It usually looks like sheets or shafts falling from a cloud. The amount of rainfall is measured with a rain gauge. Intensity can be measured according to how fast precipitation is falling or by how severely it limits visibility. Precipitation plays a major role in the water cycle since it is responsible for depositing much of the Earth's fresh water.

Air Masses

Air masses are large volumes of air in the troposphere of the Earth. They are categorized by their temperature and by the amount of water vapor they contain. Arctic and Antarctic air masses are cold, polar air masses are cool, and tropical and equatorial air masses are hot. Other types of air masses include maritime and monsoon, both of which are moist and unstable. There are also continental and superior air masses, which are dry. A weather front separates two masses of air of different densities. It is the principal cause of meteorological phenomena. Air masses are quickly and easily affected by the land they are above. They can have certain characteristics, and then develop new ones when they get blown over a different area.

Bergeron Classification System

The Bergeron classification system uses three sets of letters to identify the following characteristics of air masses: moisture content, thermal characteristics from where they originated, and the stability of the atmosphere. The first, moisture content, uses the following letters: "c" represents the dry continental air masses and "m" stands for the moist maritime air masses. The second set of abbreviations are as follows: "T" indicates the air mass is tropical in origin; "P" indicates the air mass is polar in origin; "A" indicates the air mass is Antarctic in origin; "M" stands for monsoon; "E" indicates the air mass is equatorial in origin; and "S" is used to represent superior air, which is dry air formed by a downward motion. The last set of symbols provides an indicator of the stability of the mass. "K" indicates the mass is colder than the ground below it, while "w" indicates the mass is warmer than the ground. For example, cP is a continental polar air mass, while cPk is a polar air mass blowing over the Gulf Stream, which is warmer than the mass.

High and Low-Pressure Systems

The concept of atmospheric pressure involves the idea that air exerts a force. An imaginary column of air 1 square inch in size rising through the atmosphere would exert a force of 14.7 pounds per square inch (psi). Both temperature and altitude affect atmospheric pressure. Low and high pressure systems tend to want to equalize. Air tends to move from areas of high pressure to areas of low pressure. When air moves into a low pressure system, the air that was there gets pushed up, creating lower temperatures and pressures. Water vapor condenses and forms clouds and possibly rain and snow. A barometer is used to measure air pressure.

Weather Fronts and Weather Maps

A weather front is the area between two differing masses of air that affects weather. Frontal movements are influenced by the jet stream and other high winds. Movements are determined by the type of front. Cold fronts move up to twice as fast as warm ones. It is in the turbulent frontal area that commonplace and dramatic weather events take place. This area also creates temperature changes. Weather phenomena include rain, thunderstorms, high winds, tornadoes, cloudiness, clear skies, and hurricanes. Different fronts can be plotted on weather maps using a set of designated symbols. Surface weather maps can also include symbols representing clouds, rain, temperature, air pressure, and fair weather.

COLD, WARM, STATIONARY, AND OCCLUDED FRONTS

A cold front is a mass of cold air, usually fast moving and dense, that moves into a warm air front, producing clouds. This often produces a temperature drop and rain, hail (frozen rain), thunder, and lightning. A warm front is pushed up by a fast moving cold front. It is often associated with high wispy clouds, such as cirrus and cirrostratus clouds. A stationary front forms when a warm and cold front meet, but neither is strong enough to move the other. Winds blowing parallel to the fronts keep the front stationary. The front may remain in the same place for days until the wind direction changes and both fronts become a single warm or cold front. In other cases, the entire front dissipates. An occluded front is when a cold front pushes into a warm front. The warm air rises and the two masses of cool air join. These types of fronts often occur in areas of low atmospheric pressure.

FRONT-RELATED WEATHER PHENOMENA

The following are front-related weather phenomena:

- Shearline: This evolves from a stationary front that has gotten smaller. Wind direction shifts over a short distance.
- Dry line or dew point line: This separates two warm air masses of differing moisture content. At lower altitudes, the moist air mass wedges under the drier air. At higher altitudes, the dry air wedges under the moist air. This is a frequent occurrence in the Midwest and Canada, where the dry air of the Southwest and the moister air of the Gulf of Mexico meet. This can lead to extreme weather events, including tornadoes and thunderstorms.
- Squall line: Severe thunderstorms can form at the front of or ahead of a cold front. In some cases, severe thunderstorms can also outrun cold fronts. A squall line can produce extreme weather in the form of heavy rain, hail, lightning, strong winds, tornadoes, and waterspouts.
- Tropical waves or easterly waves: These are atmospheric troughs or areas of low air pressure that travel westward in the tropics, causing clouds and thunderstorms.

FRONTAL SYSTEMS ON WEATHER MAPS

Cold fronts are represented on weather maps as a blue line. Solid blue triangles are used to indicate the direction of movement. Warm fronts are represented with a red line. Solid red semi-circles are used to indicate the direction of the front. The cold and warm front symbols are merged and alternated to point in opposite directions to indicate a stationary front. An occluded front is represented by a purple line with alternating solid purple triangles and semi-circles. A surface trough is represented by an orange dashed line. A squall or shear line is represented by a red line. Two dots and a dash are alternated to form the line. A dry line is represented by an orange line with semi-circles in outline form. A tropical wave is represented by a straight orange line. An "L" is used to indicate an area of low atmospheric pressure and an "H" is used to indicate an area of high atmospheric pressure.

SHORT AND LONG-TERM WEATHER FORECASTING

Short and long-term weather forecasting is important because the day-to-day weather greatly affects humans and human activity. Severe weather and natural events can cause devastating harm to humans, property, and sources of livelihood, such as crops. The persistence method of forecasting can be used to create both short and long-term forecasts in areas that change very little or change slowly. It assumes that the weather tomorrow will be similar to the weather today. Barometric pressure is measured because a change in air pressure can indicate the arrival of a cold front that could lead to precipitation. Long-term forecasts based on climate data are useful to help people prepare for seasonal changes and severe events such as hurricanes.

ASTRONOMY

Astronomy is the scientific study of celestial objects and their positions, movements, and structures. Celestial does not refer to the Earth by itself, but does include its movement through space. Other celestial objects include the Sun, the Moon, planets, satellites, asteroids, meteors, comets, stars, galaxies, the universe, and other space phenomena. The term astronomy has its roots in the Greek words "astro" and "nomos," which means "laws of the stars."

UNIVERSE

What can be seen of the universe is believed to be at least 93 billion light years across. To put this into perspective, the Milky Way galaxy is about 100,000 light years across. Our view of matter in the universe is that it forms into clumps which become stars, galaxies, clusters of galaxies, superclusters, and the Great Wall of galaxies. Galaxies consist of stars, some with planetary systems. Some estimates state that the universe is about 13 billion years old. It is not considered dense and is believed to consist of 73% dark energy, 23% cold dark matter, and 4% regular matter. Cosmology is the study of the universe. Interstellar medium (ISM) is the gas and dust in the interstellar space between a galaxy's stars.

ORIGIN

The universe can be said to consist of everything and nothing. The universe contains all of space, matter, energy, and time. There are likely still phenomena that have yet to be discovered. The universe can also be thought of as nothing, since a vast portion of the known universe is empty space. It is believed that the universe is expanding. The Big Bang theory, which is widely accepted among astronomers, was developed to explain the origin of the universe. There are other theories regarding the origin of the universe, such as the Steady-State theory and the Creationist theory. The Big Bang theory states that all the matter in the universe was once in one place. This matter underwent a huge explosion that spread it into space. Galaxies formed from, this material and the universe is still expanding.

GALAXIES

Galaxies consist of stars, stellar remnants, and dark matter. Dwarf galaxies contain as few as 10 million stars, while giant galaxies contain as many as 1 trillion stars. Galaxies are gravitationally bound, meaning that stars, star systems, other gases, and dust orbit the galaxy's center. The Earth exists in the Milky Way galaxy and the nearest galaxy to ours is the Andromeda galaxy. Galaxies can be classified by their visual shape into elliptical, spiral, irregular, and starburst galaxies. It is estimated that there are more than 100 billion galaxies in the universe ranging from 1,000 to 100,000 parsecs in diameter. Galaxies can be megaparsecs apart. Intergalactic space consists of a gas with an average density of less than one atom per cubic meter. Galaxies are organized into clusters which form superclusters. Dark matter may account for up to 90% of the mass of galaxies. Dark matter is still not well understood.

SOLAR SYSTEM

Our solar system is a planetary system of objects that exist in an ecliptic plane. Objects orbit around and are bound by gravity to a star called the Sun. Objects that orbit around the Sun include: planets, dwarf planets, moons, asteroids, meteoroids, cosmic dust, and comets. The definition of planets has changed. At one time, there were nine planets in the solar system, but due to the change in the definition of planets, there are now eight. Planetary objects in the solar system include four inner, terrestrial planets: Mercury, Venus, Earth, and Mars. They are relatively small, dense, rocky, lack rings, and have few or no moons. The four outer, or Jovian, planets are Jupiter, Saturn, Uranus, and Neptune, which are large and have low densities, rings, and moons. They are also known as gas giants. Between the inner and outer planets is the asteroid belt. Beyond Neptune is the Kuiper belt. Within these belts are five dwarf planets: Ceres, Pluto, Haumea, Makemake, and Eris.

Review Video: The Solar System
Visit mometrix.com/academy and enter code: 273231

SIZE

The Earth is about 12,765 km (7,934 miles) in diameter. The Moon is about 3,476 km (2,160 mi) in diameter. The distance between the Earth and the Moon is about 384,401 km (238,910 mi). The diameter of the Sun is approximately 1,390,000 km (866,000 mi). The distance from the Earth to the Sun is 149,598,000 km, also known as 1 Astronomical Unit (AU). The star that is nearest to the solar system is Proxima Centauri. It is about 270,000 AU away. Some distant galaxies are so far away that their light takes several billion years to reach the Earth. In other words, people on Earth see them as they looked billions of years ago.

FORMATION THEORIES

A planetary system consists of the various non-stellar objects orbiting a star, such as planets, dwarf planets, moons, asteroids, meteoroids, comets, and cosmic dust. The Sun, together with its planetary system, which includes Earth, is known as the solar system. The theory of how the solar system was created is that it started with the collapse of a cloud of interstellar gas and dust, which formed the solar nebula. This collapse is believed to have occurred because the cloud was disturbed. As it collapsed, it heated up and compressed at the center, forming a flatter protoplanetary disk with a protostar at the center. Planets formed as a result of accretion from the disk. Gas cooled and condensed into tiny particles of rock, metal, and ice. These particles collided and formed into larger particles, and then into object the size of small asteroids. Eventually, some became large enough to have significant gravity.

SUN

The Sun is at the center of the solar system. It is composed of 70% hydrogen (H) and 28% helium (He). The remaining 2% is made up of metals. The Sun is one of 100 billion stars in the Milky Way galaxy. Its diameter is 1,390,000 km, its mass is 1.989×10^{30} kg, its surface temperature is 5,800 K, and its core temperature is 15,600,000 K. The Sun represents more than 99.8% of the total mass of the solar system. At the core, the temperature is 15.6 million K, the pressure is 250 billion atmospheres, and the density is more than 150 times that of water. The surface is called the photosphere. The chromosphere lies above this, and the corona, which extends millions of kilometers into space, is next. Sunspots are relatively cool regions on the surface with a temperature of 3,800 K. Temperatures in the corona are over 1,000,000 K. Its magnetosphere, or heliosphere, extends far beyond Pluto.

ENERGY

The Sun's energy is produced by nuclear fusion reactions. Each second, about 700,000,000 tons of hydrogen are converted (or fused) to about 695,000,000 tons of helium and 5,000,000 tons of energy in the form of gamma rays. In nuclear fusion, four hydrogen nuclei are fused into one helium nucleus, resulting in the release of energy. In the Sun, the energy proceeds towards the surface and is absorbed and re-emitted at lower and lower temperatures. Energy is mostly in the form of visible light when it reaches the surface. It is estimated that the Sun has used up about half of the hydrogen at its core since its birth. It is expected to radiate in this fashion for another 5 billion years. Eventually, it will deplete its hydrogen fuel, grow brighter, expand to about 260 times its diameter, and become a red giant. The outer layers will ablate and become a dense white dwarf the size of the Earth.

Inner Terrestrial Planets

The four inner terrestrial planets are:

- Mercury: Mercury is the closest planet to the Sun and is also the smallest planet. It orbits the Sun every 88 days, has no satellites or atmosphere, has a Moon-like surface with craters, appears bright, and is dense and rocky with a large iron core.
- Venus: Venus is the second planet from the Sun. It orbits the Sun every 225 days, is very bright, and is similar to Earth in size, gravity, and bulk composition. It has a dense atmosphere composed of carbon dioxide and some sulfur. It is covered with reflective clouds made of sulfuric acid and exhibits signs of volcanism. Lightning and thunder have been recorded on Venus's surface.
- Earth: Earth is the third planet from the Sun. It orbits the Sun every 365 days. Approximately 71% of its surface is salt-water oceans. The Earth is rocky, has an atmosphere composed mainly of oxygen and nitrogen, has one moon, and supports millions of species. It contains the only known life in the solar system.
- Mars: Mars is the fourth planet from the Sun. It appears reddish due to iron oxide on the surface, has a thin atmosphere, has a rotational period similar to Earth's, and has seasonal cycles. Surface features of Mars include volcanoes, valleys, deserts, and polar ice caps. Mars has impact craters and the tallest mountain, largest canyon, and perhaps the largest impact crater yet discovered.

Gas Giant Planets

The four outer, gas giant planets are:

- Jupiter: Jupiter is the fifth planet from the Sun and the largest planet in the solar system. It consists mainly of hydrogen, and 25% of its mass is made up of helium. It has a fast rotation and has clouds in the tropopause composed of ammonia crystals that are arranged into bands sub-divided into lighter-hued zones and darker belts causing storms and turbulence. Jupiter has wind speeds of 100 m/s, a planetary ring, 63 moons, and a Great Red Spot, which is an anticyclonic storm.
- Saturn: Saturn is the sixth planet from the Sun and the second largest planet in the solar system. It is composed of hydrogen, some helium, and trace elements. Saturn has a small core of rock and ice, a thick layer of metallic hydrogen, a gaseous outer layer, wind speeds of up to 1,800 km/h, a system of rings, and 61 moons.
- Uranus: Uranus is the seventh planet from the Sun. Its atmosphere is composed mainly of hydrogen and helium, and also contains water, ammonia, methane, and traces of hydrocarbons. With a minimum temperature of 49 K, Uranus has the coldest atmosphere. Uranus has a ring system, a magnetosphere, and 13 moons.
- Neptune: Neptune is the eighth planet from the Sun and is the planet with the third largest mass. It has 12 moons, an atmosphere similar to Uranus, a Great Dark Spot, and the strongest sustained winds of any planet (wind speeds can be as high as 2,100 km/h). Neptune is cold (about 55 K) and has a fragmented ring system.

PHASES OF THE MOON

It takes about one month for the Moon to go through all its phases. Waxing refers to the two weeks during which the Moon goes from a new moon to a full moon. About two weeks is spent waning, going from a full moon to a new moon. The lit part of the Moon always faces the Sun.

The phases of waxing are:

- **New moon**, during which the Moon is not illuminated and rises and sets with the Sun.
- **Waxing crescent**, during which a tiny sliver is lit.
- **First quarter**, during which half the Moon is lit and the phase of the Moon is due south on the meridian.
- **Waxing gibbous**, during which more than half of the Moon is lit and has a shape similar to a football.
- **Full moon**, during which the Moon is fully illuminated, rises at sunset, and sets at sunrise.

After a full moon, the Moon is waning. The phases of waning are:

- **Waning gibbous**, during which the left side is lit and the Moon rises after sunset and sets after sunrise.
- **Third quarter**, during which the Moon is half lit and rises at midnight and sets at noon.
- **Waning crescent**, during which a tiny sliver is lit.

New moon, which starts the cycle over.

STARS

BIRTH

A nebula is a cloud of dust and gas that is composed primarily of hydrogen (97%) and helium (3%). Gravity causes parts of the nebula to clump together. This accretion continues adding atoms to the center of an unstable protostar. Equilibrium between gravity pulling atoms and gas pressure pushing heat and light away from the center is achieved. A star dies when it is no longer able to maintain equilibrium. A protostar may never become a star if it does not reach a critical core temperature. It may become a brown dwarf or a gas giant instead. If nuclear fusion of hydrogen into helium begins, a star is born. The "main sequence" of a star's life involves nuclear fusion reactions. During this time, the star contracts over billions of years to compensate for the heat and light energy lost. In the star's core, temperature, density, and pressure increase as the star contracts and the cycle continues.

LIFE CYCLE

There are different life cycle possibilities for stars after they initially form and enter into the main sequence stage. Small, relatively cold red dwarfs with relatively low masses burn hydrogen slowly, and will remain in the main sequence for hundreds of billions of years. Massive, hot supergiants will leave the main sequence after just a few million years. The Sun is a mid-sized star that may be in the main sequence for 10 billion years. After the main sequence, the star expands to become a red giant. Depending upon the initial mass of the star, it can become a black dwarf (from a medium-sized star), and then a small, cooling white dwarf. Massive stars become red supergiants (and sometimes blue supergiants), explode in a supernova, and then become neutron stars. The largest stars can become black holes.

Astronomical Unit, Light Year, and Parsec

An astronomical unit, also known as AU, is a widely used measurement in astronomy. One AU is equal to the distance from the Earth to the Sun, which is 150 million km, or 93 million miles. These distances can also be expressed as 149.60×10^9 m or 92.956×10^6 mi. A light year (ly) is the distance that light travels in a vacuum in one year. A light year is equal to about 10 trillion km, or 64,341 AU, and is used to measure large astronomical units. Also used for measuring large distances is the parsec (pc), which is the preferred unit since it is better suited for recording observational data. A parsec is the parallax of one arcsecond, and is about 31 trillion km (about 19 trillion miles), or about 3.26 light years. It is used to calculate distances by triangulation. The AU distance from the Earth to the Sun is used to form the side of a right triangle.

Sidereal Days and Solar Days

A sidereal day is four minutes shorter than a solar day. A solar day is the time it takes the Earth to complete one revolution and face the Sun again. From noon to noon is 24 hours. A sidereal day is measured against a distant "fixed" star. As the Earth completes one rotation, it has also completed part of its revolution around the Sun, so it completes a sidereal rotation in reference to the fixed star before it completes a solar rotation. The Sun travels along the ecliptic in 365.25 days. This can be tracked day after day before dawn. After one year, the stars appear back in their original positions. As a result, different constellations are viewable at different times of the year. Sidereal years are slightly longer than tropical years. The difference is caused by the precession of the equinoxes. A calendar based on the sidereal year will be out of sync with the seasons at a rate of about one day every 71 years.

Oort Cloud, the Asteroid Belt, and the Kuiper Belt

The asteroid belt is between Mars and Jupiter. The many objects contained within are composed of rock and metal similar to those found on the terrestrial planets. The Kuiper Belt is beyond Neptune's orbit, but the influence of the gas giants may cause objects from the Kuiper Belt to cross Neptune's orbit. Objects in the Kuiper Belt are still being discovered. They are thought to be composed of the frozen forms of water, ammonia, and methane, and may be the source of short-period comets. It is estimated that there are 35,000 Kuiper Belt objects greater than 100 km in diameter and perhaps 100 million objects about 20 km in diameter. There is also a hypothetical Oort Cloud that may exist far beyond the Kuiper Belt and act as a source for long-period comets.

Comets

A comet consists of frozen gases and rocky and metallic materials. Comets are usually small and typically have long tails. A comet's tail is made of ionized gases. It points away from the Sun and follows the comet as it approaches the Sun. The tail precedes the head as the comet moves away from the Sun. It is believed that as many as 100 billion comets exist. About 12 new ones are discovered each year. Their orbits are elliptical, not round. Some scientists theorize that short-period comets originate from the Kuiper Belt and long-period comets originate from the Oort Cloud, which is thought to be 100,000 AU away. Comets orbit the Sun in time periods varying from a few years to hundreds of thousands of years. A well-known comet, Halley's Comet, has an orbit of 76 years. It is 80 percent water, and consists of frozen water, carbon dioxide (dry ice), ammonia, and methane.

Meteors, Meteoroids, and Meteorites

A meteoroid is the name for a rock from space before it enters the Earth's atmosphere. Most meteoroids burn up in the atmosphere before reaching altitudes of 80 km. A meteor is the streak of light from a meteoroid in the Earth's atmosphere, and is also known as a shooting star. Meteor showers are associated with comets, happen when the Earth passes through the debris of a comet, and are associated with a higher than normal number of meteors. Meteorites are rocks that reach the Earth's surface from space. Fireballs are very bright meteors with trails that can last as long as 30 minutes. A bolide is a fireball that burns up when it enters Earth's atmosphere. There are many types of meteorites, and they are known to be composed of various materials. Iron meteorites consist of iron and nickel with a criss-cross, or Widmanstatten, internal metallic crystalline structure. Stony iron meteorites are composed of iron, nickel, and silicate materials. Stony meteorites consist mainly of silicate and also contain iron and nickel.

NATURAL SATELLITES

There are about 335 moons, or satellites, that orbit the planets and objects in the solar system. Many of these satellites have been recently discovered, a few are theoretical, some are asteroid moons (moons orbiting asteroids), some are moonlets (small moons), and some are moons of dwarf planets and objects that have not been definitively categorized, such as trans-Neptunian objects. Mercury and Venus do not have any moons. There are several moons larger than the dwarf planet Pluto and two larger than Mercury. Some consider the Earth and Moon a pair of double planets rather than a planet and a satellite. Some satellites may have started out as asteroids. They were eventually captured by a planet's gravity and became moons.

GEOMETRY OF THE EARTH-MOON-SUN SYSTEM

The Earth-Moon-Sun system is responsible for eclipses. From Earth, the Sun and the Moon appear to be about the same size. An eclipse of the Sun occurs during a new Moon, when the side of the Moon facing the Earth is not illuminated. The Moon passes in front of the Sun and blocks its view from Earth. Eclipses do not occur every month because the orbit of the Moon is at about a 5° angle to the plane of Earth's orbit. An eclipse of the Moon happens during the full Moon phase. The Moon passes through the shadow of the Earth and blocks sunlight from reaching it, which temporarily causes darkness. During a lunar eclipse, there are two parts to the shadow. The umbra is the dark, inner region. The sun is completely blocked in this area. The penumbra is a partially lighted area around the umbra. Earth's shadow is four times longer than the Moon's shadow.

REMOTE SENSING

Remote sensing refers to the gathering of data about an object or phenomenon without physical or intimate contact with the object being studied. The data can be viewed or recorded and stored in many forms (visually with a camera, audibly, or in the form of data). Gathering weather data from a ship, satellite, or buoy might be thought of as remote sensing. The monitoring of a fetus through the use of ultrasound technology provides a remote image. Listening to the heartbeat of a fetus is another example of remote sensing. Methods for remote sensing can be grouped as radiometric, geodetic, or acoustic. Examples of radiometric remote sensing include radar, laser altimeters, light detection and ranging (LIDAR) used to determine the concentration of chemicals in the air, and radiometers used to detect various frequencies of radiation. Geodetic remote sensing involves measuring the small fluctuations in Earth's gravitational field. Examples of acoustic remote sensing include underwater sonar and seismographs.

GEOSYNCHRONOUS AND GEOSTATIONARY ORBITS

A geosynchronous orbit around the Earth has an orbital period matching the Earth's sidereal rotation period. Sidereal rotation is based on the position of a fixed star, not the Sun, so a sidereal day is slightly shorter than a 24-hour solar day. A satellite in a geosynchronous orbit appears in the same place in the sky at the same time each day. Technically, any object with an orbit time period equal to the Earth's rotational period is geosynchronous. A geostationary orbit is a geosynchronous orbit that is circular and at zero inclination, which means the object is located directly above the equator. Geostationary orbits are useful for communications satellites because they are fixed in the same spot relative to the Earth. A semisynchronous orbit has an orbital period of half a sidereal day.

Notable Satellites

The first satellite to orbit the Earth was the Soviet Union's Sputnik 1 in 1957. Its two radio transmitters emitted beeps that were received by radios around the world. Analysis of the radio signals was used to gather information about the electron density of the ionosphere. Soviet success escalated the American space program. In 1958, the US put Explorer 1 into orbit. The Osumi was the first Japanese satellite, which was put into orbit in 1970. The Vanguard 1 is the satellite that has orbited the Earth the longest. It was put into orbit in 1958 and was still in orbit in June, 2009. The Mir Space Station orbited Earth for 11 years, and was assembled in space starting in 1986. It was almost continuously occupied until 1999. The International Space Station began being assembled in orbit in 1998. At 43,000 cubic feet, it is the largest manned object sent into space. It circles the Earth every 90 minutes.

Piloted Space Missions

The Soviet space program successfully completed the first space flight by orbiting Yuri Gagarin in 1961 on Vostok 1. His orbit lasted 1 hour, 48 minutes. Later in 1961, the US completed its first piloted space flight by launching Alan Shepard into space in the Mercury-Redstone 3. This space mission was suborbital. The first woman in space was Valentina Tereshkova, who orbited the Earth 48 times aboard Vostok 6 in 1963. The first space flight with more than one person and also the first that didn't involve space suits took place on the Voskhod in 1964. The first person on the Moon was American Neil Armstrong. In 1969, he traveled to the Moon on Apollo 11, which was the 11th manned space flight completed in the Apollo program, which was conducted from 1968 to 1972. In 2003, Yang Liwei became the first person from China to go into space. He traveled onboard the Shenzhou 5. The Space Shuttle Orbiter has included piloted space shuttles from 1981 until the present. The program was suspended after two space shuttle disasters: Challenger in 1986 and Columbia in 2003.

Unpiloted Space Missions

The first artificial object to reach another space object was Luna 2. It crashed on the Moon in 1959. The first automatic landing was by Luna 9. It landed on the Moon in 1966. Mariner 2's flyby of Venus in 1962 was the first successful interplanetary flyby. Venera 7 landing on and transmitting data from Venus was the first interplanetary surface landing, which took place in 1970. The first soft landing on Mars was in 1971. Unpiloted spacecraft have also made successful soft landings on the asteroids Eros and Itokawa, as well as Titan, a moon of Saturn. The first flyby of Jupiter was in 1973 by Pioneer 10. Pioneer 10 was also the first craft of its kind to leave the solar system. The first flyby of Mercury was in 1974 by Mariner. The first flyby of Saturn was in 1979 by Pioneer 11. The first flyby of Uranus was in 1986 by Voyager 2, which also flew by Neptune in 1989.

Limitations of Space Exploration

There are many limitations of space exploration. The main limitation is knowledge. Space exploration is currently time-consuming, dangerous, and costly. Manned and unmanned missions, even within the solar system, take years of planning and years to complete. The associated financial costs are great. Interstellar travel and intergalactic is not yet realistically feasible. Technological advances are needed before these types of missions can be carried out. By some estimates, it would take more than 70 years to travel to Proxima Centauri (the nearest star) using the fastest rocket technology available. It would take much longer using less advanced technologies. Space travel is dangerous for many reasons. Rocket fuel is highly explosive. Non-Earth environments are uninhabitable for humans. Finally, astronauts are exposed to larger than usual amounts of radiation.

Life Sciences

The Cell

Cell Theory

The basic tenets of cell theory are that all living things are made up of cells and that cell are the basic units of life. Cell theory has evolved over time and is subject to interpretation. The development of cell theory is attributed to Matthias Schleiden and Theodor Schwann, who developed the theory in the early 1800s. Early cell theory was comprised of four statements: all organisms (living things) are made of cells; new cells are formed from pre-existing cells; all cells are similar; and cells are the most basic units of life. Other concepts related to classic and modern cell theory include statements such as: cells provide the basic units of functionality and structure in living things; cells are both distinct stand-alone units and basic building blocks; energy flow occurs within cells; cells contain genetic information in the form of DNA; and all cells consist of mostly the same chemicals.

Cell Structures

Cell structures are listed and described below:

- Cytosol: This is the liquid material in the cell. It is mostly water, but also contains some floating molecules.
- Cytoplasm: This is a general term that refers to cytosol and the substructures (organelles) found within the plasma membrane, but not within the nucleus.
- Cell membrane (plasma membrane): This defines the cell by acting as a barrier. It helps keeps cytoplasm in and substances located outside the cell out. It also determines what is allowed to enter and exit the cell.
- Endoplasmic reticulum: The two types of endoplasmic reticulum are rough (has ribosomes on the surface) and smooth (does not have ribosomes on the surface). It is a tubular network that comprises the transport system of a cell. It is fused to the nuclear membrane and extends through the cytoplasm to the cell membrane.
- Mitochondrion (pl. mitochondria): These cell structures vary in terms of size and quantity. Some cells may have one mitochondrion, while others have thousands. This structure performs various functions such as generating ATP, and is also involved in cell growth and death. Mitochondria contain their own DNA that is separate from that contained in the nucleus.
- Ribosomes: Ribosomes are involved in synthesizing proteins from amino acids. They are numerous, making up about one quarter of the cell. Some cells contain thousands of ribosomes. Some are mobile and some are embedded in the rough endoplasmic reticulum.
- Golgi complex (Golgi apparatus): This is involved in synthesizing materials such as proteins that are transported out of the cell. It is located near the nucleus and consists of layers of membranes.
- Vacuoles: These are sacs used for storage, digestion, and waste removal. There is one large vacuole in plant cells. Animal cells have small, sometimes numerous vacuoles.

- Vesicle: This is a small organelle within a cell. It has a membrane and performs varying functions, including moving materials within a cell.
- Cytoskeleton: This consists of microtubules that help shape and support the cell.
- Microtubules: These are part of the cytoskeleton and help support the cell. They are made of protein.

Review Video: Cell Structure
Visit mometrix.com/academy and enter code: 591293

PLANT VS. ANIMAL CELLS

The functions of plant and animal cells vary greatly, and the functions of different cells within a single organism can also be vastly different. Animal and plant cells are similar in structure in that they are eukaryotic, which means they contain a nucleus. The nucleus is a round structure that controls the activities of the cell and contains chromosomes. Both types of cells have cell membranes, cytoplasm, vacuoles, and other structures. The main difference between the two is that plant cells have a cell wall made of cellulose that can handle high levels of pressure within the cell, which can occur when liquid enters a plant cell. Plant cells have chloroplasts that are used during the process of photosynthesis, which is the conversion of sunlight into food. Plant cells usually have one large vacuole, whereas animal cells can have many smaller ones. Plant cells have a regular shape, while the shapes of animal cells can vary.

Plant cells can be much larger than animal cells, ranging from 10 to 100 micrometers. Animal cells are 10 to 30 micrometers in size. Plant cells can have much larger vacuoles that occupy a large portion of the cell. They also have cell walls, which are thick barriers consisting of protein and sugars. Animal cells lack cell walls. Chloroplasts in plants that perform photosynthesis absorb sunlight and convert it into energy. Mitochondria produce energy from food in animal cells. Plant and animal cells are both eukaryotic, meaning they contain a nucleus. Both plant and animal cells duplicate genetic material, separate it, and then divide in half to reproduce. Plant cells build a cell plate between the two new cells, while animal cells make a cleavage furrow and pinch in half. Microtubules are components of the cytoskeleton in both plant and animal cells. Microtubule organizing centers (MTOCs) make microtubules in plant cells, while centrioles make microtubules in animal cells.

ANIMAL CELL STRUCTURES

The following structures are unique to animal cells:

- Centrosome: This is comprised of the pair of centrioles located at right angles to each other and surrounded by protein. The centrosome is involved in mitosis and the cell cycle.
- Centriole: These are cylinder-shaped structures near the nucleus that are involved in cellular division. Each cylinder consists of nine groups of three microtubules. Centrioles occur in pairs.
- Lysosome: This digests proteins, lipids, and carbohydrates, and also transports undigested substances to the cell membrane so they can be removed. The shape of a lysosome depends on the material being transported.
- Cilia (singular: cilium): These are appendages extending from the surface of the cell, the movement of which causes the cell to move. They can also result in fluid being moved by the cell.
- Flagella: These are tail-like structures on cells that use whip-like movements to help the cell move. They are similar to cilia, but are usually longer and not as numerous. A cell usually only has one or a few flagella.

PLANT CELL STRUCTURES

The following structures are unique to plant cells:

- Cell wall: Made of cellulose and composed of numerous layers, the cell wall provides plants with a sturdy barrier that can hold fluid within the cell. The cell wall surrounds the cell membrane.
- Chloroplast: This is a specialized organelle that plant cells use for photosynthesis, which is the process plants use to create food energy from sunlight. Chloroplasts contain chlorophyll, which has a green color.
- Plastid: This is a membrane-bound organelle found in plant cells that is used to make chemical compounds and store food. It can also contain pigments used during photosynthesis. Plastids can develop into more specialized structures such as chloroplasts, chromoplasts (make and hold yellow and orange pigments), amyloplasts (store starch), and leucoplasts (lack pigments, but can become differentiated).
- Plasmodesmata (sing. plasmodesma): These are channels between the cell walls of plant cells that allow for transport between cells.

EUKARYOTIC AND PROKARYOTIC CELLS

The main difference between eukaryotic and prokaryotic cells is that eukaryotic cells have a nucleus and prokaryotic cells do not. Eukaryotic cells are considered more complex, while prokaryotic cells are smaller and simpler. Eukaryotic cells have membrane-bound organelles that perform various functions and contribute to the complexity of these types of cells. Prokaryotic cells do not contain membrane-bound organelles. In prokaryotic cells, the genetic material (DNA) is not contained within a membrane-bound nucleus. Instead, it aggregates in the cytoplasm in a nucleoid. In eukaryotic cells, DNA is mostly contained in chromosomes in the nucleus, although there is some DNA in mitochondria and chloroplasts. Prokaryotic cells usually divide by binary fission and are haploid. Eukaryotic cells divide by mitosis and are diploid. Prokaryotic structures include plasmids, ribosomes, cytoplasm, a cytoskeleton, granules of nutritional substances, a plasma membrane, flagella, and a few others. Prokaryotic cells are single celled organisms, such as bacteria, which are classified as prokaryotes.

The following are nuclear parts of a eukaryotic cell:

- Nucleus (pl. nuclei): This is a small structure that contains the chromosomes and regulates the DNA of a cell. The nucleus is the defining structure of eukaryotic cells, and all eukaryotic cells have a nucleus. The nucleus is responsible for the passing on of genetic traits between generations. The nucleus contains a nuclear envelope, nucleoplasm, a nucleolus, nuclear pores, chromatin, and ribosomes.
- Chromosomes: These are highly condensed, threadlike rods of DNA. Short for deoxyribonucleic acid, DNA is the genetic material that stores information about the plant or animal.
- Chromatin: This consists of the DNA and protein that make up chromosomes.
- Nucleolus (nucleole): This structure contained within the nucleus consists of protein. It is small, round, does not have a membrane, is involved in protein synthesis, and synthesizes and stores RNA (ribonucleic acid).
- Nuclear envelope: This encloses the structures of the nucleus. It consists of inner and outer membranes made of lipids.
- Nuclear pores: These are involved in the exchange of material between the nucleus and the cytoplasm.
- Nucleoplasm: This is the liquid within the nucleus, and is similar to cytoplasm.

Cellular Respiration

Cellular respiration refers to a set of metabolic reactions that convert chemical bonds into energy stored in the form of ATP. Respiration includes many oxidation and reduction reactions that occur thanks to the electron transport system within the cell. Oxidation is a loss of electrons and reduction is a gain of electrons. Electrons in C-H (carbon/hydrogen) and C-C (carbon/carbon) bonds are donated to oxygen atoms. Processes involved in cellular respiration include glycolysis, the Krebs cycle, the electron transport chain, and chemiosmosis. The two forms of respiration are aerobic and anaerobic. Aerobic respiration is very common, and oxygen is the final electron acceptor. In anaerobic respiration, the final electron acceptor is not oxygen. Aerobic respiration results in more ATP than anaerobic respiration. Fermentation is another process by which energy is converted.

Sizes of Cells and Organelles

The size of the nucleus in a eukaryotic cell is about 6 micrometers (μm). It occupies about 10 percent of the cell. A chloroplast is about 1 μm. Plant and animal cell sizes range from about 10 μm to 100 μm, while the sizes of bacteria range from about 1 μm to 10 μm. Atoms have a size of about 0.1 nanometers.

Cell Division

Cell division is performed in organisms so they can grow and replace cells that are old, worn out, or damaged.

- Chromatids: During cell division, the DNA is replicated, and chromatids are the two identical replicated pieces of chromosome that are joined at the centromere to form an "X."
- Gametes: These are cells used by organisms to reproduce sexually. Gametes in humans are haploid, meaning they contain only half of the organism's genetic information (23 chromosomes). Other human cells contain all 46 chromosomes.
- Haploid/diploid: Haploid means there is one set of chromosomes. Diploid means there are two sets of chromosomes (one set from each parent).
- Cytokinesis: This is the splitting of a cell (including the cytoplasm) into two cells. Some believe this occurs following telophase. Others say it occurs from anaphase, as the cell begins to furrow, through telophase, when the cell actually splits into two.

Metabolism, Macromolecules, Metabolic Pathways, and Anabolic and Catabolic Reactions

Metabolism is all of the chemical reactions that take place within a living organism. These chemical changes convert nutrients to energy and macromolecules. Macromolecules are large and complex, and play an important role in cell structure and function. Metabolic pathways refer to a series of reactions in which the product of one reaction is the substrate for the next. These pathways are dependent upon enzymes that act as catalysts. An anabolic reaction is one that builds larger and more complex molecules (macromolecules) from smaller ones. Catabolic reactions are the opposite. Larger molecules are broken down into smaller, simpler molecules. Catabolic reactions release energy, while anabolic ones require energy. The four basic organic macromolecules produced by anabolic reactions are carbohydrates (polysaccharides), nucleic acids, proteins, and lipids. The four basic building blocks involved in catabolic reactions are monosaccharides (glucose), amino acids, fatty acids (glycerol), and nucleotides.

Glycolysis

In glycolysis, glucose is converted into pyruvate and energy stored in ATP bonds is released. Glycolysis can involve various pathways. Various intermediates are produced that are used in other processes, and the pyruvic acid produced by glycolysis can be further used for respiration by the Krebs cycle or in fermentation. Glycolysis occurs in both aerobic and anaerobic organisms. Oxidation of molecules produces reduced coenzymes, such as NADH. The coenzymes relocate hydrogens to the electron transport chain. The proton is transported through the cell membrane and the electron is transported down the chain by proteins. At the end of the chain, water is formed when the final acceptor releases two electrons that combine with oxygen. The protons are pumped back into the cell or organelle by the ATP synthase enzyme, which uses energy produced to add a phosphate to ADP to form ATP. The proton motive force is produced by the protons being moved across the membrane.

Krebs Cycle

The Krebs cycle is also called the citric acid cycle or the tricarboxylic acid cycle (TCA). It is a catabolic pathway in which the bonds of glucose and occasionally fats or lipids are broken down and reformed into ATP. It is a respiration process that uses oxygen and produces carbon dioxide, water, and ATP. Cells require energy from ATP to synthesize proteins from amino acids and replicate DNA. The cycle is acetyl CoA, citric acid, isocitric acid, ketoglutaric acid (products are amino acids and CO_2), succinyl CoA, succinic acid, fumaric acid, malic acid, and oxaloacetic acid. One of the products of the Krebs cycle is NADH, which is then used in the electron chain transport system to manufacture ATP. From glycolysis, pyruvate is oxidized in a step linking to the Krebs cycle. After the Krebs cycle, NADH and succinate are oxidized in the electron transport chain.

Cell Cycle

The term cell cycle refers to the process by which a cell reproduces, which involves cell growth, the duplication of genetic material, and cell division. Complex organisms with many cells use the cell cycle to replace cells as they lose their functionality and wear out. The entire cell cycle in animal cells can take 24 hours. The time required varies among different cell types. Human skin cells, for example, are constantly reproducing. Some other cells only divide infrequently. Once neurons are mature, they do not grow or divide. The two ways that cells can reproduce are through meiosis and mitosis. When cells replicate through mitosis, the "daughter cell" is an exact replica of the parent cell. When cells divide through meiosis, the daughter cells have different genetic coding than the parent cell. Meiosis only happens in specialized reproductive cells called gametes.

Mitosis

The primary events that occur during mitosis are:

- Interphase: The cell prepares for division by replicating its genetic and cytoplasmic material. Interphase can be further divided into G_1, S, and G_2.
- Prophase: The chromatin thickens into chromosomes and the nuclear membrane begins to disintegrate. Pairs of centrioles move to opposite sides of the cell and spindle fibers begin to form. The mitotic spindle, formed from cytoskeleton parts, moves chromosomes around within the cell.
- Metaphase: The spindle moves to the center of the cell and chromosome pairs align along the center of the spindle structure.
- Anaphase: The pairs of chromosomes, called sisters, begin to pull apart, and may bend. When they are separated, they are called daughter chromosomes. Grooves appear in the cell membrane.

- Telophase: The spindle disintegrates, the nuclear membranes reform, and the chromosomes revert to chromatin. In animal cells, the membrane is pinched. In plant cells, a new cell wall begins to form.
- Cytokinesis: This is the physical splitting of the cell (including the cytoplasm) into two cells. Some believe this occurs following telophase. Others say it occurs from anaphase, as the cell begins to furrow, through telophase, when the cell actually splits into two.

Review Video: Mitosis
Visit mometrix.com/academy and enter code: 849894

Meiosis

Meiosis has the same phases as mitosis, but they happen twice. In addition, different events occur during some phases of meiosis than mitosis. The events that occur during the first phase of meiosis are interphase (I), prophase (I), metaphase (I), anaphase (I), telophase (I), and cytokinesis (I). During this first phase of meiosis, chromosomes cross over, genetic material is exchanged, and tetrads of four chromatids are formed. The nuclear membrane dissolves. Homologous pairs of chromatids are separated and travel to different poles. At this point, there has been one cell division resulting in two cells. Each cell goes through a second cell division, which consists of prophase (II), metaphase (II), anaphase (II), telophase (II), and cytokinesis (II). The result is four daughter cells with different sets of chromosomes. The daughter cells are haploid, which means they contain half the genetic material of the parent cell. The second phase of meiosis is similar to the process of mitosis. Meiosis encourages genetic diversity.

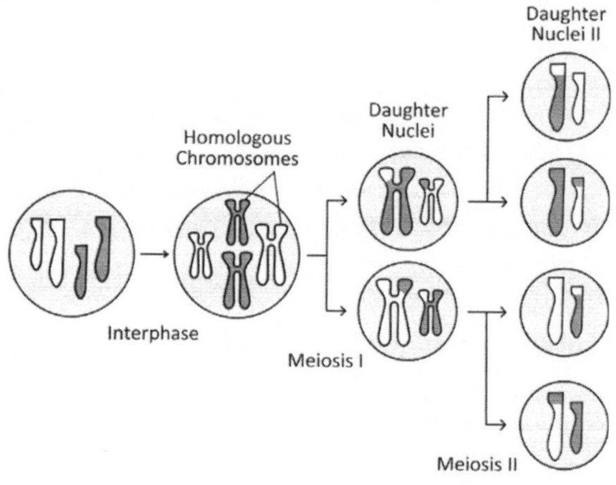

Homeostasis

Homeostasis is the ability and tendency of an organism, cell, or body to adjust to environmental changes to maintain equilibrium. One way an organism, such as a human body, can maintain homeostasis is through the release of hormones. Some hormones work in pairs. When a condition reaches an upper limit, a hormone is released to correct the condition. When a condition reaches the other end of the spectrum, another hormone is released. Hormones that work in this way are termed antagonistic. Insulin and glucagon are a pair of antagonistic hormones that help regulate the level of glucose in the blood.

Negative and Positive Feedback Loops and Hormone Pairs

Positive feedback loops actually tend to destabilize systems by increasing changes. A negative feedback loop acts to make a system more stable by buffering changes. The hormones insulin and glucagon (an antagonistic pair of hormones) are involved in negative feedback loops in the liver's control of blood sugar levels. Alpha cells secrete glucagon when the concentration of blood glucose decreases. Glucagon is broken down and fatty acids and amino acids are converted to glucose. Once there is more glucose, glucagon secretion is reduced. Beta cells secrete insulin when the concentration of blood glucose increases. This leads to the liver absorbing glucose. Glucose is converted to glycogen, and fat and the concentration of glucose decrease. Insulin production is then reduced. Hormones work in other ways aside from antagonistically. For example, follicle stimulating hormone (FSH) increases the production of estrogen. Once estrogen reaches a certain level, it suppresses FSH production. In some cases, a single hormone can increase or decrease the level of a substance.

DNA

Chromosomes consist of genes, which are single units of genetic information. Genes are made up of deoxyribonucleic acid (DNA). DNA is a nucleic acid located in the cell nucleus. There is also DNA in the mitochondria. DNA replicates to pass on genetic information. The DNA in almost all cells is the same. It is also involved in the biosynthesis of proteins. The model or structure of DNA is described as a double helix. A helix is a curve, and a double helix is two congruent curves connected by horizontal members. The model can be likened to a spiral staircase. It is right-handed. The British scientist Rosalind Elsie Franklin is credited with taking the x-ray diffraction image in 1952 that was used by Francis Crick and James Watson to formulate the double-helix model of DNA and speculate about its important role in carrying and transferring genetic information.

Structure

DNA has a double helix shape, resembles a twisted ladder, and is compact. It consists of nucleotides. Nucleotides consist of a five-carbon sugar (pentose), a phosphate group, and a nitrogenous base. Two bases pair up to form the rungs of the ladder. The "side rails" or backbone consists of the covalently bonded sugar and phosphate. The bases are attached to each other with hydrogen bonds, which are easily dismantled so replication can occur. Each base is attached to a phosphate and to a sugar. There are four types of nitrogenous bases: adenine (A), guanine (G), cytosine (C), and thymine (T). There are about 3 billion bases in human DNA. The bases are mostly the same in everybody, but their order is different. It is the order of these bases that creates diversity in people. Adenine (A) pairs with thymine (T), and cytosine (C) pairs with guanine (G).

Gene, Genotype, Phenotype, and Allele

A gene is a portion of DNA that identifies how traits are expressed and passed on in an organism. A gene is part of the **genetic code**. Collectively, all genes form the **genotype** of an individual. The genotype includes genes that may not be expressed, such as **recessive genes**. The **phenotype** is the physical, visual manifestation of genes. It is determined by the basic genetic information and how genes have been affected by their environment.

An **allele** is a variation of a gene. Also known as a trait, it determines the manifestation of a gene. This manifestation results in a specific physical appearance of some facet of an organism, such as eye color or height. For example, the genetic information for eye color is a gene. The gene variations responsible for blue, green, brown, or black eyes are called alleles. **Locus** (pl. loci) refers to the location of a gene or alleles.

Review Video: Genotype vs Phenotype
Visit mometrix.com/academy and enter code: 922853

Mendel's Laws and Punnett Squares

Mendel's laws are the law of segregation (the first law) and the law of independent assortment (the second law). The law of segregation states that there are two alleles and that half of the total number of alleles are contributed by each parent organism. The law of independent assortment states that traits are passed on randomly and are not influenced by other traits. The exception to this is linked traits. A Punnett square can illustrate how alleles combine from the contributing genes to form various phenotypes. One set of a parent's genes are put in columns, while the genes from the other parent are placed in rows. The allele combinations are shown in each cell. When two different alleles are present in a pair, the dominant one is expressed. A Punnett square can be used to predict the outcome of crosses.

Dominant and Recessive

Gene traits are represented in pairs with an upper-case letter for the dominant trait (A) and a lower-case letter for the recessive trait (a). Genes occur in pairs (AA, Aa, or aa). There is one gene on each chromosome half supplied by each parent organism. Since half the genetic material is from each parent, the offspring's traits are represented as a combination of these. A dominant trait only requires one gene of a gene pair for it to be expressed in a phenotype, whereas a recessive trait requires both genes in order to be manifested. For example, if the mother's genotype is Dd and the father's is dd, the possible combinations are Dd and dd. The dominant trait will be manifested if the genotype is DD or Dd. The recessive trait will be manifested if the genotype is dd. Both DD and dd are homozygous pairs. Dd is heterozygous.

Major Processes and Systems of Plants

Plants are autotrophs, which means they make their own food. In a sense, they are self sufficient. Three major processes used by plants are photosynthesis, transpiration, and respiration. Photosynthesis involves using sunlight to make food for plants. Transpiration evaporates water out of plants. Respiration is the utilization of food that was produced during photosynthesis. Two major systems in plants are the shoot and the root system. The shoot system includes leaves, buds, and stems. It also includes the flowers and fruits in flowering plants. The shoot system is located above the ground. The root system is the component of the plant that is underground, and includes roots, tubers, and rhizomes. Meristems form plant cells by mitosis. Cells then differentiate into cell types to form the three types of plant tissues, which are dermal, ground, and vascular. Dermal refers to tissues that form the covering or outer layer of a plant. Ground tissues consist of parenchyma, collenchyma, and/or sclerenchyma cells.

Photosynthesis

Photosynthesis is the conversion of sunlight into energy in plant cells, and also occurs in some types of bacteria and protists. Carbon dioxide and water are converted into glucose during photosynthesis, and light is required during this process. Cyanobacteria are thought to be the descendants of the first organisms to use photosynthesis about 3.5 billion years ago. Photosynthesis is a form of cellular respiration. It occurs in chloroplasts that use thylakoids, which are structures in the membrane that contain light reaction chemicals. Chlorophyll is a pigment that absorbs light. During the process, water is used and oxygen is released. The equation for the chemical reaction that occurs during photosynthesis is $6H_2O + 6CO_2 \rightarrow C_6H_{12}O_6 + 6O_2$. During photosynthesis, six molecules of water and six molecules of carbon dioxide react to form one molecule of sugar and six molecules of oxygen.

Sexual Reproduction, Seed Formation, and Germination in Flowering Plants

There are at least 230,000 species of flowering plants. They represent about 90 percent of all plants. Angiosperms have a sexual reproduction phase that includes flowering. When growing plants, one may think they develop in the following order: seeds, growth, flowers, and fruit. The reproductive cycle has the following order: flowers, fruit, and seeds. In other words, seeds are the products of successful reproduction. The colors and scents of flowers serve to attract pollinators. Flowers and other plants can also be pollinated by wind. When a pollen grain meets the ovule and is successfully fertilized, the ovule develops into a seed. A seed consists of three parts: the embryo, the endosperm, and a seed coat. The embryo is a small plant that has started to develop, but this development is paused. Germination is when the embryo starts to grow again. The endosperm consists of proteins, carbohydrates, or fats. It typically serves as a food source for the embryo. The seed coat provides protection from disease, insects, and water.

Extrinsic and Hormones

Extrinsic refers to homeostatic systems that are controlled from outside the body. In higher animals, the nervous system and endocrine system help regulate body functions by responding to stimuli. Hormones in animals regulate many processes, including growth, metabolism, reproduction, and fluid balance. The names of hormones tend to end in "-one." Endocrine hormones are proteins or steroids. Steroid hormones (anabolic steroids) help control the manufacture of protein in muscles and bones.

Vertebrates, Invertebrates, Endoskeletons and Exoskeletons

Invertebrates do not have a backbone, whereas vertebrates do. The great majority of animal species (an estimated 98 percent) are invertebrates, including worms, jellyfish, mollusks, slugs, insects, and spiders. They comprise 30 phyla in all. Vertebrates belong to the phylum Chordata. The vertebrate body has two cavities. The thoracic cavity holds the heart and lungs and the abdominal cavity holds the digestive organs. Animals with exoskeletons have skeletons on the outside. Examples are crabs and turtles. Animals with endoskeletons have skeletons on the inside. Examples are humans, tigers, birds, and reptiles.

Major Organ Systems

The 11 major organ systems are skeletal, muscular, nervous, digestive, respiratory, circulatory, skin, excretory, immune, endocrine, and reproductive.

Skeletal

This consists of the bones and joints. The skeletal system provides support for the body through its rigid structure, provides protection for internal organs, and works to make organisms motile. Growth hormone affects the rate of reproduction and the size of body cells, and also helps amino acids move through membranes.

Muscular

This includes the muscles. The muscular system allows the body to move and respond to its environment.

Nervous

This includes the brain, spinal cord, and nerves. The nervous system is a signaling system for intrabody communications among systems, responses to stimuli, and interaction within an environment. Signals are electrochemical. Conscious thoughts, memories, and sense interpretation occur in the nervous system. It also controls involuntary muscles and functions, such as breathing and the beating of the heart.

DIGESTIVE

This includes the mouth, pharynx, esophagus, stomach, intestines, rectum, anal canal, teeth, salivary glands, tongue, liver, gallbladder, pancreas, and appendix. The system helps change food into a form that the body can process and use for energy and nutrients. Food is eventually eliminated as solid waste. Digestive processes can be mechanical, such as chewing food and churning it in the stomach, and chemical, such as secreting hydrochloric acid to kill bacteria and converting protein to amino acids. The overall system converts large food particles into molecules so the body can use them. The small intestine transports the molecules to the circulatory system. The large intestine absorbs nutrients and prepares the unused portions of food for elimination.

RESPIRATORY

This includes the nose, pharynx, larynx, trachea, bronchi, and lungs. It is involved in gas exchange, which occurs in the alveoli. Fish have gills instead of lungs.

CIRCULATORY

This includes the heart, blood, and blood vessels, such as veins, arteries, and capillaries. Blood transports oxygen and nutrients to cells and carbon dioxide to the lungs.

SKIN (INTEGUMENTARY)

This includes skin, hair, nails, sense receptors, sweat glands, and oil glands. The skin is a sense organ, provides an exterior barrier against disease, regulates body temperature through perspiration, manufactures chemicals and hormones, and provides a place for nerves from the nervous system and parts of the circulation system to travel through. Skin has three layers: epidermis, dermis, and subcutaneous. The epidermis is the thin, outermost, waterproof layer. The dermis has the sweat glands, oil glands, and hair follicles. The subcutaneous layer has connective tissue. Also, this layer has adipose (i.e., fat) tissue, nerves, arteries, and veins.

Review Video: Integumentary System
Visit mometrix.com/academy and enter code: 655980

Excretory

This includes the kidneys, ureters, bladder, and urethra. The excretory system helps maintain the amount of fluids in the body. Wastes from the blood system and excess water are removed in urine. The system also helps remove solid waste. Immune: This includes the lymphatic system, lymph nodes, lymph vessels, thymus, and spleen. Lymph fluid is moved throughout the body by lymph vessels that provide protection against disease. This system protects the body from external intrusions, such as microscopic organisms and foreign substances. It can also protect against some cancerous cells.

REPRODUCTIVE

In the male, this system includes the testes, vas deferens, urethra, prostate, penis, and scrotum. In the female, this system includes the ovaries, fallopian tubes (oviduct and uterine tubes), cervix, uterus, vagina, vulva, and mammary glands. Sexual reproduction helps provide genetic diversity as gametes from each parent contribute half the DNA to the zygote offspring. The system provides a method of transporting the male gametes to the female. It also allows for the growth and development of the embryo. Hormones involved are testosterone, interstitial cell stimulating hormone (ICSH), luteinizing hormone (LH), follicle stimulating hormone (FSH), and estrogen. Estrogens secreted from the ovaries include estradiol, estrone, and estriol. They encourage growth, among other things. Progesterone helps prepare the endometrium for pregnancy.

Differences between RNA and DNA

RNA and DNA differ in terms of structure and function. RNA has a different sugar than DNA. It has **ribose** rather than **deoxyribose** sugar. The RNA nitrogenous bases are adenine (A), guanine (G), cytosine (C), and uracil (U). **Uracil** is found only in RNA and **thymine** in found only in DNA. RNA consists of a single strand and DNA has two strands. If straightened out, DNA has two side rails. RNA only has one "backbone," or strand of sugar and phosphate group components. RNA uses the fully hydroxylated sugar **pentose**, which includes an extra oxygen compared to deoxyribose, which is the sugar used by DNA. RNA supports the functions carried out by DNA. It aids in gene expression, replication, and transportation.

> **Review Video: DNA vs. RNA**
> Visit mometrix.com/academy and enter code: 184871

RNA acts as a helper to DNA and carries out a number of other functions. Types of RNA include ribosomal RNA (rRNA), transfer RNA (tRNA), and messenger RNA (mRNA). Viruses can use RNA to carry their genetic material to DNA. Ribosomal RNA is not believed to have changed much over time. For this reason, it can be used to study relationships in organisms. Messenger RNA carries a copy of a strand of DNA and transports it from the nucleus to the cytoplasm. Transcription is the process in which RNA polymerase copies DNA into RNA. DNA unwinds itself and serves as a template while RNA is being assembled. The DNA molecules are copied to RNA. Translation is the process whereby ribosomes use transcribed RNA to put together the needed protein. Transfer RNA is a molecule that helps in the translation process, and is found in the cytoplasm. Ribosomal RNA is in the ribosomes.

Codons

Codons are groups of three nucleotides on the messenger RNA, and can be visualized as three rungs of a ladder. A **codon** has the code for a single amino acid. There are 64 codons but 20 amino acids. More than one combination, or triplet, can be used to synthesize the necessary amino acids. For example, AAA (adenine-adenine-adenine) or AAG (adenine-adenine-guanine) can serve as codons for lysine. These groups of three occur in strings, and might be thought of as frames. For example, AAAUCUUCGU, if read in groups of three from the beginning, would be AAA, UCU, UCG, which are codons for lysine, serine, and serine, respectively. If the same sequence was read in groups of three starting from the second position, the groups would be AAU (asparagine), CUU (proline), and so on. The resulting amino acids would be completely different. For this reason, there are **start and stop codons** that indicate the beginning and ending of a sequence (or frame). **AUG** (methionine) is the start codon. **UAA**, **UGA**, and **UAG**, also known as ocher, opal, and amber, respectively, are stop codons.

> **Review Video: Codons**
> Visit mometrix.com/academy and enter code: 978172

DNA Replication

Pairs of chromosomes are composed of DNA, which is tightly wound to conserve space. When replication starts, it unwinds. The steps in DNA replication are controlled by enzymes. The enzyme helicase instigates the deforming of hydrogen bonds between the bases to split the two strands. The splitting starts at the A-T bases (adenine and thymine) as there are only two hydrogen bonds. The cytosine-guanine base pair has three bonds. The term "origin of replication" is used to refer to where the splitting starts. The portion of the DNA that is unwound to be replicated is called the replication fork. Each strand of DNA is transcribed by an mRNA. It copies the DNA onto itself, base by base, in a complementary manner. The exception is that uracil replaces thymine.

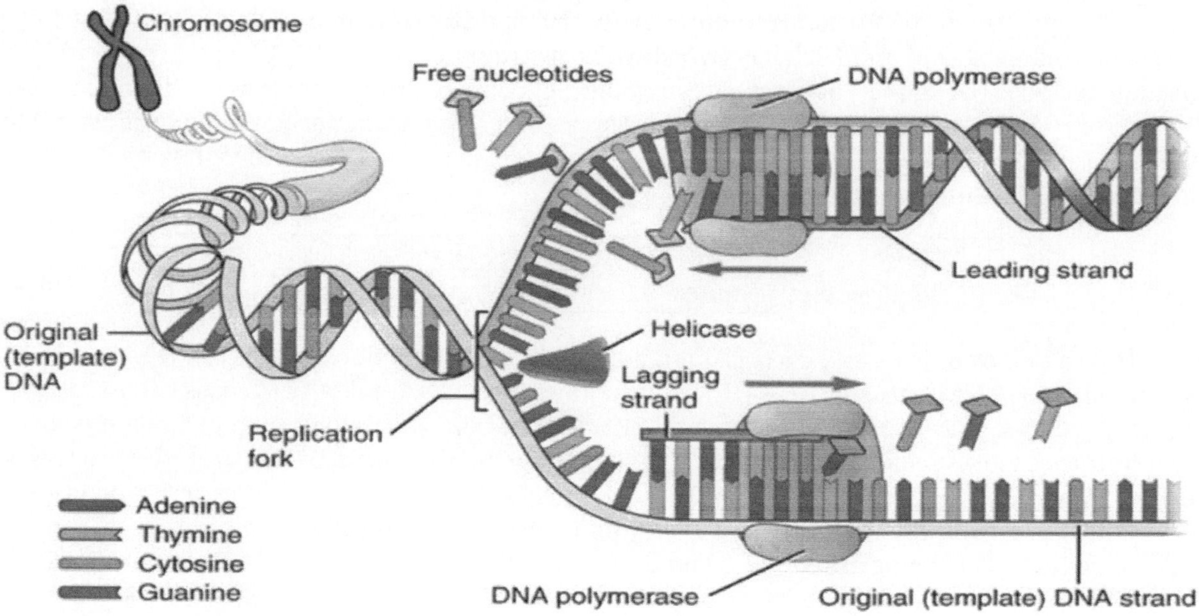

FUNCTIONS OF PROTEINS

Many proteins are involved in the replication of DNA, and each has a specific function. Helicase is a protein that facilitates the unwinding of the double helix structure of DNA. Single strand binding (SSB) proteins attach themselves to each strand to prevent the DNA strands from joining back together. After DNA is unwound, there are leading and lagging strands. The leading strand is synthesized continuously and the lagging strand is synthesized in Okazaki fragments. Primase, an RNA polymerase (catalyzing enzyme), acts as a starting point for replication by forming short strands, or primers, of RNA. The DNA clamp, or sliding clamp, helps prevent DNA polymerase from coming apart from the strand. DNA polymerase helps form the DNA strand by linking nucleotides. As the process progresses, RNase H removes the primers. DNA ligase then links the existing shorter strands into a longer strand.

MUTATIONS

Gene disorders are the result of DNA mutations. DNA mutations lead to unfavorable gene disorders, but also provide genetic variability. This diversity can lead to increased survivability of a species. Mutations can be neutral, beneficial, or harmful. Mutations can be hereditary, meaning they are passed from parent to child. Polymorphism refers to differences in humans, such as eye and hair color, that may have originally been the result of gene mutations, but are now part of the normal variation of the species. Mutations can be de novo, meaning they happen either only in sex cells or shortly after fertilization. They can also be acquired, or somatic. These are the kinds that happen as a result of DNA changes due to environmental factors or replication errors. Mosaicism is when a mutation happens in a cell during an early embryonic stage. The result is that some cells will have the mutation and some will not.

DNA MUTATION

A DNA mutation occurs when the normal gene sequence is altered. Mutations can happen when DNA is damaged as a result of environmental factors, such as chemicals, radiation, or ultraviolet rays from the sun. It can also happen when errors are made during DNA replication. The phosphate-sugar side rail of DNA can be damaged if the bonds between oxygen and phosphate groups are disassociated. Translocation happens when the broken bonds attempt to bond with other DNA. This repair can cause a mutation. The nucleotide itself can be altered. A C, for example, might look like a T. During replication, the damaged C is replicated as a T and paired with a G, which is incorrect base pairing. Another way mutations can occur is if an error is made by the DNA polymerase while replicating a base. This happens about once for every 100,000,000 bases. A repair protein proofreads the code, however, so the mistake is usually repaired.

Translocation

Translocation is a genetic mutation in which one piece of a chromosome is transferred to another chromosome. Burkitt's lymphoma, chronic myelogenous leukemia, and Down syndrome are all examples. Trisomy 21, or Down syndrome, occurs when a copy of chromosome 21 attaches to chromosome 14. Most Down syndrome cases are caused by a pair of chromosomes (the 21st) that does not split during meiosis. Both divided cells will have an abnormal number of chromosomes. One will have 22 and the other will have 24. When this egg gets fertilized, it will have three copies of chromosome 21 instead of two. Down syndrome can also be caused by translocation between the 14th and 21st chromosomes. In these instances, genetic material is swapped. There are 200 to 250 genes on the 21st chromosome. The overexpression of the gene results in the following Down syndrome traits: premature aging, decreased immune system function, heart defects, skeletal abnormalities, disruption of DNA synthesis and repair, intellectual disability, and cataracts.

Random Mutations, Nonrandom Mating, and Gene Migration

Random mutations are genetic changes caused by DNA errors or environmental factors such as chemicals and radiation. Mutations can be beneficial or harmful. Nonrandom mating refers to the fact that the probability of two individuals mating in a population is not the same for all pairs. Nonrandom mating can be caused by geographical isolation, small populations, and other factors. Nonrandom mating can lead to inbreeding (mating with a relative), which can lead to a decline in physical fitness as seen in a phenotype and the reduction of allele frequency and occurrence. Also known as gene flow, gene migration is the movement of alleles to another population. This can occur through immigration, when individuals of a species move into an area, or through emigration, when individuals of a species move out of an area.

Monohybrid and Hybrid Crosses

Genetic crosses are the possible combinations of alleles, and can be represented using Punnett squares. A monohybrid cross refers to a cross involving only one trait. Typically, the ratio is 3:1 (DD, Dd, Dd, dd), which is the ratio of dominant gene manifestation to recessive gene manifestation. This ratio occurs when both parents have a pair of dominant and recessive genes. If one parent has a pair of dominant genes (DD) and the other has a pair of recessive (dd) genes, the recessive trait can not be expressed in the next generation because the resulting crosses all have the Dd genotype. A dihybrid cross refers to one involving more than one trait, which means more combinations are possible. The ratio of genotypes for a dihybrid cross is 9:3:3:1 when the traits are not linked. The ratio for incomplete dominance is 1:2:1, which corresponds to dominant, mixed, and recessive phenotypes.

Heredity and Environment

The non-Mendelian concept of polygenetic inheritance takes into account environmental factors on phenotypes. For example, an individual inherits genes that help determine height, but a diet lacking in certain nutrients could limit that individual's ability to reach that height. Another example is the concept of genetic disposition, which is a propensity for a certain disease that is genetically inherited, but not necessarily manifested. For example, individuals with certain skin types are more likely to develop skin cancer. If they limit their exposure to solar radiation, however, this will not necessarily occur.

Blood Typing

There are four possible blood types: A, B, AB, and O. These types are produced by combinations of the three alleles. AA and AO lead to type A blood. BB and BO lead to type B blood. AB leads to type AB blood because the alleles are co-dominant. AB has both A protein and antigens and B protein and antigens. The O allele is recessive. OO leads to blood type O, which lacks proteins and blood-surface antigens. Blood donors with an O blood type are known as universal donors because they do not have the type of antigens that can trigger immune system responses. Blood donors with type AB blood are known as universal recipients because they do not have the antibodies that will attack A and B antigen molecules. If parents have AB and O blood, offspring have a 50% chance of having type A blood and a 0% chance of having type O blood.

Recombinant DNA and Gene Splicing

Recombinant DNA (rDNA) refers to manipulating sequences of DNA. One portion of DNA is removed and replaced with another. Gene splicing is a way to recombine DNA. In gene splicing, base pairs of DNA are chemically cleaved. Restriction enzymes are used to perform the cutting part of gene splicing. Once base pairs are separated, different additional genetic information can be added by a vector. DNA ligase (an enzyme) is used to put the pieces back together. The process of DNA recombination happens naturally and incrementally as a result of evolution. Use of recombinant DNA produced through genetic engineering has been used in the laboratory in diagnostic, medical forensic and agricultural applications.

Applications of Genetic Engineering

Diagnostic and medical applications include treating diabetes with insulin, producing human proteins, treating hemophilia, anemia, and blood clots, and manufacturing hepatitis B vaccine. Gene therapy has been used to replace defective alleles with normal alleles. For example, if a patient has a condition caused by an enzyme deficiency, replacing the defective allele enables the person to produce that enzyme. Medical forensic applications involving DNA analysis include using it to identify individuals and solve criminal cases. Agricultural applications include crop modification to develop types of wheat, cotton, and soybeans that resist weed controlling herbicides. Plants can be altered to make them grow bigger or vaccinated to make them resistant to plant viruses and insects.

Allele Frequency

The gene pool refers to all alleles of a gene and their combinations. The Hardy-Weinberg principle (or Castle-Hardy Weinberg principle) postulates that the allele frequency for dominant and recessive alleles will remain the same in a population through successive generations if certain conditions exist. These conditions are: no mutations, large populations, random mating, no migration, and equal genotypes. This is an ideal and not how most population's function. Changes in the frequency and types of alleles in a gene pool can be caused by gene flow, random mutation, nonrandom mating, and genetic drift. In organisms that reproduce by sexual reproduction, reproduction isolation is defined as something that acts as a barrier to two species reproducing. These barriers are classified as prezygotic and postzygotic.

Prezygotic Barriers to Reproduction

The following are prezygotic barriers to reproduction:

- Spatial: This refers to species that are separated by a distance that prevents them from mating.
- Geographical: This is when species are physically separated by a barrier. A barrier can divide a population, which is known as vicariance. If a population crosses a barrier to create two species, it is known as dispersal.
- Habitat: This refers to species that live in different habitats in the same area.
- Temporal: This refers to the fact that species reach sexual maturity at different times. An example is plants that flower at different times of the year.
- Behavioral: This refers to the fact that mating rituals distinguish interaction between sexes. For example, many species of crickets are morphologically (structurally) the same, yet a female of one species will only respond to the mating rituals of males within her species.
- Mechanical: This refers to physiological structural differences that prevent mating or the transfer of gametes.
- Gametic isolation: This refers to the fact that fertilization may not occur when gametes of different species are not compatible.

Postzygotic Barriers to Reproduction

The following are postzygotic barriers to reproduction:

- Hybrid viability: This is when a hybrid zygote does not reach maturity.
- Hybrid sterility: This is also known as hybrid infertility. It occurs when two species produce a hybrid offspring that reaches maturity, but is sterile. An example of this is the mule. Mules are the result of a horse and a donkey mating. Mules, however, can not reproduce.
- Hybrid breakdown: This is when the first generation is not only viable, but also reaches maturity and can reproduce. Subsequent generations, however, are neither viable nor fertile.
- Hybrid zygote abnormality: This is when two species produce a zygote that does not survive to birth or germination, does not develop normally or reach sexual maturity, and cannot reproduce.
- Allopatric speciation: This refers to speciation that occurs because of geographical factors, such as physical barriers or dispersal.
- Sympatric speciation: This refers to speciation that happens within parent populations.
- Parapatric speciation: This refers to speciation that occurs because of an extreme change in habitat.

Viruses

Viruses are microorganisms that replicate in the cells of other organisms, including plants, animals, bacteria, and other microorganisms. All viruses have a head. Some also have a tail consisting of protein. The tail is used to attach to a host cell and enter it. This is one way in which viruses introduce their genetic material to the host. The head of a virus, also called a protein capsid, contains genetic material in the form of DNA, RNA, or enzymes. The adenovirus and the herpes virus are both DNA viruses. The HIV retrovirus, influenza, and the rotavirus are RNA viruses. The number of virus types is thought to be in the millions. Virology is a branch of microbiology that is devoted to the study of viruses. Viruses can be transmitted to other organisms in a number of ways, such as by insects, by air, and through direct contact.

Origin of Life on Earth

One theory of how life originated on Earth is that life developed from nonliving materials. The first stage of this transformation happened when abiotic (nonliving) synthesis took place, which is the formation of monomers like amino acids and nucleotides. Next, monomers joined together to create polymers such as proteins and nucleic acids. These polymers are then believed to have formed into protobionts. The last stage was the development of the process of heredity. Supporters of this theory believe that RNA was the first genetic material. Another theory postulates that hereditary systems came about before the origination of nucleic acids. Another theory is that life, or the precursors for it, were transported to Earth from a meteorite or other object from space. There is no real evidence to support this theory.

Evolution

Supporting Evidence

Scientific evidence supporting the theory of evolution can be found in biogeography, comparative anatomy and embryology, the fossil record, and molecular evidence. Biogeography studies the geographical distribution of animals and plants. Evidence of evolution related to the area of biogeography includes species that are well suited for extreme environments. The fossil record shows that many species lived only for a short time period before becoming extinct. The fossil record can also show the succession of plants and animals. Living fossils are existing species that have not changed much morphologically and are very similar to ancient examples in the fossil record. Examples include the horseshoe crab and ginkgo. Comparative embryology studies how species are similar in the embryonic stage, but become increasingly specialized and diverse as they age. Vestigial organs are those that still exist, but become nonfunctional. Examples include the hind limbs of whales and the wings of birds that can no longer fly, such as ostriches.

Types and Mechanisms of Evolution and Species, Speciation, and BSC

The three types of evolution are divergent, convergent, and parallel. Divergent evolution refers to two species that become different over time. This can be caused by one of the species adapting to a different environment. Convergent evolution refers to two species that start out fairly different but evolve to share many similar traits. Parallel evolution refers to species that are not similar and do not become more or less similar over time. Mechanisms of evolution include descent (the passing on of genetic information), mutation, migration, natural selection, and genetic variation and drift. The biological definition of species refers to a group of individuals that can mate and reproduce. Speciation refers to the evolution of a new biological species. The biological species concept (BSC) basically states that a species is a community of individuals that can reproduce and have a niche in nature.

Rate of Evolution

The rate of evolution is affected by the variability of a population. Variability increases the likelihood of evolution. Variability in a population can be increased by mutations, immigration, sexual reproduction (as opposed to asexual reproduction), and size. Natural selection, emigration, and smaller populations can lead to decreased variability. Sexual selection affects evolution. If fewer genes are available, it will limit the number of genes passed on to subsequent generations. Some animal mating behaviors are not as successful as others. A male that does not attract a female because of a weak mating call or dull feathers, for example, will not pass on its genes. Mechanical isolation, which refers to sex organs that do not fit together very well, can also decrease successful mating.

Organism and Microbe

An organism is a living thing. A unicellular organism is an organism that has only one cell. Examples of unicellular organisms are bacteria and paramecium. A multicellular organism is one that consists of many cells. Humans are a good example. By some estimates, the human body is made up of billions of cells. Others think the human body has more than 75 trillion cells. The term microbe refers to small organisms that are only visible through a microscope. Examples include viruses, bacteria, fungi, and protozoa. Microbes are also referred to as microorganisms. Bacteria can be rod shaped, round (cocci), or spiral (spirilla). These shapes are used to differentiate among types of bacteria. Bacteria can be identified by staining them. This particular type of stain is called a gram stain. If bacteria are gram-positive, they absorb the stain and become purple. If bacteria are gram-negative, they do not absorb the stain and become a pinkish color.

Classification

The most widely accepted system for taxonomy is the three-domain classification system; sometimes called the six-kingdom classification system. The three domains are Archaea, Bacteria, and Eukarya. Both Archaea and Bacteria are made of prokaryotic cells, while Eukarya are made of eukaryotic cells. The domains of Bacteria and Archaea each have a single kingdom Eubacteria and Archaebacteria, respectively. The domain Eukarya has four kingdoms: Protista, Fungi, Plantae, and Animalia. Kingdom Protista includes about 250,000 species of unicellular protozoans and unicellular and multicellular algae. Kingdom Fungi includes about 100,000 species. Kingdom Plantae includes about 320,000 species. Kingdom Animalia is estimated to include more than 1,500,000 species. The groupings in this system, in descending order from broadest to most specific, are: domain, kingdom, phylum/division, class, order, family, genus, and species. A memory aid for this is: Dear King Philip Came Over For Good Soup. According to the three-domain classification system, humans are: domain Eukarya, kingdom Animalia, phylum Chordata, subphylum Vertebrata, class Mammalia, order Primate, family Hominidae, genus Homo, and species Sapiens.

Protista Kingdom

Organisms in the Protista kingdom are classified according to their methods of locomotion, their methods of reproduction, and how they get their nutrients. Protists can move by the use of a flagellum, cilia, or pseudopod. Flagellates have flagellum, which are long tails or whip-like structures that are rotated to help the protist move. Ciliates use cilia, which are smaller hair-like structures on the exterior of a cell that wiggle to help move the surrounding matter. Amoeboids use pseudopodia to move. Bacteria reproduce either sexually or asexually. Binary fission is a form of asexual reproduction whereby bacteria divide in half to produce two new organisms that are clones of the parent. In sexual reproduction, genetic material is exchanged. When kingdom members are categorized according to how they obtain nutrients, the three types of protists are photosynthetic, consumers, and saprophytes. Photosynthetic protists convert sunlight into energy. Organisms that use photosynthesis are considered producers. Consumers, also known as heterotrophs, eat or consume other organisms. Saprophytes consume dead or decaying substances.

Fungi Kingdom

Kingdoms Fungi and Plantae

Mycology is the study of fungi. The Fungi kingdom includes about 100,000 species. They are further delineated as mushrooms, yeasts, molds, rusts, mildews, stinkhorns, puffballs, and truffles. Fungi are characterized by cell walls that have chitin, a long chain polymer carbohydrate. Fungi are different from species in the Plant kingdom, which have cell walls consisting of cellulose. Fungi are thought to have evolved from a single ancestor. Although they are often thought of as a type of plant, they are more similar to animals than plants. Fungi are typically small and numerous, and have a diverse morphology among species. They can have bright red cups and be orange jellylike masses, and their shapes can resemble golf balls, bird nests with eggs, starfish, parasols, and male genitalia. Some members of the stinkhorn family emit odors similar to dog scat to attract flies that help transport spores that are involved in reproduction. Fungi of this family are also consumed by humans.

Review Video: Kingdom Plantae Characteristics
Visit mometrix.com/academy and enter code: 710084

PLANTS

Major plant phyla: Chlorophyta are green algae. Bryophyta are nonvascular mosses and liverworts. They have root-like parts called rhizoids. Since they do not have the vascular structures to transport water, they live in moist environments. Lycophyta are club mosses. They are vascular plants. They use spores and need water to reproduce. Equisetopsida (sphenophyta) are horsetails. Like lycophyta, they need water to reproduce with spores. They have rhizoids and needle-like leaves. The pteridophytes (filicopsida) are ferns. They have stems (rhizomes). Spermatopsida are the seed plants. Gymnosperms are a conifer, which means they have cones with seeds that are used in reproduction. Plants with seeds require less water. Cycadophyta are cone-bearing and look like palms. Gnetophyta are plants that live in the desert. Coniferophyta are pine trees, and have both cones and needles. Ginkgophyta are ginkgos. Anthophyta is the division with the largest number of plant species, and includes flowering plants with true seeds.

Vascular, nonvascular, seed bearing, and pteridophytes: Only plants in the division bryophyta (mosses and liverworts) are nonvascular, which means they do not have xylem to transport water. All of the plants in the remaining divisions are vascular, meaning they have true roots, stems, leaves, and xylem. Pteridophytes are plants that use spores and not seeds to reproduce. They include the following divisions: Psilophyta (whisk fern), Lycophyta (club mosses), Sphenophyta (horsetails), and Pterophyta (ferns). Spermatophytes are plants that use seeds to reproduce. Included in this category are gymnosperms, which are flowerless plants that use naked seeds, and angiosperms, which are flowering plants that contain seeds in or on a fruit. Gymnosperms include the following divisions: cycadophyta (cycads), ginkgophyta (maidenhair tree), gnetophyta (ephedra and welwitschia), and coniferophyta (which includes pinophyta conifers). Angiosperms comprise the division anthophyta (flowering plants).

ANIMAL KINGDOM

KINGDOM ANIMALIA

The animal kingdom is comprised of more than one million species in about 30 phyla. There about 800,000 species of insects alone, representing half of all animal species. The characteristics that distinguish members of the animal kingdom from members of other kingdoms are that they are multicellular, are heterotrophic, reproduce sexually (there are some exceptions), have cells that do not contain cell walls or photosynthetic pigments, can move at some stage of life, and can rapidly respond to the environment as a result of specialized tissues like nerve and muscle. Heterotrophic refers to the method of getting energy by eating food that has energy releasing substances. Plants, on the other hand, are autotrophs, which mean they make their own energy. During reproduction, animals have a diploid embryo in the blastula stage. This structure is unique to animals. The blastula resembles a fluid-filled ball.

Subdivisions: The animal kingdom includes about one million species. Metazoans are multicellular animals. Food is ingested and enters a mesoderm-lined coelom (body cavity). Phylum porifera and coelenterate are exceptions. The taxonomy of animals involves grouping them into phyla according to body symmetry and plan, as well as the presence of or lack of segmentation. The more complex phyla that have a coelom and a digestive system are further classified as protostomes or deuterostomes according to blastula development. In protostomes, the blastula's blastopore (opening) forms a mouth. In deuterostomes, the blastopore forms an anus. Taxonomy schemes vary, but there are about 36 phyla of animals. The corresponding term for plants at this level is division. The most notable phyla include chordata, mollusca, porifera, cnidaria, platyhelminthes, nematoda, annelida, arthropoda, and echinodermata, which account for about 96 percent of all animal species.

Animal Phyla

These four animal phyla lack a coelom or have a pseudocoelom:

- Porifera: These are sponges. They lack a coelom and get food as water flows through them. They are usually found in marine and sometimes in freshwater environments. They are perforated and diploblastic, meaning there are two layers of cells.
- Cnidaria: Members of this phylum are hydrozoa, jellyfish, and obelia. They have radial symmetry, sac-like bodies, and a polyp or medusa (jellyfish) body plan. They are diploblastic, possessing both an ectoderm and an endoderm. Food can get in through a cavity, but members of this phylum do not have an anus.
- Platyhelminthes: These are also known as flatworms. Classes include turbellaria (planarian) and trematoda (which include lung, liver, and blood fluke parasites). They have organs and bilateral symmetry. They have three layers of tissue: an ectoderm, a mesoderm, and an endoderm.
- Nematoda: These are roundworms. Hookworms and many other parasites are members of this phylum. They have a pseudocoelom, which means the coelom is not completely enclosed within the mesoderm. They also have a digestive tract that runs directly from the mouth to the anus. They are nonsegmented.

Members of the protostomic phyla have mouths that are formed from blastopores:

- Mollusca: Classes include bivalvia (organisms with two shells, such as clams, mussels, and oysters), gastropoda (snails and slugs), cephalopoda (octopus, squid, and chambered nautilus), scaphopoda, amphineura (chitons), and monoplacophora.
- Annelida: This phylum includes the classes oligochaeta (earthworms), polychaeta (clam worms), and hirudinea (leeches). They have true coeloms enclosed within the mesoderm. They are segmented, have repeating units, and have a nerve trunk.
- Arthropoda: This phylum is diverse and populous. Members can be found in all types of environments. They have external skeletons, jointed appendages, bilateral symmetry, and nerve cords. They also have open circulatory systems and sense organs. Subphyla include crustacea (lobster, barnacles, pill bugs, and daphnia), hexapoda (all insects, which have three body segments, six legs, and usual wings), myriapoda (centipedes and millipedes), and chelicerata (the horseshoe crab and arachnids). The subphylum crustacea includes shrimps, crabs, and even pill bugs, which have gills. Bees, ants, and wasps belong to the order hymenoptera. Like several other insect orders, they undergo complete metamorphosis.

Members of the deuterostomic phyla have anuses that are formed from blastopores:

- Echinodermata: Members of this phylum have radial symmetry, are marine organisms, and have a water vascular system. Classes include echinoidea (sea urchins and sand dollars), crinoidea (sea lilies), asteroidea (starfish), ophiuroidea (brittle stars), and holothuroidea (sea cucumbers).
- Chordata: This phylum includes humans and all other vertebrates, as well as a few invertebrates (urochordata and cephalochordata). Members of this phylum include agnatha (lampreys and hagfish), gnathostomata, chondrichthyes (cartilaginous fish-like sharks, skates, and rays), osteichthyes (bony fishes, including ray-finned fish that humans eat), amphibians (frogs, salamanders, and newts), reptiles (lizards, snakes, crocodiles, and dinosaurs), birds, and mammals.

ANIMAL CLASSIFICATION BASED ON FOOD SOURCES AND REQUIREMENTS

As heterotrophs, animals can be further classified as carnivores, herbivores, omnivores, and parasites. Predation refers to a predator that feeds on another organism, which results in its death. Detritivory refers to heterotrophs that consume organic dead matter. Carnivores are animals that are meat eaters. Herbivores are plant eaters, and omnivores eat both meat and plants. A parasite's food source is its host. A parasite lives off of a host, which does not benefit from the interaction. Nutrients can be classified as carbohydrates, fats, fiber, minerals, proteins, vitamins, and water. Each supply a specific substance required for various species to survive, grow, and reproduce. A calorie is a measurement of heat energy. It can be used to represent both how much energy a food can provide and how much energy an organism needs to live.

ANIMAL TISSUE TYPES

Animals have four main tissues types: epithelial, connective, muscle, and bone. Epithelial tissue is found on body surfaces (like skin) and lining body cavities (like the stomach). Its function is to form and protect various glands. The three types of epithelial tissue are squamous (flattened), cuboidal (cube-shaped), and columnar (elongated). It can be further classified as simple (a single layer) or stratified (more than one layer). Epithelial cells move substances in, around, and out of the body. They can also have protective and secretory functions. Glands comprised of epithelial tissue can be unicellular or multicellular. Connective tissue is used to bind, support, protect, form blood, store fat, and fill space. The two kinds of connective tissue are loose and fibrous. In the human body, cartilage, bone, tendons, ligaments, blood, and protective layers on muscle, nerve, and blood vessels are types of connective tissue. The three types of muscle tissue are skeletal (striated), smooth, and cardiac.

SYSTEMS AND STRUCTURES IN ANIMALS

Systems in animals have developed to perform various functions, including providing physical protection and obtaining food. Some animals have internal or external skeletons, shells, or skin that provide protection and support. Skin helps prevent water loss. Muscle systems enable movement. Brains and nervous systems help animals respond to external stimuli by processing incoming and outgoing signals. The main systems in animals are skeletal, muscular, nervous, digestive, respiratory, reproductive, and circulatory. The human stomach, for example, aids in the process of turning consumed food sources into energy. It has many tissue types: smooth muscle tissue, loose connective tissue, nervous tissue, blood, and columnar epithelial tissue. Many animals have a stomach or digestive chamber with two openings. These are known as metazoans.

Muscle in Mammals

Skeletal muscle is strong, quick, and capable of voluntary contraction. Skeletal muscle fibers are striated and cylinder shaped. They have about 25 nuclei that are located to the side of the cell. Skeletal muscle consists of myofibrils that contain two types of filaments (myofilaments) made of proteins. The two types of filaments are actin and myosin. These filaments are aligned, giving the appearance of striation. During contraction, they slide against each other and become more overlapped. Smooth muscle is weak, slow, and usually contracts involuntarily. Examples in humans can be found in the gastrointestinal tract, blood vessels, bladder, uterus, hair follicles, and parts of the eye. Smooth muscle fibers are not striated, but spindle shaped. They are somewhat long and a little wider in the center. Each cell contains one nucleus that is centrally located. Smooth muscle cells also contain myofibrils, but they are not aligned. Cardiac muscle is strong, quick, and continuously contracts involuntarily. It is found in the myocardium of the heart.

Endocrine System

The endocrine system includes the pituitary gland, pineal gland, hypothalamus, thyroid gland, parathyroids, thymus, adrenals, pancreas, ovaries, and testes. It controls systems and processes by secreting hormones into the blood system. Exocrine glands are those that secrete fluid into ducts. Endocrine glands secrete hormones directly into the blood stream without the use of ducts. Prostaglandin (tissue hormones) diffuses only a short distance from the tissue that created it, and influences nearby cells only. Adrenal glands are located above each kidney. The cortex secretes some sex hormones, as well as mineralocorticoids and glucocorticoids involved in immune suppression and stress response. The medulla secretes epinephrine and norepinephrine. Both elevate blood sugar, increase blood pressure, and accelerate heart rate. Epinephrine also stimulates heart muscle. The islets of Langerhans are clumped within the pancreas and secrete glucagon and insulin, thereby regulating blood sugar levels. The four parathyroid glands at the rear of the thyroid secrete parathyroid hormone.

Reproductive Systems in Animals

Based on whether or not and when an organism uses meiosis or mitosis, the three possible cycles of reproduction are haplontic, diplontic, and haplodiplontic. Fungi, green algae, and protozoa are haplontic. Animals and some brown algae and fungi are diplontic. Plants and some fungi are haplodiplontic. Diplontic organisms, like multicelled animals, have a dominant diploid life cycle. The haploid generation is simply the egg and sperm. Monoecious species are bisexual (hermaphroditic). In this case, the individual has both male and female organs: sperm-bearing testicles and egg-bearing ovaries. Hermaphroditic species can self fertilize. Some worms are hermaphroditic. Cross fertilization is when individuals exchange genetic information. Most animal species are dioecious, meaning individuals are distinctly male or female.

Nutritional Requirements in Animals and Humans

Carbohydrates are the primary source of energy as they can be easily converted to glucose. Fats (oils or lipids) are usually not very water soluble, and vitamins A, D, E, and K are fat soluble. Fats are needed to help process these vitamins and can also store energy. Fats have the highest calorie value per gram (9,000 calories). Dietary fiber, or roughage, helps the excretory system. In humans, fiber can help regulate blood sugar levels, reduce heart disease, help food pass through the digestive system, and add bulk. Dietary minerals are chemical elements that are involved with biochemical functions in the body. Proteins consist of amino acids. Proteins are broken down in the body into amino acids that are used for protein biosynthesis or fuel. Vitamins are compounds that are not made by the body, but obtained through the diet. Water is necessary to prevent dehydration since water is lost through the excretory system and perspiration.

Social Behaviors

The following are social behaviors:

- Territoriality: This refers to members of a species protecting areas from other members of their species and from other species. Species members claim specific areas as their own.
- Dominance: This refers to the species in a community that is the most populous.
- Altruism: This is when a species or individual in a community exhibits behaviors that benefit another individual at a cost to itself. In biology, altruism does not have to be a conscious sacrifice.
- Threat display: This refers to behavior by an organism that is intended to intimidate or frighten away members of its own or another species.

Population

Population is a measure of how many individuals exist in a specific area. It can be used to measure the size of human, plant, or animal groups. Population growth depends on many factors. Factors that can limit the number of individuals in a population include lack of resources such as food and water, space, habitat destruction, competition, disease, and predators. Exponential growth refers to an unlimited rising growth rate. This kind of growth can be plotted on a chart in the shape of a J. Carrying capacity is the population size that can be sustained. The world's population as of 2020 is about 7.75 billion and growing. The human population has not yet reached its carrying capacity. Population dynamics refers to how a population changes over time and the factors that cause changes. An S-shaped curve shows that population growth has leveled off. Biotic potential refers to the maximum reproductive capacity of a population given ideal environmental conditions.

Species Interactions

Predation, parasitism, commensalism, and mutualism are all types of species interactions that affect species populations. Intraspecific relationships are relationships among members of a species. Interspecific relationships are relationships between members of different species.

Predation: This is a relationship in which one individual feeds on another (the prey), causing the prey to die. **Mimicry** is an adaptation developed as a response to predation. It refers to an organism that has a similar appearance to another species, which is meant to fool the predator into thinking the organism is more dangerous than it really is. Two examples are the drone fly and the Io moth. The fly looks like a bee, but cannot sting. The Io moth has markings on its wings that make it look like an owl. The moth can startle predators and gain time to escape. Predators can also use mimicry to lure their prey.

Natural Selection, Gradualism, and Punctuated Equilibrium

Natural selection, developed by Darwin, states that traits that help give a species a survival advantage are passed on to subsequent generations. Members of a species that do not have the advantageous trait die before they reproduce. Darwin's four principles are: from generation to generation, there are various individuals within a species; genes determine variations; more individuals are born than survive to maturation; and specific genes enable an organism to better survive. Gradualism can be contrasted with punctuationism. It is an idea that evolution proceeds at a steady pace and does not include sudden developments of new species or features from one generation to the next. Punctuated equilibrium can be contrasted with gradualism. It is the idea in evolutionary biology that states that evolution involves long time periods of no change (stasis) accompanied by relatively brief periods (hundreds of thousands of years) of rapid change.

Vascular and Nonvascular Plants

Vascular plants have vascular tissue in the form of xylem and phloem. These make up the parts of the plants, such as the roots, stems, and leaves that are involved in transporting minerals and water throughout the plant. This capability enables vascular plants to grow tall. Food/energy that is converted by photosynthesis in the leaves is brought down to the roots, while water is brought to the top of the plant. Nonvascular (or avascular) plants lack true leaves, stems, and roots. Nonvascular plants do not develop vascular tissue, such as xylem and phloem. They tend to be small, and individual cells are adjacent to their environment.

Root System and Transportation System in Plants

Plant roots include zones where cell differentiation, elongation and division, and meristem formation occur. Primary meristems include protoderms, ground meristems, procambiums, and apical meristems. There is also a root cap. A tuber is an underground stem that is enlarged and used for food storage. A rhizome is an underground stem of sorts that sends out roots and shoots from its nodes (bulging or swelling points). Vascular tissues include xylem and phloem. Xylem can be scattered throughout a pith or formed into rings. Phloem allows for food transport down a plant. The food travels from where it was produced through photosynthesis to other structures, such as roots, that require the food. Phloem can be made up of bundles of sieve tubes. It is usually located outside the xylem.

Transpiration, Respiration, and Phylogenetic

Transpiration is the movement of water through a vascular plant. It is also the method by which water is evaporated out of plants. Transpiration mainly happens during the process of photosynthesis, when water and minerals travel up through the xylem and are used and water is released through stomata (flattened oval-shaped openings). During transpiration, water is drawn up a plant. This process also helps cool leaves. Respiration refers to the process of metabolizing sugars to provide plants with the energy they need for growth and reproduction. The chemical equation is $C_6H_{12}O_6 + 6O_2 \rightarrow 6CO_2 + 6H_2O$ + energy. During the process of respiration, sugars are burned, energy is released, oxygen is used, and water and carbon dioxide are produced. Respiration can occur as a light or dark reaction. Phylogenetic refers to organisms that are related because of their evolutionary history.

Reproduction Methods of Plants

Bryophytes are seedless plants. They include liverworts, hornworts, and mosses. They use spores that form into gametophytes to reproduce. Sperm are flagellated, meaning they require at least some water to swim to the egg. Some bryophytes are plants that are one sex or the other, but other bryophytes have both sexes on the same plant. Ferns also have flagellated sperm and require water for the same reason as bryophytes. Both ferns and bryophytes undergo alternation of generations. These plants spend about half of their reproductive cycles as sporophytes, making haploid spores through meiosis during this stage. The other half of the cycle is spent as a haploid gametophyte. At this point, male and female gametes join to form one zygote. Seed plants use seeds to reproduce. Flowering plants use flowers and seeds.

Flowering Plants

Sexual Parts

Flowering plants can be categorized sexually according to which organs they have. Flowers can be bisexual or unisexual. Species can be dioecious, which means male and female flowers are contained on different individual plants. Monoecious means that both male and female flowers are on one individual. Bisexual flowers are those that have all of the following: sepal, petal, stamen, and pistil. If they have all of these parts, they are considered complete. They have both the male stamen and the female counterpart, the pistil. Unisexual flowers only have a pistil or a stamen, not both. Incomplete flowers do not have all four parts. The flower rests upon a pedicel and is contained with the receptacle. The carpal is made up of the stigma at the tip, a style, and the ovary at the base. The ovary contains the ovules (eggs). Carpels are sometimes formed as a single pistil. The stamen includes the anther and the filament, and produces the male pollen.

POLLINATION

The anthers of the stamens (male parts) have microsporangia that form into a pollen grain, which consists of a small germ cell within a larger cell. The pollen grain is released and lands on a stigma (female) portion of the pistil. It grows a pollen tube the length of the style and ends up at the ovule. The pollen grain releases the sperm and fertilization occurs. In double fertilization, one of the sperm joins with the egg to become a diploid zygote. The other sperm becomes the endosperm nucleus. Seeds are formed. One cotyledon (monocot) or two cotyledons (dicot) also form to store food and surround the embryo. Correspondingly, monocots produce one seed leaf, while dicots produce two. The seed matures and becomes dormant, and fruits typically form.

TROPISM, GEOTROPIC, PLAGIOTROPIC, PHOTOTROPISM, AND THIGMOTROPISM

Tropism refers to the fact that plants grow in response to specific stimuli. Seeds are geotropic (or gravitropic), meaning they grow as a response to gravity. Roots are positively geotropic and grow towards gravity. Stems are negatively geotropic and grow away from the force of gravity. A seed planted upside down will still grow roots and stems in the right direction. Plagiotropic refers to the fact that secondary branches and roots grow at right angles to gravity. Phototropism refers to the fact that a plant bends or grows toward a light source. Thigmotropism refers to how plants respond to contact. Plant hormones are organic compounds that usually influence changes in plants. They can cause fruit to ripen or instigate plant growth.

PLANT HORMONES

Five major groups of hormones are auxins, gibberellins, ethylenes, cytokinins, and abscisic acids. Auxins occur naturally and can be synthesized. They affect plant cell elongation, apical dominance, and rooting. Gibberellins affect plant height. Ethylenes help fruit ripen. Cytokinins are involved in cell division. Abscisic acids inhibit other hormones.

IMPORTANT TERMS

Homeostasis — This describes the ability and tendency of an organism, cell, or body to adjust to environmental changes to maintain equilibrium.
Gene expression — This refers to the use of information in a gene, usually during the processes of transcription and translation, that result in a protein product.
Transcription — This refers to the synthesis of RNA. Information is provided by DNA.
Translation — This is the decoding of mRNA (messenger RNA) used in the fabrication of protein. It occurs after transcription.
Cellular differentiation — This is the process by which a less specialized cell becomes a more specialized cell.
Lethal allele — This is when a mutation in an essential gene results in the death of the organism. Cystic fibrosis and Tay-Sachs disease are examples of lethal recessive alleles.
Pleiotropy — This refers to a gene that affects more than one trait.
Epistasis — This refers to the situation in which two or more genes determine a single phenotype.
Karyotype — This is a picture of genes based on a sample of blood or skin.
Community — **Community:** A community is any number of species interacting within a given area. A **niche** is the role of a species within a community. **Species diversity** refers to the number of

species within a community and their populations. A **biome** refers to an area in which species are associated because of climate. The six major biomes in North America are desert, tropical rain forest, grassland, coniferous forest, deciduous forest, and tundra.

Biotic — Biotic factors are the living factors, such as other organisms, that affect a community or population. Abiotic factors are nonliving factors that affect a community or population, such as facets of the environment.

Ecology — Ecology is the study of plants, animals, their environments, and how they interact.

Ecosystem — An ecosystem is a community of species and all of the environment factors that affect them.

Physical Sciences

ATOMS AND MOLECULES

Elements from the periodic table such as hydrogen, carbon, iron, helium, mercury, and oxygen are atoms. Atoms combine to form molecules. For example, two atoms of hydrogen (H) and one atom of oxygen (O) combine to form one molecule of water (H_2O).

STRUCTURE OF ATOMS

All matter consists of atoms. Atoms consist of a nucleus and electrons. The nucleus consists of protons and neutrons. The properties of these are measurable; they have mass and an electrical charge. The nucleus is positively charged due to the presence of protons. Electrons are negatively charged and orbit the nucleus. The nucleus has considerably more mass than the surrounding electrons. Atoms can bond together to make molecules. Atoms that have an equal number of protons and electrons are electrically neutral. If the number of protons and electrons in an atom is not equal, the atom has a positive or negative charge and is an ion.

Review Video: Structure of Atoms
Visit mometrix.com/academy and enter code: 905932

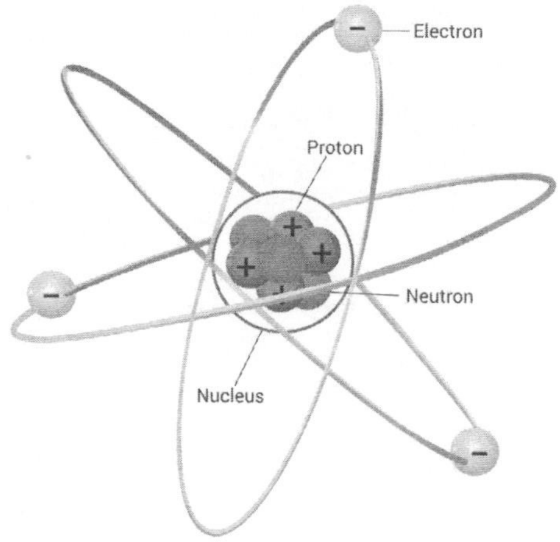

FORMATION OF MOLECULES

Electrons in an atom can orbit different levels around the nucleus. They can absorb or release energy, which can change the location of their orbit or even allow them to break free from the atom. The outermost layer is the valence layer, which contains the valence electrons. The valence layer tends to have or share eight electrons. Molecules are formed by a chemical bond between atoms, a bond that occurs at the valence level. Two basic types of bonds are covalent and ionic. A covalent bond is formed when atoms share electrons. An ionic bond is formed when an atom transfers an electron to another atom. A cation or positive ion is formed when an atom loses one or more electrons. An anion or negative ion is formed when an atom gains one or more electrons. A hydrogen bond is a weak bond between a hydrogen atom of one molecule and an electronegative atom (such as nitrogen, oxygen, or fluorine) of another molecule. The Van der Waals force is a weak force between molecules. This type of force is much weaker than actual chemical bonds between atoms.

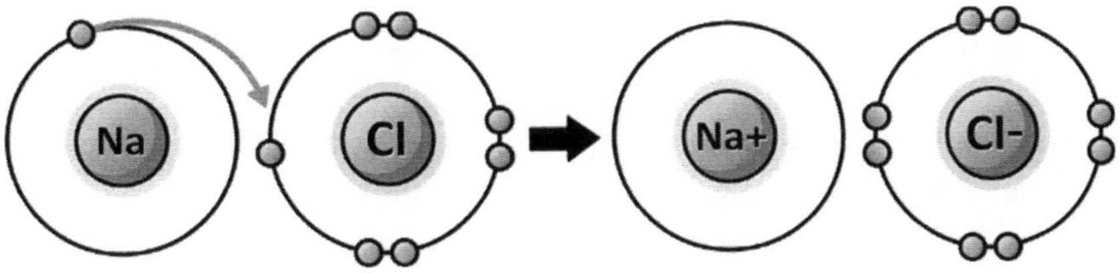

Review Video: Ionic Bonding
Visit mometrix.com/academy and enter code: 116546

Models of Atoms

Atoms are extremely small. A hydrogen atom is about 5×10^{-8} mm in diameter. According to some estimates, five trillion hydrogen atoms could fit on the head of a pin. Atomic radius refers to the average distance between the nucleus and the outermost electron. Models of atoms that include the proton, nucleus, and electrons typically show the electrons very close to the nucleus and revolving around it, similar to how the Earth orbits the sun. However, another model relates the Earth as the nucleus and its atmosphere as electrons, which is the basis of the term "electron cloud." Another description is that electrons swarm around the nucleus. It should be noted that these atomic models are not to scale. A more accurate representation would be a nucleus with a diameter of about 2 cm in a stadium. The electrons would be in the bleachers. This model is similar to the not-to-scale solar system model. In reference to the periodic table, atomic radius increases as energy levels are added and decreases as more protons are added (because they pull the electrons closer to the nucleus). Essentially, atomic radius increases toward the left and toward the bottom of the periodic table (i.e., Francium (Fr) has the largest atomic radius while Helium (He) has the smallest).

Isotope

The number of protons in an atom determines the element of that atom. For instance, all helium atoms have exactly two protons, and all oxygen atoms have exactly eight protons. If two atoms have the same number of protons, then they are the same element. However, the number of neutrons in two atoms can be different without the atoms being different elements. Isotope is the term used to distinguish between atoms that have the same number of protons but a different number of neutrons. The names of isotopes have the element name with the mass number. Recall that the mass number is the number of protons plus the number of neutrons. For example, carbon-12 refers to an atom that has 6 protons, which makes it carbon, and 6 neutrons. In other words, 6 protons + 6 neutrons = 12. Carbon-13 has six protons and seven neutrons, and carbon-14 has six protons and eight neutrons. Isotopes can also be written with the mass number in superscript before the element symbol. For example, carbon-12 can be written as ^{12}C.

Atomic Mass and Atomic Weight

Atomic mass: This is also known as the mass number. The atomic mass is the total number of protons and neutrons in the nucleus of an atom. It is referred to as "A." The atomic mass (A) is equal to the number of protons (Z) plus the number of neutrons (N). This can be represented by the equation $A = Z + N$. The mass of electrons in an atom is basically insignificant because it is so small.

Atomic weight: This may sometimes be referred to as "relative atomic mass," but should not be confused with atomic mass. Atomic weight is the ratio of the average mass per atom of a sample (which can include various isotopes of an element) to 1/12 of the mass of an atom of carbon-12.

Electrons

Electrons are subatomic particles that orbit the nucleus at various levels commonly referred to as layers, shells, or clouds. The orbiting electron or electrons account for only a fraction of the atom's mass. They are much smaller than the nucleus, are negatively charged, and exhibit wave-like characteristics. Electrons are part of the lepton family of elementary particles. Electrons can occupy orbits that are varying distances away from the nucleus, and tend to occupy the lowest energy level they can. If an atom has all its electrons in the lowest available positions, it has a stable electron arrangement. The outermost electron shell of an atom in its uncombined state is known as the valence shell. The electrons there are called valence electrons, and it is their number that determines bonding behavior. Atoms tend to react in a manner that will allow them to fill or empty their valence shells.

Interaction of Atoms to Form Compounds

Atoms interact by transferring or sharing the electrons furthest from the nucleus. Known as the outer or valence electrons, they are responsible for the chemical properties of an element. Bonds between atoms are created when electrons are paired up by being transferred or shared. If electrons are transferred from one atom to another, the bond is ionic. If electrons are shared, the bond is covalent. Atoms of the same element may bond together to form molecules or crystalline solids. When two or more different types of atoms bind together chemically, a compound is made. The physical properties of compounds reflect the nature of the interactions among their molecules. These interactions are determined by the structure of the molecule, including the atoms they consist of and the distances and angles between them.

Matter

Matter refers to substances that have mass and occupy space (or volume). The traditional definition of matter describes it as having three states: solid, liquid, and gas. These different states are caused by differences in the distances and angles between molecules or atoms, which result in differences in the energy that binds them. Solid structures are rigid or nearly rigid and have strong bonds. Molecules or atoms of liquids move around and have weak bonds, although they are not weak enough to readily break. Molecules or atoms of gases move almost independently of each other, are typically far apart, and do not form bonds. The current definition of matter describes it as having four states. The fourth is plasma, which is an ionized gas that has some electrons that are described as free because they are not bound to an atom or molecule.

Ions and Ionization

Most atoms are neutral since the positive charge of the protons in the nucleus is balanced by the negative charge of the surrounding electrons. Electrons are transferred between atoms when they come into contact with each other. This creates a molecule or atom in which the number of electrons does not equal the number of protons, which gives it a positive or negative charge. A negative ion is created when an atom gains electrons, while a positive ion is created when an atom loses electrons. An ionic bond is formed between ions with opposite charges. The resulting compound is neutral. Ionization refers to the process by which neutral particles are ionized into charged particles. Gases and plasmas can be partially or fully ionized through ionization.

Physical and Chemical Properties and Changes

Both physical changes and chemical reactions are everyday occurrences. Physical changes do not result in different substances. For example, when water becomes ice it has undergone a physical change, but not a chemical change. It has changed its form, but not its composition. It is still H_2O. Chemical properties are concerned with the constituent particles that make up the physicality of a substance. Chemical properties are apparent when chemical changes occur. The chemical properties of a substance are influenced by its electron configuration, which is determined in part by the number of protons in the nucleus (the atomic number). Carbon, for example, has 6 protons and 6 electrons. It is an element's outermost valence electrons that mainly determine its chemical properties. Chemical reactions may release or consume energy.

PERIODIC TABLE

The periodic table groups elements with similar chemical properties together. The grouping of elements is based on atomic structure. It shows periodic trends of physical and chemical properties and identifies families of elements with similar properties. It is a common model for organizing and understanding elements. In the periodic table, each element has its own cell that includes varying amounts of information presented in symbol form about the properties of the element. Cells in the table are arranged in rows (periods) and columns (groups or families). At minimum, a cell includes the symbol for the element and its atomic number. The cell for hydrogen, for example, which appears first in the upper left corner, includes an "H" and a "1" above the letter. Elements are ordered by atomic number, left to right, top to bottom.

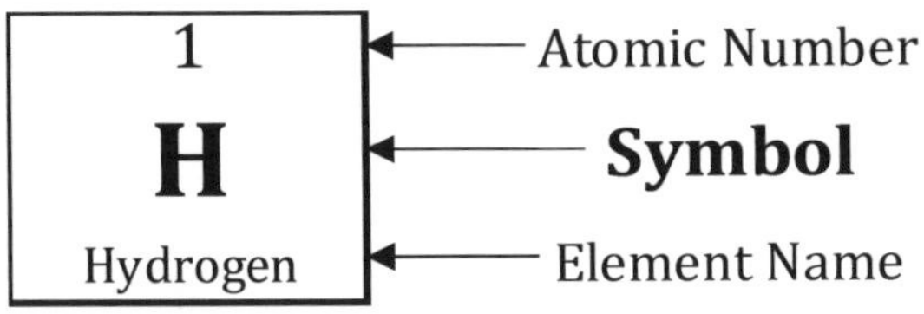

GROUPS

In the periodic table, the groups are the columns numbered 1 through 18 that group elements with similar outer electron shell configurations. Since the configuration of the outer electron shell is one of the primary factors affecting an element's chemical properties, elements within the same group have similar chemical properties. Previous naming conventions for groups have included the use of Roman numerals and upper-case letters. Currently, the periodic table groups are: Group 1, alkali metals; Group 2, alkaline earth metals; Groups 3-12, transition metals; Group 13, boron family; Group 14; carbon family; Group 15, pnictogens; Group 16, chalcogens; Group 17, halogens; Group 18, noble gases.

PERIODS, BLOCKS, AND ELECTRONS

In the periodic table, there are seven periods (rows), and within each period there are blocks that group elements with the same outer electron subshell (more on this in the next section). The number of electrons in that outer shell determines which group an element belongs to within a given block. Each row's number (1, 2, 3, etc.) corresponds to the highest number electron shell that is in use. For example, row 2 uses only electron shells 1 and 2, while row 7 uses all shells from 1-7.

ATOMIC AND IONIC RADII, ELECTRONEGATIVITY, IONIZATION ENERGY, ELECTRON AFFINITY, AND PHYSICAL PROPERTIES

Atomic radii will decrease from left to right across a period (row) on the periodic table. In a group (column), there is an increase in the atomic radii of elements from top to bottom. Ionic radii will be smaller than the atomic radii for metals, but the opposite is true for non-metals. From left to right, electronegativity, or an atom's likeliness of taking another atom's electrons, increases. In a group, electronegativity decreases from top to bottom. Ionization energy, or the amount of energy needed to get rid of an atom's outermost electron, increases across a period and decreases down a group. Electron affinity will become more negative across a period but will not change much within a group. The melting point decreases from top to bottom in the metal groups and increases from top to bottom in the non-metal groups.

Separation and Decomposition

Decomposition is considered a chemical reaction whereby a single compound breaks down into component parts or simpler compounds. When a compound or substance separates into these simpler substances, the byproducts are often substances that are different from the original. Decomposition can be viewed as the opposite of combination reactions. Most decomposition reactions are endothermic. Heat needs to be added for the chemical reaction to occur. Separation processes can be mechanical or chemical, and usually involve re-organizing a mixture of substances without changing their chemical nature. The separated products may differ from the original mixture in terms of chemical or physical properties. Types of separation processes include filtration, crystallization, distillation, and chromatography. Basically, decomposition breaks down one compound into two or more compounds or substances that are different from the original; separation sorts the substances from the original mixture into like substances.

Chemical Reactions

Chemical reactions measured in human time can take place quickly or slowly. They can take a fraction of a second or billions of years. The rates of chemical reactions are determined by how frequently reacting atoms and molecules interact. Rates are also influenced by the temperature and various properties (such as shape) of the reacting materials. Catalysts accelerate chemical reactions, while inhibitors decrease reaction rates. Some types of reactions release energy in the form of heat and light. Some types of reactions involve the transfer of either electrons or hydrogen ions between reacting ions, molecules, or atoms. In other reactions, chemical bonds are broken down by heat or light to form reactive radicals with electrons that will readily form new bonds. Processes such as the formation of ozone and greenhouse gases in the atmosphere and the burning and processing of fossil fuels are controlled by radical reactions.

Review Video: Understanding Chemical Reactions
Visit mometrix.com/academy and enter code: 579876

Oxidation/Reduction Reactions

One way to organize chemical reactions is to sort them into two categories: oxidation/reduction reactions (also called redox reactions) and metathesis reactions (which include acid/base reactions). Oxidation/reduction reactions can involve the transfer of one or more electrons, or they can occur as a result of the transfer of oxygen, hydrogen, or halogen atoms. The species that loses electrons is oxidized and is referred to as the reducing agent. The species that gains electrons is reduced and is referred to as the oxidizing agent. The element undergoing oxidation experiences an increase in its oxidation number, while the element undergoing reduction experiences a decrease in its oxidation number. Single replacement reactions are types of oxidation/reduction reactions. In a single replacement reaction, electrons are transferred from one chemical species to another. The transfer of electrons results in changes in the nature and charge of the species.

Metathesis (Acid/Base) Reactions

Double replacement reactions are metathesis reactions. In a **double replacement reaction**, the chemical reactants exchange ions. However, the oxidation state stays the same. One of the signs of this is the building of a solid precipitate. In acid/base reactions, an acid is a compound that can donate a proton. A base is a compound that can accept a proton. In these types of reactions, the acid and base react to make salt and water. When the proton is donated, the base becomes water. So, the remaining ions make a salt. One way to know if a reaction is a redox or a metathesis reaction is to note the oxidation number of atoms in the reaction. It does not change during a metathesis reaction.

Electron Shells

There are seven electron shells. One is closest to the nucleus and seven is the farthest away. Electron shells can also be identified with the letters K, L, M, N, O, P, and Q. Traditionally, there were four subshells identified by the first letter of their descriptive name: s (sharp), p (principal), d (diffuse), and f (fundamental). The maximum number of electrons for each subshell is as follows: s is 2, p is 6, d is 10, and f is 14. Every shell has an s subshell, the second shell and those above also have a p subshell, the third shell and those above also have a d subshell, and so on. Each subshell contains atomic orbitals, which describes the wave-like characteristics of an electron or a pair of electrons expressed as two angles and the distance from the nucleus. Atomic orbital is a concept used to express the likelihood of an electron's position in accordance with the idea of wave-particle duality.

Chemical Bonds

Chemical bonds involve a negative-positive attraction between an electron or electrons and the nucleus of an atom or nuclei of more than one atom. The attraction keeps the atom cohesive, but also enables the formation of bonds among other atoms and molecules. Each of the seven energy levels (or shells) of an atom has a maximum number of electrons it can contain. The farther away from the nucleus an electron is, the more energy it has. The first shell, or K-shell, holds a maximum of 2 electrons; the second, L, holds 8; the third, M, holds 18; the fourth, N, holds 32; the fifth, O, holds 60; the sixth, P, holds 82; the seventh, Q, holds 108. The shells also have subshells. Chemical bonds form and break between atoms when atoms gain, lose, or share an electron in the outer (valence) shell.

Electron Configuration and Notation

Electron configuration: This is a trend whereby electrons fill shells and subshells in an element in a particular order and with a particular number of electrons. The chemical properties of the elements reflect their electron configurations. Energy levels (shells) do not have to be completely filled before the next one begins to be filled. An example of electron configuration notation is $1s^2 2s^2 2p^5$, where the first number is the row (period), or shell. The letter refers to the subshell of the shell, and the number in superscript is the number of electrons in the subshell. A common shorthand method for electron configuration notation is to use a noble gas (in a bracket) to abbreviate the shells that elements have in common. For example, the electron configuration for neon is $1s^2 2s^2 2p^6$. The configuration for phosphorus is $1s^2 2s^2 2p^6 3s^2 3p^2$, which can be written as $[Ne]3s^2 3p^2$. Subshells are filled in the following manner: 1s, 2s, 2p, 3s, 3p, 4s, 3d, 4p, 5s, 4d, 5p, 6s, 4f, 5d, 6p, 7s, 5f, 6d, and 7p.

Kinetic Theory of Gases

The kinetic theory of gases assumes that gas molecules are small compared to the distances between them and that they are in constant random motion. The attractive and repulsive forces between gas molecules are negligible. Their kinetic energy does not change with time as long as the temperature remains the same. The higher the temperature is, the greater the motion will be. As the temperature of a gas increases, so does the kinetic energy of the molecules. In other words, gas will occupy a greater volume as the temperature is increased and a lesser volume as the temperature is decreased. In addition, the same amount of gas will occupy a greater volume as the temperature increases, but pressure remains constant. At any given temperature, gas molecules have the same average kinetic energy. The ideal gas law is derived from the kinetic theory of gases.

Mole and Avogadro's Number

Atomic mass unit (amu) is the smallest unit of mass, and is equal to 1/12 of the mass of the carbon isotope carbon-12. A mole (mol) is a measurement of molecular weight that is equal to the molecule's amu in grams. For example, carbon has an amu of 12, so a mole of carbon weighs 12 grams. One mole is equal to about 6.0221415×10^{23} elementary entities, which are usually atoms or molecules. This amount is also known as the Avogadro constant or Avogadro's number (NA). Another way to say this is that one mole of a substance is the same as one Avogadro's number of that substance. One mole of chlorine, for example, is 6.0221415×10^{23} chlorine atoms. The charge on one mole of electrons is referred to as a Faraday.

Inorganic and Organic Molecules

The terms inorganic and organic have become less useful over time as their definitions have changed. Historically, inorganic molecules were defined as those of a mineral nature that were not created by biological processes. Organic molecules were defined as those that were produced biologically by a "life process" or "vital force." It was then discovered that organic compounds could be synthesized without a life process. Currently, molecules containing carbon are considered organic. Carbon is largely responsible for creating biological diversity, and is more capable than all other elements of forming large, complex, and diverse molecules of an organic nature. Carbon often completes its valence shell by sharing electrons with other atoms in four covalent bonds, which is also known as tetravalence.

Inorganic Compounds

The main trait of **inorganic compounds** is that they lack carbon. Inorganic compounds include mineral salts, alloys, non-metallic compounds such as phosphate, and metal complexes. A metal complex has a central atom (or ion) bonded to surrounding ligands (molecules or anions). The ligands sacrifice the donor atoms (in the form of at least one pair of electrons) to the central atom. Many inorganic compounds are ionic, meaning they form ionic bonds rather than share electrons. They may have high melting points because of this. They may also be colorful, but this is not an absolute identifier of an inorganic compound. Salts, which are inorganic compounds, are an example of inorganic bonding of cations (positive ions) and anions (negative ions). Some examples of salts are magnesium chloride ($MgCl_2$) and sodium oxide (Na_2O). Oxides, carbonates, sulfates, and halides are classes of inorganic compounds. They are typically poor conductors, are very water soluble, and crystallize easily. Minerals and silicates are also inorganic compounds.

Organic Compounds

Two of the main characteristics of organic compounds are that they include carbon and are formed by covalent bonds. Carbon can form long chains, double and triple bonds, and rings. While inorganic compounds tend to have high melting points, organic compounds tend to melt at temperatures below 300° C. They also tend to boil, sublimate, and decompose below this temperature. Unlike inorganic compounds, they are not very water soluble. Organic molecules are organized into functional groups based on their specific atoms, which helps determine how they will react chemically. A few groups are alkanes, nitro, alkenes, sulfides, amines, and carbolic acids. The hydroxyl group (-OH) consists of alcohols. These molecules are polar, which increases their solubility. By some estimates, there are more than 16 million organic compounds.

Review Video: Organic Compounds
Visit mometrix.com/academy and enter code: 264922

Nomenclature

Nomenclature refers to the manner in which a compound is named. First, it must be determined whether the compound is ionic (formed through electron transfer between cations and anions) or molecular (formed through electron sharing between molecules). When dealing with an ionic compound, the name is determined using the standard naming conventions for ionic compounds. This involves indicating the positive element first (the charge must be defined when there is more than one option for the valency) followed by the negative element plus the appropriate suffix. The rules for naming a molecular compound are as follows: write elements in order of increasing group number and determine the prefix by determining the number of atoms. Exclude mono for the first atom. The name for CO_2, for example, is carbon dioxide. The end of oxygen is dropped and "ide" is added to make oxide, and the prefix "di" is used to indicate there are two atoms of oxygen.

Molecular Formula and Molecular Compounds

Elements are represented in upper case letters. If there is no subscript, it indicates there is only one atom of the element. Otherwise, the subscript indicates the number of atoms. In molecular formulas, elements are organized according to the Hill system. Carbon is first, hydrogen comes next, and the remaining elements are listed in alphabetical order. If there is no carbon, all elements are listed alphabetically. There are a couple of exceptions to these rules. First, oxygen is usually listed last in oxides. Second, in ionic compounds the positive ion is listed first, followed by the negative ion. In CO_2, for example, C indicates 1 atom of carbon and O_2 indicates 2 atoms of oxygen. The compound is carbon dioxide. The formula for ammonia (an ionic compound) is NH_3, which is one atom of nitrogen and three of hydrogen. H_2O is two atoms of hydrogen and one of oxygen. Sugar is $C_6H_{12}O_6$, which is 6 atoms of carbon, 12 of hydrogen, and 6 of oxygen.

Chemical Equations

Chemical equations describe chemical reactions. The reactants are on the left side before the arrow. The products are on the right side after the arrow. The arrow is the mark that points to the reaction or change. The coefficient is the number before the element. This gives the ratio of reactants to products in terms of moles.

The equation for making water from hydrogen and oxygen is $2H_{2(g)} + O_{2(g)} \rightarrow 2H_2O_{(l)}$. The number 2 before hydrogen and water is the coefficient. This means that there are 2 moles of hydrogen and 2 of water. There is 1 mole of oxygen. This does not need to have the number 1 before the symbol for the element. For additional information, the following subscripts are often included to indicate the state of the substance: (g) stands for gas, (l) stands for liquid, (s) stands for solid, and (aq) stands for aqueous. Aqueous means the substance is dissolved in water. Charges are shown by superscript for individual ions, not for ionic compounds. Polyatomic ions are separated by parentheses. This is done so the kind of ion will not be confused with the number of ions.

Balancing Equations

An **unbalanced equation** is one that does not follow the **law of conservation of mass**, which states that matter can only be changed, not created or destroyed. If an equation is unbalanced, the numbers of atoms indicated by the stoichiometric coefficients on each side of the arrow will not be equal. Start by writing the formulas for each species in the reaction. Count the atoms on each side and determine if the number is equal. Coefficients must be whole numbers. Fractional amounts, such as half a molecule, are not possible. Equations can be balanced by adjusting the coefficients of each part of the equation to the smallest possible whole number coefficient. $H_2 + O_2 \rightarrow H_2O$ is an example of an unbalanced equation. The balanced equation is $2H_2 + O_2 \rightarrow 2H_2O$, which indicates that it takes two moles of hydrogen and one of oxygen to produce two moles of water.

Review Video: Balancing Chemical Equations
Visit mometrix.com/academy and enter code: 341228

Combination and Decomposition Reactions

Combination, or synthesis, reactions: In a combination reaction, two or more reactants combine to make one product. This can be seen in the equation $A + B \rightarrow AB$. These reactions are also known as synthesis or addition reactions. An example is burning hydrogen in air to produce water. The equation is $2H_2\ (g) + O_2\ (g) \rightarrow 2H_2O\ (l)$. Another example is when water and sulfur trioxide react to form sulfuric acid. The equation is $H_2O + SO_3 \rightarrow H_2SO_4$. Decomposition (or desynthesis, decombination, or deconstruction) reactions: In a decomposition reaction, a reactant is broken down into two or more products. This can be seen in the equation $AB \rightarrow A + B$. These reactions are also called analysis reactions. Thermal decomposition is caused by heat. Electrolytic decomposition is due to electricity. An example of this type of reaction is the decomposition of water into hydrogen and oxygen gas. The equation is $2H_2O \rightarrow 2H_2 + O_2$.

Properties of Water

The important properties of water (H_2O) are high polarity, hydrogen bonding, cohesiveness, adhesiveness, high specific heat, high latent heat, and high heat of vaporization. Water is vital to life as we know it. The reason is that water is one of the main parts of many living things.

Water is a liquid at room temperature. The high specific heat of water means that it does not easily break its hydrogen bonds. Also, it resists heat and motion. This is why it has a high boiling point and high vaporization point.

Most substances are denser in their solid forms. However, water is different because its solid-state floats in its liquid state. Water is cohesive. This means that it is drawn to itself. It is also adhesive. This means that it draws in other molecules. If water will attach to another substance, the substance is said to be hydrophilic. Because of its cohesive and adhesive properties, water makes a good solvent. Substances with polar ions and molecules easily dissolve in water.

Review Video: Properties of Water
Visit mometrix.com/academy and enter code: 279526

Solutions

A solution is a homogeneous mixture. A mixture is two or more different substances that are mixed together, but not combined chemically. Homogeneous mixtures are those that are uniform in their composition. Solutions consist of a solute (the substance that is dissolved) and a solvent (the substance that does the dissolving). An example is sugar water. The solvent is the water and the solute is the sugar. The intermolecular attraction between the solvent and the solute is called solvation. Hydration refers to solutions in which water is the solvent. Solutions are formed when the forces between the molecules of the solute and the solvent are as strong as the forces holding the solute together. An example is that salt (NaCl) dissolves in water to create a solution. The Na^+ and the Cl^- ions in salt interact with the molecules of water and vice versa to overcome the intramolecular forces of the solute.

Review Video: Pure Substances and Mixtures
Visit mometrix.com/academy and enter code: 100384

Ideal Gas Law

The ideal gas law is used to explain the properties of a gas under ideal pressure, volume, and temperature conditions. It is best suited for describing monatomic gases (gases in which atoms are not bound together) and gases at high temperatures and low pressures. It is not well-suited for instances in which a gas or its components are close to their condensation point. All collisions are perfectly elastic and there are no intermolecular attractive forces at work. The ideal gas law is a way to explain and measure the macroscopic properties of matter. It can be derived from the kinetic theory of gases, which deals with the microscopic properties of matter. The equation for the ideal gas law is $PV = nRT$, where "P" is absolute pressure, "V" is absolute volume, and "T" is absolute temperature. "R" refers to the universal gas constant, which is 8.3145 J/mol Kelvin, and "n" is the number of moles.

Properties of Acids

When they are dissolved in aqueous solutions, some properties of acids are that they conduct electricity, change blue litmus paper to red, have a sour taste, react with bases to neutralize them, and react with active metals to free hydrogen. A weak acid is one that does not donate all of its protons or disassociate completely. Strong acids include hydrochloric, hydriodic, hydrobromic, perchloric, nitric, and sulfuric. They ionize completely. Superacids are those that are stronger than 100 percent sulfuric acid. They include fluoroantimonic, magic, and perchloric acids. Acids can be used in pickling, a process used to remove rust and corrosion from metals. They are also used as catalysts in the processing of minerals and the production of salts and fertilizers. Phosphoric acid (H_3PO_4) is added to sodas and other acids are added to foods as preservatives or to add taste.

Properties of Bases

When they are dissolved in aqueous solutions, some properties of bases are that they conduct electricity, change red litmus paper to blue, feel slippery, and react with acids to neutralize their properties. A weak base is one that does not completely ionize in an aqueous solution, and usually has a low pH. Strong bases can free protons in very weak acids. Examples of strong bases are hydroxide compounds such as potassium, barium, and lithium hydroxides. Most are in the first and second groups of the periodic table. A superbase is extremely strong compared to sodium hydroxide and cannot be kept in an aqueous solution. Superbases are organized into organic, organometallic, and inorganic classes. Bases are used as insoluble catalysts in heterogeneous reactions and as catalysts in hydrogenation.

Review Video: Properties of Acids and Bases
Visit mometrix.com/academy and enter code: 645283

Properties of Salts

Some properties of salts are that they are formed from acid base reactions, are ionic compounds consisting of metallic and nonmetallic ions, dissociate in water, and are comprised of tightly bonded ions. Some common salts are sodium chloride ($NaCl$), sodium bisulfate, potassium dichromate ($K_2Cr_2O_7$), and calcium chloride ($CaCl_2$). Calcium chloride is used as a drying agent, and may be used to absorb moisture when freezing mixtures. Potassium nitrate (KNO_3) is used to make fertilizer and in the manufacture of explosives. Sodium nitrate ($NaNO_3$) is also used in the making of fertilizer. Baking soda (sodium bicarbonate) is a salt, as are Epsom salts [magnesium sulfate ($MgSO_4$)]. Salt and water can react to form a base and an acid. This is called a hydrolysis reaction.

pH and pH Scale

The potential of hydrogen (pH) is a measurement of the concentration of hydrogen ions in a substance in terms of the number of moles of H^+ per liter of solution. A lower pH indicates a higher H^+ concentration, while a higher pH indicates a lower H^+ concentration. Pure water has a neutral pH, which is 7. Anything with a pH lower than water (less than 7) is considered acidic. Anything with a pH higher than water (greater than 7) is a base. Drain cleaner, soap, baking soda, ammonia, egg whites, and sea water are common bases. Urine, stomach acid, citric acid, vinegar, hydrochloric acid, and battery acid are acids. A pH indicator is a substance that acts as a detector of hydrogen or hydronium ions. It is halochromic, meaning it changes color to indicate that hydrogen or hydronium ions have been detected.

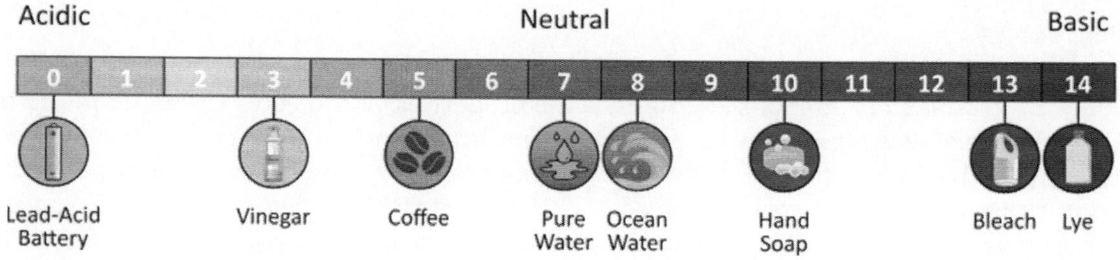

Stable and Radioactive Isotopes

Stable isotopes: Isotopes that have not been observed to decay are stable, or non-radioactive, isotopes. It is not known whether some stable isotopes may have such long decay times that observing decay is not possible. Currently, 80 elements have one or more stable isotopes. There are 256 known stable isotopes in total. Carbon, for example, has three isotopes. Two (carbon-12 and carbon-13) are stable and one (carbon-14) is radioactive.

Radioactive isotopes: These have unstable nuclei and can undergo spontaneous nuclear reactions, which results in particles or radiation being emitted. It can not be predicted when a specific nucleus will decay, but large groups of identical nuclei decay at predictable rates. Knowledge about rates of decay can be used to estimate the age of materials that contain radioactive isotopes.

Most Abundant Elements

Aside from dark energy and dark matter, which are thought to account for all but four percent of the universe, the two most abundant elements in the universe are hydrogen (H) and helium (He). After hydrogen and helium, the most abundant elements are oxygen, neon, nitrogen, carbon, silicon, and magnesium. The most abundant isotopes in the solar system are hydrogen-1 and helium-4. Measurements of the masses of elements in the Earth's crust indicate that oxygen (O), silicon (Si), and aluminum (Al) are the most abundant on Earth. Hydrogen in its plasma state is the most abundant chemical element in stars in their main sequences, but is relatively rare on planet Earth.

Past Atomic Models and Theories

There have been many revisions to theories regarding the structure of atoms and their particles. Part of the challenge in developing an understanding of matter is that atoms and their particles are too small to be seen. It is believed that the first conceptualization of the atom was developed by Democritus in 400 B.C. Some of the more notable models are the solid sphere or billiard ball model postulated by John Dalton, the plum pudding or raisin bun model by J.J. Thomson, the planetary or nuclear model by Ernest Rutherford, the Bohr or orbit model by Niels Bohr, and the electron cloud or quantum mechanical model by Louis de Broglie and Erwin Schrodinger. Rutherford directed the alpha scattering experiment that discounted the plum pudding model. The shortcoming of the Bohr model was the belief that electrons orbited in fixed rather than changing ecliptic orbits.

Conservation of Matter and Atomic Theory

Atomic theory is concerned with the characteristics and properties of atoms that make up matter. It deals with matter on a microscopic level as opposed to a macroscopic level. Atomic theory, for instance, discusses the kinetic motion of atoms in order to explain the properties of macroscopic quantities of matter. John Dalton (1766-1844) is credited with making many contributions to the field of atomic theory that are still considered valid. This includes the notion that all matter consists of atoms and that atoms are indestructible. In other words, atoms can be neither created nor destroyed. This is also the theory behind the conservation of matter, which explains why chemical reactions do not result in any detectable gains or losses in matter. This holds true for chemical reactions and smaller scale processes. When dealing with large amounts of energy, however, atoms can be destroyed by nuclear reactions. This can happen in particle colliders or atom smashers.

Conservation of Mass Number and Charge in Nuclear Reactions

Mass number is the sum of neutrons and protons in the nucleus ($A = N + Z$). The conservation of mass number is a concept related to nuclear reactions. Two conditions are required to balance a nuclear reaction. They are conservation of mass number and conservation of nuclear charge. In a nuclear equation, the mass numbers should be equal on each side of the arrow. In this type of equation, the mass number is in superscript in front of the element and the atomic number is in subscript. The total number of nucleons is the same even though the product elements are different. For example, when a specific isotope of uranium decays into thorium and helium, the original mass number of uranium is 238. After the reaction, the mass number of thorium is 234 and the mass number of helium is 4 ($238 = 234 + 4$). The mass number is the same on both sides of the equation.

Electronegativity

Electronegativity is a measure of how capable an atom is of attracting a pair of bonding electrons. It refers to the fact that one atom exerts slightly more force in a bond than another, creating a dipole. If the electronegative difference between two atoms is small, the atoms will form a polar covalent bond. If the difference is large, the atoms will form an ionic bond. When there is no electronegativity, a pure nonpolar covalent bond is formed. Electronegativity can be discussed as a trend in the periodic table. Fluorine (F) has the greatest electronegativity, and elements to the left and below fluorine have lower levels of electronegativity. This property of elements is often measured using the Pauling scale, which ranges from 4.0 (fluorine) to 0.7 (francium). Elements with high electronegativity are highly reactive because they can capture electrons. The symbols δ^+ (delta plus) and δ^- (delta minus) stand for fractional charges.

Review Video: Electronegativity
Visit mometrix.com/academy and enter code: 823348

Oxidation State and Oxidation Number

Oxidation state and oxidation number are usually the same number. Even though they have different meanings, they are frequently used interchangeably. Oxidation numbers are Roman numerals in parentheses that are used as part of the naming scheme for inorganic compounds. Oxidation state refers to the hypothetical charge on an atom if all of its bonds are 100 percent ionic. They are integers that can occasionally be fractional numbers. Oxidation state is increased through oxidation (loss of electrons) and decreased through reduction (gain of electrons). The number for an oxidation state refers to a single atom or ion, and is a way to keep track of electrons. When using Lewis diagrams, shared electrons are generally assigned to the more electronegative element. In bonds involving two atoms of the same element, electrons are split between them. Lone pairs of electrons are assigned to the atom they are with.

Lewis Formulas and Kekulé Diagrams

Lewis formulas show the bonding or nonbonding tendency of specific pairs of valence electrons. Lewis dot diagrams use dots to represent valence electrons. Dots are paired around an atom. When an atom forms a covalent bond with another atom, the elements share the dots as they would electrons. Double and triple bonds are indicated with additional adjacent dots. Methane (CH_4), for instance, would be shown as a C with 2 dots above, below, and to the right and left and an H next to each set of dots. In structural formulas, the dots are single lines. Kekulé diagrams, like Lewis dot diagrams, are two-dimensional representations of chemical compounds. Covalent bonds are shown as lines between elements. Double and triple bonds are shown as two or three lines and unbonded valence electrons are shown as dots.

Crystals

The crystalline structure of crystals is also known as a lattice. Crystal particles have symmetrical arrangements. Solidification may result in the formation of a single crystal or a group of crystals, which is known as a polycrystalline structure. The symmetry of a crystal is used to determine its classification. Although they are organized, structured, and symmetrical, crystals are imperfect and can have defects. Some may also have specific electrical properties. Crystal systems are grouped in accordance with their axial systems (there are three axes). The unique systems of crystals are cubic, hexagonal, rhombohedral, orthorhombic, monoclinic, and triclinic. Crystals in the cubic system are the most symmetric. The unit cell is the spatial arrangement of atoms. The spacing between unit cells is known as the lattice parameters. Salts form in cubic crystals. Common table salt (NaCl), for instance, forms a cubic lattice through ionic bonding. Rapid evaporation of a salt water solution results in small crystals, while slower evaporation leads to larger crystals.

Isomerization and Neutralization Reactions

Isomerization, or rearrangement, is the process of forming a compound's isomer. Within a compound, bonds are reformed. The reactant and product have the same molecular formula, but different structural formulas and different properties ($A \rightarrow B$ or $A \rightarrow A'$). For example, butane (C_4H_{10}) is a hydrocarbon consisting of four carbon atoms in a straight chain. Heating it to 100° C or higher in the presence of a catalyst forms isobutane (methylpropane), which has a branched-chain structure. Boiling and freezing points are greatly different for butane and isobutane. A rearrangement reaction occurs within the molecule. A neutralization, acid-base, or proton transfer reaction is when one compound acquires H^+ from another. These types of reactions are also usually double displacement reactions. The acid has an H^+ that is transferred to the base and neutralized to form a salt.

Single and Double Substitution Reactions

Single substitution, displacement, or replacement reactions occur when one reactant is displaced by another to form the final product ($A + BC \rightarrow AB + B$). Single substitution reactions can be cationic or anionic. When a piece of copper (Cu) is placed into a solution of silver nitrate ($AgNO_3$), the solution turns blue. The copper appears to be replaced with a silvery-white material. The equation is $2AgNO_3 + Cu \rightarrow Cu\ (NO_3)_2 + 2Ag$. When this reaction takes place, the copper dissolves and the silver in the silver nitrate solution precipitates (becomes a solid), resulting in copper nitrate and silver. Copper and silver have switched places in the nitrate. Double displacement, double replacement, substitution, metathesis, or ion exchange reactions occur when ions or bonds are exchanged by two compounds to form different compounds ($AC + BD \rightarrow AD + BC$). An example of this is that silver nitrate and sodium chloride form two different products (silver chloride and sodium nitrate) when they react. The formula for this reaction is $AgNO_3 + NaCl \rightarrow AgCl + NaNO_3$.

Review Video: What is a Single-Replacement Reaction?
Visit mometrix.com/academy and enter code: 442975

Binary compounds

Binary compounds refer to compounds that contain only two elements. They can be ionic or covalent. Binary ionic compounds are formed by cations (metallic positive ions) and anions (nonmetal negative ions). Ionic compounds are not molecules. The suffix "ide" is used if there is one anion, as in the case of cuprous oxide, for example. Another example is that fluorine is an element, while fluoride is the negative ion of fluorine. The binary compound barium fluoride would be written as BaF_2. This is because one barium ion has a charge of +2 and one fluoride ion has a charge of -1, so it would take two fluoride ions to balance out the one barium ion. If there is no charge symbol, it is assumed that the charge is 1. The suffixes "ate" or "ite" are used when there is more than one anion, as in the case of mercurous nitrate, for example. A ternary compound is one formed of three elements.

Hydrogen bonds

Hydrogen bonds are weaker than covalent and ionic bonds, and refer to the type of attraction in an electronegative atom such as oxygen, fluorine, or nitrogen. Hydrogen bonds can form within a single molecule or between molecules. A water molecule is polar, meaning it is partially positively charged on one end (the hydrogen end) and partially negatively charged on the other (the oxygen end). This is because the hydrogen atoms are arranged around the oxygen atom in a close tetrahedron. Hydrogen is oxidized (its number of electrons is reduced) when it bonds with oxygen to form water. Hydrogen bonds tend not only to be weak but also short-lived. They also tend to be numerous. Hydrogen bonds give water many of its important properties, including its high specific heat and high heat of vaporization, its solvent qualities, its adhesiveness and cohesiveness, its hydrophilic qualities, and its ability to float in its solid form. Hydrogen bonds are also an important component of proteins, nucleic acids, and DNA.

Polar and nonpolar solutes and solvents

For solvation to occur, bonds of similar strength must be broken and formed. Nonpolar substances are usually soluble in nonpolar solvents. Ionic and polar matter is usually soluble in polar solvents. Water is a polar solvent. Oil is nonpolar. Therefore, the saying "oil and water don't mix" is quite true. Heptane (C_7H_{16}) is another nonpolar liquid that is said to be immiscible in water, meaning it can't combine with water. The hydrogen bonds of the water molecules are stronger than the London dispersion forces of the heptane. Polar molecules such as NH_3 (ammonia), SO_2 (sulfur dioxide), and H_2S (hydrogen sulfide) are termed hydrophilic, meaning they readily combine with water. Nonpolar molecules, including the noble gases and other gases such as He (helium), Ne (neon), and CO_2 (carbon dioxide) are termed hydrophobic, meaning they repel or do not readily combine with water. One way to remember this is that "like dissolves like." Polar solvents dissolve polar solutes, while nonpolar solvents dissolve nonpolar solutes.

Effect of temperature and pressure on solubility

Solids tend to dissolve faster when the temperature is increased. Higher temperatures help break bonds through an increase in kinetic energy. Solubility tends to increase for solids being dissolved in water as the temperature approaches 100 °C, but at higher temperatures ionic solutes tend to become less soluble. Gases tend to be less soluble at higher temperatures. When solutions are saturated at high temperatures, the solute will precipitate (return to solid form) and "fall out of the solution" as the solution cools. Melting points can be lowered by using a solvent such as salt on icy roads, which lowers the freezing point of ice. Adding salt to water when making ice cream also lowers the melting point of the water. A solution's melting point is usually lower than the melting point of the solvent alone. Pressure has little effect on the solubility of liquid solutions. In gas solutions, an increase in pressure increases solubility, and vice versa.

MOLARITY, MOLALITY, AND COLLIGATIVE PROPERTIES

The concentration of a solution is measured in terms of molarity. One molar (M) is equal to a quantity of moles of solute per liter of solution. Adding one mole of a substance to one liter of solution would most likely result in a molarity greater than one. The amount of substance should be measured into a small amount of solution, and then more solution should be added to reach a volume of one liter to ensure accuracy. Molality refers to the concentration or ratio of moles of solute per kilogram of solvent. Colligative properties refer to how a solvent acts when it becomes a solution. Colligative properties are determined by the number of solute molecules rather than their exact characteristics. Some examples of colligative properties are that a solution's osmotic pressure and boiling point increase and its melting point decreases when the amount of solute is increased. As the amount of solute is increased, vapor will decrease above the solution when it is composed of a solid, nonvolatile solute dissolved in a liquid.

SOLUTIONS

A syrup is a solution of water and sugar. A brine is a solution of table salt, or sodium chloride (NaCl), and water. A saline solution is a sterilized concentration of sodium chloride in water. A seltzer is a solution of carbon dioxide in water. The term dilute is used when there is less solute. Adding more solvent is known as diluting a solution, as is removing a portion of the solute. Concentrated is the term used when there is more solute. Adding more solute makes a solution more concentrated, as does removing a portion of the solvent.

Properties of solutions include: they have a maximum particle size of one nm, they do not separate when allowed to stand or when poured through a fiber filter, they are clear and do not scatter light, and their boiling points increase while their melting points decrease when the amount of solute is increased.

MIXTURES, SUSPENSIONS, COLLOIDS, EMULSIONS, AND FOAMS

A mixture is a combination of two or more substances that are not bonded. Suspensions are mixtures of heterogeneous materials. Particles are usually larger than those found in true solutions. Dirt mixed vigorously with water is an example of a suspension. The dirt is temporarily suspended in water, but the two separate once the mixing is ceased. A mixture of large (1 nm to 500 nm) particles is called a colloidal suspension. The particles are termed dispersants and the dispersing medium is similar to the solvent in a solution. Sol refers to a liquid or a solid that also has solids dispersed through it, such as milk or gelatin. An aerosol spray is a colloid suspension of gas and the solid or liquid being dispersed. An emulsion refers to a liquid or a solid that has a liquid dispersed through it. A foam is a liquid that has gas dispersed through it.

EFFECTS OF CATALYSTS ON REACTIONS

Catalysts, substances that help change the rate of reaction without changing their form, can increase reaction rate by decreasing the number of steps it takes to form products. The mass of the catalyst should be the same at the beginning of the reaction as it is at the end. The activation energy is the minimum amount required to get a reaction started. Activation energy causes particles to collide with sufficient energy to start the reaction. A catalyst enables more particles to react, which lowers the activation energy. Examples of catalysts in reactions are manganese oxide (MnO_2) in the decomposition of hydrogen peroxide, iron in the manufacture of ammonia using the Haber process, and concentrate of sulfuric acid in the nitration of benzene.

Review Video: Catalysts
Visit mometrix.com/academy and enter code: 288189

Buffer

A buffer is a solution whose pH remains relatively constant when a small amount of an acid or a base is added. It is usually made of a weak acid and its conjugate base (proton receiver) or one of its soluble salts. It can also be made of a weak base and its conjugate acid (proton donator) or one of its salts. A constant pH is necessary in living cells because some living things can only live within a certain pH range. If that pH changes, the cells could die. Blood is an example of a buffer. A pKa is a measure of acid dissociation or the acid dissociation constant. Buffer solutions can help keep enzymes at the correct pH. They are also used in the fermentation process, in dyeing fabrics, and in the calibration of pH meters. An example of a buffer is HC_2H_3O (a weak acid) and $NaC_2H_3O_2$ (a salt containing the $C_2H_3O_2^-$ ion).

Nuclear Reactions

The particles of an atom's nucleus (the protons and neutrons) are bound together by nuclear force, also known as residual strong force. Unlike chemical reactions, which involve electrons, nuclear reactions occur when two nuclei or nuclear particles collide. This results in the release or absorption of energy and products that are different from the initial particles. The energy released in a nuclear reaction can take various forms, including the release of kinetic energy of the product particles and the emission of very high energy photons known as gamma rays. Some energy may also remain in the nucleus. Radioactivity refers to the particles emitted from nuclei as a result of nuclear instability. There are many nuclear isotopes that are unstable and can spontaneously emit some kind of radiation. The most common types of radiation are alpha, beta, and gamma radiation, but there are several other varieties of radioactive decay.

Heat, Energy, Work, and Thermal Energy

Heat is the transfer of energy from a body or system as a result of thermal contact. Heat consists of random motion and the vibration of atoms, molecules, and ions. The higher the temperature is, the greater the atomic or molecular motion will be. Energy is the capacity to do work. Work is the quantity of energy transferred by one system to another due to changes in a system that is the result of external forces, or macroscopic variables. Another way to put this is that work is the amount of energy that must be transferred to overcome a force. Lifting an object in the air is an example of work. The opposing force that must be overcome is gravity. Work is measured in joules (J). The rate at which work is performed is known as power. Thermal energy is the energy present in a system due to temperature.

THERMAL CONTACT

Thermal contact refers to energy transferred to a body by a means other than work. A system in thermal contact with another can exchange energy with it through the process of heat transfer.

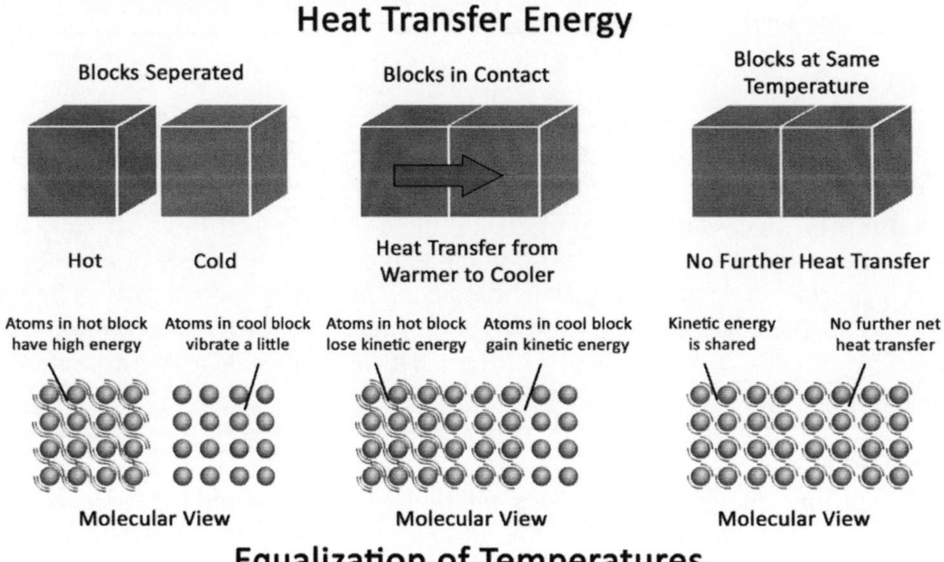

Thermal contact does not necessarily involve direct physical contact. Heat is energy that can be transferred from one body or system to another without work being done. Everything tends to become less organized and less useful over time (entropy). In all energy transfers, therefore, the overall result is that the heat is spread out so that objects are in thermodynamic equilibrium and the heat can no longer be transferred without additional work.

ENERGY TYPES

Some discussions of energy consider only two types of energy: kinetic energy (the energy of motion) and potential energy (which depends on relative position or orientation). There are, however, other types of energy. Electromagnetic waves, for example, are a type of energy contained by a field. Another type of potential energy is electrical energy, which is the energy it takes to pull apart positive and negative electrical charges. Chemical energy refers to the manner in which atoms form into molecules, and this energy can be released or absorbed when molecules regroup. Solar energy comes in the form of visible light and non-visible light, such as infrared and ultraviolet rays. Sound energy refers to the energy in sound waves.

CONDUCTION

A conductor is a material that provides little resistance to heat transfer between its particles. An insulator is a material that provides resistance to heat transfer between its particles. When studying atoms at a microscopic level, it can be seen that some materials such as metals have properties that allow electrons to flow easily. Metals are good conductors of electricity because their valence electrons are loosely held in a network of atoms. This is because the valence shells of metal atoms have weak attractions to their nuclei. This results in a "sea of electrons," and electrons can flow between atoms with little resistance. In insulating materials such as glass, they hardly flow at all. In between materials can be called semiconducting materials, and have intermediate conducting behavior. At low temperatures, some materials become superconductors and offer no resistance to the flow of electrons. Thermal conductivity refers to a material's capacity to conduct heat.

ENDOTHERMIC AND EXOTHERMIC REACTIONS

Endothermic reactions are chemical reactions that absorb heat and exothermic reactions are chemical reactions that release heat. Reactants are the substances that are consumed during a reaction, while products are the substances that are produced or formed. A balanced equation is one that uses reactants, products, and coefficients in such a way that the number of each type of atom (law of conservation of mass) and the total charge remains the same. The reactants are on the left side of the arrow and the products are on the right. The heat difference between endothermic and exothermic reactions is caused by bonds forming and breaking. If more energy is needed to break the reactant bonds than is released when they form, the reaction is endothermic. Heat is absorbed and the environmental temperature decreases. If more energy is released when product bonds form than is needed to break the reactant bonds, the reaction is exothermic. Heat is released and the environmental temperature increases.

EFFECT OF TEMPERATURE ON REACTION RATE

The collision theory states that for a chemical reaction to occur, atoms or molecules have to collide with each other with a certain amount of energy. A certain amount of energy is required to breach the activation barrier. Heating a mixture will raise the energy levels of the molecules and the rate of reaction (the time it takes for a reaction to complete). Generally, the rate of reaction is doubled for every 10 degrees Celsius temperature increase. However, the increase needed to double a reaction rate increases as the temperature climbs. This is due to the increase in collision frequency that occurs as the temperature increases. Other factors that can affect the rate of reaction are surface area, concentration, pressure, and the presence of a catalyst.

NUCLEAR FISSION AND NUCLEAR FUSION

Nuclear fission and nuclear fusion are similar in that they occur in the nucleus of an atom, can release great amounts of energy, and result in the formation of different elements (known as nuclear transmutation). They are different in that one breaks apart a nucleus and the other joins nuclei. Nuclear fission is the splitting of a large nucleus into smaller pieces. Nuclear fusion is the joining of two nuclei, which occurs under extreme temperatures and pressures. Fusion occurs naturally in stars, and is the process responsible for the release of great amounts of energy. When fusion occurs, many atomic nuclei with like charges are joined together, forming a heavier nucleus. When this occurs, energy can be absorbed and/or released.

RADIOISOTOPES, RADIOACTIVE DECAY, AND RADIOACTIVITY

Radioisotopes, also known as radionuclides or radioactive isotopes, are atoms that have an unstable nucleus. This is a nucleus that has excess energy and the potential to make radiation particles within the nucleus (subatomic particles) or undergo radioactive decay, which can result in the emission of gamma rays. Radionuclides may occur naturally, but can also be artificially produced. Radioactive decay occurs when an unstable atomic nucleus spontaneously loses energy by emitting ionizing particles and radiation. Decay is a form of energy transfer, as energy is lost. It also results in different products. Before decay there is one type of atom, called the parent nuclide. After decay there are one or more different products, called the daughter nuclide(s). Radioactivity refers to particles that are emitted from nuclei as a result of nuclear instability.

RADIOACTIVE HALF-LIFE AND RADIATION

Radioactive half-life is the time it takes for half of the radioactive nuclei in a sample to undergo radioactive decay. Radioactive decay rates are usually expressed in terms of half-lives. The different types of radioactivity lead to different decay paths, which transmute the nuclei into other chemical elements. Decay products (or daughter nuclides) make radioactive dating possible. Decay chains are a series of decays that result in different products. For example, uranium-238 is often found in granite. Its decay chain includes 14 daughter products. It eventually becomes a stable isotope of lead, which is why lead is often found with deposits of uranium ore. Its first half-life is equivalent to the approximate age of the earth, about 4.5 billion years. One of its products is radon, a radioactive gas. Radiation occurs when energy is emitted by one body and absorbed by another. Nuclear weapons, nuclear reactors, and radioactive substances are all examples of things that involve ionizing radiation. Acoustic and electromagnetic radiation are other types of radiation.

Alpha Particles, Beta Particles, and Gamma Rays

Ionizing radiation is that which can cause an electron to detach from an atom. It occurs in radioactive reactions and comes in three types: alpha (α), beta (β), and gamma (γ). Alpha rays are positive, beta rays are negative, and gamma rays are neutral. Alpha particles are larger than beta particles and can cause severe damage if ingested. Because of their large mass, however, they can be stopped easily. Even paper can protect against this type of radiation. Beta particles can be beta-minus or beta-plus. Beta-minus particles contain an energetic electron, while beta-plus particles are emitted by positrons and can result in gamma photons. Beta particles can be stopped with thin metal. Gamma rays are a type of high energy electromagnetic radiation consisting of photons. Gamma radiation rids the decaying nucleus of excess energy after it has emitted either alpha or beta radiation. Gamma rays can cause serious damage when absorbed by living tissue, and it takes thick lead to stop them. Alpha, beta, and gamma radiation can also have positive applications.

Energy Transformations

The following are types of energy transformation:

- Heat to mechanical: An example of a heat to mechanical energy transformation is a steam engine, such as the type used on a steam locomotive. A heat source such as coal is used to boil water. The steam produced turns a shaft, which eventually turns the wheels.
- Kinetic to potential and potential to kinetic: A pendulum swinging is an example of both a kinetic to potential and a potential to kinetic energy transformation. When a pendulum is moved from its center point (the point at which it is closest to the ground) to the highest point before it returns, it is an example of a kinetic to potential transformation. When it swings from its highest point toward the center, it is considered a potential to kinetic transformation. The sum of the potential and kinetic energy is known as the total mechanical energy.
- Potential to kinetic: Stretching a rubber band gives it potential energy. That potential energy becomes kinetic energy when the rubber band is released.
- Electric to mechanical: Ceiling fan
- Chemical to heat: A familiar example of a chemical to heat energy transformation is the internal combustion engine, which transforms the chemical energy (a type of potential energy) of gas and oxygen into heat. This heat is transformed into propulsive energy, which is kinetic. Lighting a match and burning coal are also examples of chemical to heat energy transformations.
- Chemical to light: Phosphorescence and luminescence (which allow objects to glow in the dark) occur because energy is absorbed by a substance (charged) and light is re-emitted comparatively slowly. This process is different from the one involved with glow sticks. They glow due to chemiluminescence, in which an excited state is created by a chemical reaction and transferred to another molecule.
- Heat to electricity: Examples include thermoelectric, geothermal, and ocean thermal.
- Nuclear to heat: Examples include nuclear reactors and power plants.
- Mechanical to sound: Playing a violin or almost any instrument

- Sound to electric: Microphone
- Light to electric: Solar panels
- Electric to light: Light bulbs

Laws of Thermodynamics

The laws of thermodynamics are generalized principles dealing with energy and heat.

- The zeroth law of thermodynamics states that two objects in thermodynamic equilibrium with a third object are also in equilibrium with each other. Being in thermodynamic equilibrium basically means that different objects are at the same temperature.
- The first law deals with conservation of energy. It states that neither mass nor energy can be destroyed; only converted from one form to another.
- The second law states that the entropy (the amount of energy in a system that is no longer available for work or the amount of disorder in a system) of an isolated system can only increase. The second law also states that heat is not transferred from a lower-temperature system to a higher-temperature one unless additional work is done.
- The third law of thermodynamics states that as temperature approaches absolute zero, entropy approaches a constant minimum. It also states that a system cannot be cooled to absolute zero.

First Law of Thermodynamics

The laws of thermodynamics state that energy can be exchanged between physical systems as heat or work, and that systems are affected by their surroundings. It can be said that the total amount of energy in the universe is constant. The first law is mainly concerned with the conservation of energy and related concepts, which include the statement that energy can only be transferred or converted, not created or destroyed. The formula used to represent the first law is $\Delta U = Q - W$, where ΔU is the change in total internal energy of a system, Q is the heat added to the system, and W is the work done by the system. Energy can be transferred by conduction, convection, radiation, mass transfer, and other processes such as collisions in chemical and nuclear reactions. As transfers occur, the matter involved becomes less ordered and less useful. This tendency towards disorder is also referred to as entropy.

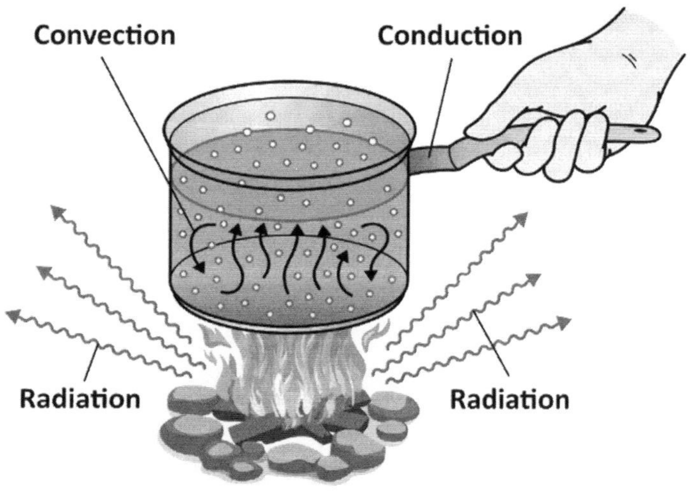

Second Law of Thermodynamics

The second law of thermodynamics explains how energy can be used. In particular, it states that heat will not transfer spontaneously from a cold object to a hot object. Another way to say this is that heat transfers occur from higher temperatures to lower temperatures. Also covered under this law is the concept that systems not under the influence of external forces tend to become more disordered over time. This type of disorder can be expressed in terms of entropy. Another principle covered under this law is that it is impossible to make a heat engine that can extract heat and convert it all to useful work. A thermal bottleneck occurs in machines that convert energy to heat and then use it to do work. These types of machines are less efficient than ones that are solely mechanical.

Review Video: Heat Transfer at the Molecular Level
Visit mometrix.com/academy and enter code: 451646

HEAT AND TEMPERATURE

Heat is energy transfer (other than direct work) from one body or system to another due to thermal contact. Everything tends to become less organized and less orderly over time (entropy). In all energy transfers, therefore, the overall result is that the energy is spread out uniformly. This transfer of heat energy from hotter to cooler objects is accomplished by conduction, radiation, or convection. Temperature is a measurement of an object's stored heat energy. More specifically, temperature is the average kinetic energy of an object's particles. When the temperature of an object increases and its atoms move faster, kinetic energy also increases. Temperature is not energy since it changes and is not conserved. Thermometers are used to measure temperature.

TEMPERATURE SCALES

There are three main scales for measuring temperature. Celsius uses the base reference points of water freezing at 0 degrees and boiling at 100 degrees. Fahrenheit uses the base reference points of water freezing at 32 degrees and boiling at 212 degrees. Celsius and Fahrenheit are both relative temperature scales since they use water as their reference point. The Kelvin temperature scale is an absolute temperature scale. Its zero mark corresponds to absolute zero. Water's freezing and boiling points are 273.15 Kelvin and 373.15 Kelvin, respectively. Where Celsius and Fahrenheit are measured in degrees, Kelvin does not use degree terminology.

- Converting Celsius to Fahrenheit: $°\text{F} = \frac{9}{5}°\text{C} + 32$
- Converting Fahrenheit to Celsius: $°\text{C} = \frac{5}{9}(°\text{F} - 32)$
- Converting Celsius to Kelvin: $K = °\text{C} + 273.15$
- Converting Kelvin to Celsius: $°\text{C} = K - 273.15$

HEAT CAPACITY AND SPECIFIC HEAT CAPACITY

Heat capacity, also known as thermal mass, refers to the amount of heat energy required to raise the temperature of an object, and is measured in Joules per Kelvin or Joules per degree Celsius. The equation for relating heat energy to heat capacity is $Q = C\Delta T$, where Q is the heat energy transferred, C is the heat capacity of the body, and ΔT is the change in the object's temperature. Specific heat capacity, also known as specific heat, is the heat capacity per unit mass. Every element and compound has its own specific heat. For example, it takes different amounts of heat energy to raise the temperature of the same amounts of magnesium and lead by one degree. The equation for relating heat energy to specific heat capacity is $Q = mc\Delta T$, where m represents the mass of the object, and c represents its specific heat capacity.

HEAT TRANSFER AT THE MOLECULAR LEVEL

Conduction is a form of heat transfer that occurs at the molecular level. It is the result of molecular agitation that occurs within an object, body, or material while the material stays motionless. An example of this is when a frying pan is placed on a hot burner. At first, the handle is not hot. As the pan becomes hotter due to conduction, the handle eventually gets hot too. In this example, energy is being transferred down the handle toward the colder end because the higher speed particles collide with and transfer energy to the slower ones. When this happens, the original material becomes cooler and the second material becomes hotter until equilibrium is reached. Thermal conduction can also occur between two substances such as a cup of hot coffee and the colder surface it is placed on. Heat is transferred, but matter is not.

Convection, Radiation, and Latent Heat

Convection refers to heat transfer that occurs through the movement or circulation of fluids (liquids or gases). Some of the fluid becomes or is hotter than the surrounding fluid, and is less dense. Heat is transferred away from the source of the heat to a cooler, denser area. Examples of convection are boiling water and the movement of warm and cold air currents in the atmosphere and the ocean. Forced convection occurs in convection ovens, where a fan helps circulate hot air. Radiation is heat transfer that occurs through the emission of electromagnetic waves, which carry energy away from the emitting object. All objects with temperatures above absolute zero radiate heat. Latent heat refers to the amount of heat required for a substance to undergo a phase (state) change (from a liquid to a solid, for example).

Motion and Displacement

Motion is a change in the location of an object and is the result of an unbalanced net force acting on the object. Understanding motion requires an understanding of three basic quantities: displacement, velocity, and acceleration. When something moves from one place to another, it has undergone *displacement*. Displacement along a straight line is a very simple example of a vector quantity. If an object travels from position $x = -5$ cm to $x = 5$ cm, it has undergone a displacement of 10 cm. If it traverses the same path in the opposite direction, its displacement is -10 cm. A vector that spans the object's displacement in the direction of travel is known as a displacement vector.

Gravitational Force

Gravitational force is a universal force that causes every object to exert a force on every other object. The gravitational force between two objects can be described by the formula, $F = Gm_1m_2/r^2$, where m_1 and m_2 are the masses of two objects, r is the distance between them, and G is the gravitational constant, $G = 6.674 \times 10^{-11}$ N-m^2/kg^2. In order for this force to have a noticeable effect, one or both of the objects must be extremely large, so the equation is generally only used in problems involving planetary bodies. For problems involving objects on the earth being affected by earth's gravitational pull, the force of gravity is simply calculated as $F = mg$, where g is 9.81 m/s^2 toward the ground.

Electrical Force

Electrical force is a universal force that exists between any two electrically charged objects. Opposite charges attract one another and like charges repel one another. The magnitude of the force is directly proportional to the magnitude of the charges (q) and inversely proportional to the square of the distance (r) between the two objects:

$F = kq_1q_2/r^2$, where $k = 9 \times 10^9$ N-m^2/C^2. Magnetic forces operate on a similar principle.

Velocity and Acceleration

There are two types of velocity to consider: average velocity and instantaneous velocity. Unless an object has a constant velocity or we are explicitly given an equation for the velocity, finding the instantaneous velocity of an object requires the use of calculus. If we want to calculate the average velocity of an object, we need to know two things: the displacement, or the distance it has covered, and the time it took to cover this distance. The formula for average velocity is simply the distance traveled divided by the time required. In other words, the average velocity is equal to the change in position divided by the change in time. Average velocity is a vector and will always point in the same direction as the displacement vector (since time is a scalar and always positive). Acceleration is the change in the velocity of an object. On most test questions, the acceleration will be a constant value. Like position and velocity, acceleration is a vector quantity and will therefore have both magnitude and direction.

Acceleration of Object Thrown Upward

When an object is thrown upward the acceleration throughout its flight is 9.8 meters per second squared (m/s^2) downward. This is Earth's gravity (g) close to its surface. It is the acceleration of all objects when there is no resistance, such as that of air.

Work

Work can be thought of as the amount of energy expended in accomplishing some goal. The simplest equation for mechanical work (W) is $W = Fd$, where F is the force exerted and d is the displacement of the object on which the force is exerted. This equation requires that the force be applied in the same direction as the displacement. If this is not the case, then the work may be calculated as $W = Fd\cos(\theta)$, where θ is the angle between the force and displacement vectors. If force and displacement have the same direction, then work is positive; if they are in opposite directions, then work is negative; and if they are perpendicular, the work done by the force is zero.

Example Calculation of Work

If a man pushes a block horizontally across a surface with a constant force of 10 N for a distance of 20 m, the work done by the man is 200 N-m or 200 J. If instead the block is sliding and the man tries to slow its progress by pushing against it, his work done is -200 J, since he is pushing in the direction opposite the motion. If the man pushes vertically downward on the block while it slides, his work done is zero, since his force vector is perpendicular to the displacement vector of the block.

Review Video: Push and Pull Forces
Visit mometrix.com/academy and enter code: 104731

Work Done upon a Stationary Object

If an object is held stationary, there is no work performed. This is because the formula for work performed is equal to the force times distance, or displacement ($W = F * d[\cos\Theta]$). Displacement is a vector measurement, and there must be displacement for work to be done. If an object is being held up, forces are at work, but are canceling each other out. No work is being done.

Mechanics, Vectors, and Scalars

Mechanics is the study of matter and motion, and the topics related to matter and motion, such as force, energy, and work. Discussions of mechanics will often include the concepts of vectors and scalars. Vectors are quantities with both magnitude and direction, while scalars have only magnitude. Scalar quantities include length, area, volume, mass, density, energy, work, and power. Vector quantities include displacement, velocity, acceleration, momentum, and force.

Effect of Mass on Acceleration of Falling Object

The weight of an object is the force of gravity on the object, and may be defined as the mass times the acceleration of gravity: w = mg. Mass is the amount of matter an object contains. When an object falls, it will accelerate at the same speed regardless of its mass, provided that gravity is the only force working on the object. Where mass can come into play is when there is significant air resistance. The force due to air resistance is a function of the object's size, shape, and velocity, but not mass. Thus, the air resistance force on two identically sized and shaped objects of different masses will be the same, but the heavier object will not be as affected, since it requires a greater force to overcome its momentum.

Newton's Laws of Motion

Newton's First Law of Motion

An object at rest or in motion will remain at rest or in motion unless acted upon by an external force.

This phenomenon is commonly referred to as inertia, the tendency of a body to remain in its present state of motion. In order for the body's state of motion to change, it must be acted on by an unbalanced force.

Newton's Second Law of Motion

An object's acceleration is directly proportional to the net force acting on the object, and inversely proportional to the object's mass.

This law is generally written in equation form F=ma, where F is the net force acting on a body, *m* is the mass of the body, and *a* is its acceleration. Note that since the mass is always a positive quantity, the acceleration is always in the same direction as the force.

Newton's Third Law of Motion

Newton's third law - For every force, there is an equal and opposite force. When a hammer strikes a nail, the nail hits the hammer just as hard. If we consider two objects, *A* and *B*, then we may express any contact between these two bodies with the equation $F_{AB} = -F_{BA}$, where the order of the subscripts denotes which body is exerting the force. At first glance, this law might seem to forbid any movement at all since every force is being countered with an equal opposite force, but these equal opposite forces are acting on different bodies with different masses, so they will not cancel each other out.

Simple Machines

Simple machines include the inclined plane, lever, wheel and axle, and pulley. These simple machines have no internal source of energy. More complex or compound machines can be formed from them. Simple machines provide a force known as a mechanical advantage and make it easier to accomplish a task. The inclined plane enables a force less than the object's weight to be used to push an object to a greater height. A lever enables a multiplication of force. The wheel and axle allows for movement with less resistance. Single or double pulleys allow for easier direction of force. The wedge and screw are forms of the inclined plane. A wedge turns a smaller force working over a greater distance into a larger force. The screw is similar to an incline that is wrapped around a shaft.

Inclined Plane

A certain amount of work is required to move an object. The amount cannot be reduced, but by changing the way the work is performed a mechanical advantage can be gained. A certain amount of work is required to raise an object to a given vertical height. By getting to a given height at an angle, the effort required is reduced, but the distance that must be traveled to reach a given height is increased. An example of this is walking up a hill. One may take a direct, shorter, but steeper route, or one may take a more meandering, longer route that requires less effort. Examples of wedges include doorstops, axes, plows, zippers, and can openers.

Lever

A lever consists of a bar or plank and a pivot point or fulcrum. Work is performed by the bar, which swings at the pivot point to redirect the force. There are three types of levers: first, second, and third class. Examples of a first-class lever include balances, see-saws, nail extractors, and scissors (which also use wedges). In a second-class lever the fulcrum is placed at one end of the bar and the work is performed at the other end. The weight or load to be moved is in between. The closer to the fulcrum the weight is, the easier it is to move. Force is increased, but the distance it is moved is decreased. Examples include pry bars, bottle openers, nutcrackers, and wheelbarrows. In a third-class lever the fulcrum is at one end and the positions of the weight and the location where the work is performed are reversed. Examples include fishing rods, hammers, and tweezers.

Wheel and axle work

The center of a wheel and axle can be likened to a fulcrum on a rotating lever. As it turns, the wheel moves a greater distance than the axle, but with less force. Obvious examples of the wheel and axle are the wheels of a car, but this type of simple machine can also be used to exert a greater force. For instance, a person can turn the handles of a winch to exert a greater force at the turning axle to move an object. Other examples include steering wheels, wrenches, faucets, waterwheels, windmills, gears, and belts. Gears work together to change a force. The four basic types of gears are spur, rack and pinion, bevel, and worm gears. The larger gear turns slower than the smaller, but exerts a greater force. Gears at angles can be used to change the direction of forces.

Pulley

A single pulley consists of a rope or line that is run around a wheel. This allows force to be directed in a downward motion to lift an object. This does not decrease the force required, just changes its direction. The load is moved the same distance as the rope pulling it. When a combination pulley is used, such as a double pulley, the weight is moved half the distance of the rope pulling it. In this way, the work effort is doubled. Pulleys are never 100% efficient because of friction. Examples of pulleys include cranes, chain hoists, block and tackles, and elevators.

Kinetic and potential energy

The two types of energy most important in mechanics are potential and kinetic energy. Potential energy is the amount of energy an object has stored within itself because of its position or orientation. There are many types of potential energy, but the most common is gravitational potential energy. It is the energy that an object has because of its height (h) above the ground. It can be calculated as $PE = mgh$, where m is the object's mass and g is the acceleration of gravity. Kinetic energy is the energy of an object in motion, and is calculated as $KE = mv^2/2$, where v is the magnitude of its velocity. When an object is dropped, its potential energy is converted into kinetic energy as it falls. These two equations can be used to calculate the velocity of an object at any point in its fall.

Archimedes's principle

Archimedes's principle states that a buoyant (upward) force on a submerged object is equal to the weight of the liquid displaced by the object. Water has a density of one gram per cubic centimeter. Anything that floats in water has a lower effective density, and anything that sinks has a higher effective density. This principle of buoyancy can also be used to calculate the volume of an irregularly shaped object. The mass of the object (m) minus its apparent mass in the water (m_a) divided by the density of water (ρ_w), gives the object's volume: $V = (m-m_a)/\rho_w$.

FLOATING OBJECTS

A key determiner as to whether an object will float or sink in water is its density. The general rule is that if an object is less dense than water, it floats; if it is denser than water, it sinks. The density of an object is equal to its mass divided by its volume (d = m/v). It is important to note the difference between an object's density and a material's density. Water has a density of one gram per cubic centimeter, while steel has a density approximately eight times that. Despite having a much higher material density, an object made of steel may still float. A hollow steel sphere, for instance, will float easily because the density of the object includes the air contained within the sphere. An object may also float only in certain orientations. An ocean liner that is placed in the water upside down, for instance, may not remain afloat. An object will float only if it can displace a mass of water equal to its own mass.

ELECTRIC CHARGES

The attractive force between the electrons and the nucleus is called the electric force. A positive (+) charge or a negative (-) charge creates a field of sorts in the empty space around it, which is known as an electric field. The direction of a positive charge is away from the electric field and the direction of a negative charge is towards it. An electron within the force of the field is pulled towards a positive charge because an electron has a negative charge. A particle with a positive charge is pushed away, or repelled, by another positive charge. Like charges repel each other and opposite charges attract. Lines of force show the paths of charges. The electric force between two objects is directly proportional to the product of the charge magnitudes and inversely proportional to the square of the distance between the two objects. Electric charge is measured with the unit Coulomb (C). It is the amount of charge moved in one second by a steady current of one ampere (1C = 1A × 1s).

MODELS FOR THE FLOW OF ELECTRIC CHARGE

Models that can be used to explain the flow of electric current, potential, and circuits include water, gravity, and roller coasters. For example, just as gravity is a force and a mass can have a potential for energy based on its location, so can a charge within an electrical field. Just as a force is required to move an object uphill, a force is also required to move a charge from a low to high potential. Another example is water. Water does not flow when it is level. If it is lifted to a point and then placed on a downward path, it will flow. A roller coaster car requires work to be performed to transport it to a point where it has potential energy (the top of a hill). Once there, gravity provides the force for it to flow (move) downward. If either path is broken, the flow or movement stops or is not completed.

FRICTION

Friction is a force that arises as a resistance to motion where two surfaces are in contact. The maximum magnitude of the frictional force (f)can be calculated as $f = F_c\mu$, where F_c is the contact force between the two objects and μ is a coefficient of friction based on the surfaces' material composition. Two types of friction are static and kinetic. To illustrate these concepts, imagine a book resting on a table. The force of its weight (W) is equal and opposite to the force of the table on the book, or the normal force (N). If we exert a small force (F) on the book, attempting to push it to one side, a frictional force (f) would arise, equal and opposite to our force. At this point, it is a *static frictional force* because the book is not moving. If we increase our force on the book, we will eventually cause it to move. At this point, the frictional force opposing us will be a *kinetic frictional force*. Generally, the kinetic frictional force is lower than static frictional force (because the frictional coefficient for static friction is larger), which means that the amount of force needed to maintain the movement of the book will be less than what was needed to start it moving.

A glass rod and a plastic rod can illustrate the concept of static electricity due to friction. Both start with no charge. A glass rod rubbed with silk produces a positive charge, while a plastic rod rubbed with fur produces a negative charge. The electron affinity of a material is a property that helps determine how easily it can be charged by friction. Materials can be sorted by their affinity for electrons into a triboelectric series. Materials with greater affinities include celluloid, sulfur, and rubber. Materials with lower affinities include glass, rabbit fur, and asbestos. In the example of a glass rod and a plastic one, the glass rod rubbed with silk acquires a positive charge because glass has a lower affinity for electrons than silk. The electrons flow to the silk, leaving the rod with fewer electrons and a positive charge. When a plastic rod is rubbed with fur, electrons flow to the rod and result in a negative charge.

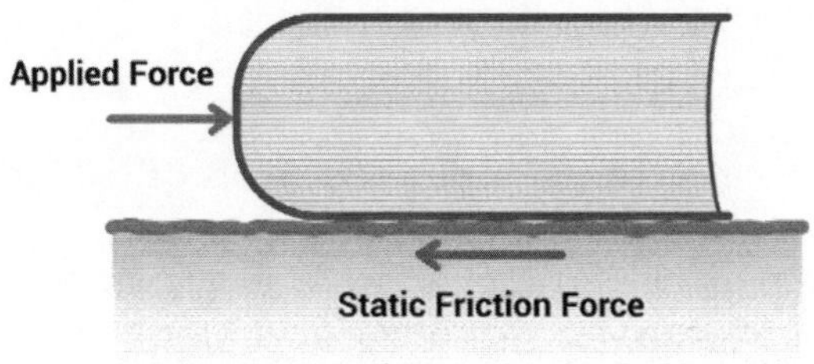

INDUCTION

Insulators are materials that prevent the movement of electrical charges, while conductors are materials that allow the movement of electrical charges. This is because conductive materials have free electrons that can move through the entire volume of the conductor. This allows an external charge to change the charge distribution in the material. In induction, a neutral conductive material, such as a sphere, can become charged by a positively or negatively charged object, such as a rod. The charged object is placed close to the material without touching it. This produces a force on the free electrons, which will either be attracted to or repelled by the rod, polarizing (or separating) the charge. The sphere's electrons will flow into or out of it when touched by a grounded object. The sphere is now charged. The charge will be opposite that of the charging rod.

CONDUCTION AND THE LAW OF CONSERVATION OF CHARGE

Charging by conduction is similar to charging by induction, except that the material transferring the charge actually touches the material receiving the charge. A negatively or positively charged object is touched to an object with a neutral charge. Electrons will either flow into or out of the neutral object and it will become charged. Insulators cannot be used to conduct charges. Charging by conduction can also be called charging by contact. The law of conservation of charge states that the total number of units before and after a charging process remains the same. No electrons have been created. They have just been moved around. The removal of a charge on an object by conduction is called grounding.

ELECTRIC POTENTIAL

Electric potential, or electrostatic potential or voltage, is an expression of potential energy per unit of charge. It is measured in volts (V) as a scalar quantity. The formula used is $V = E/Q$, where V is voltage, E is electrical potential energy, and Q is the charge. Voltage is typically discussed in the context of electric potential difference between two points in a circuit. Voltage can also be thought of as a measure of the rate at which energy is drawn from a source in order to produce a flow of electric charge.

Electric Current

Electric current is the sustained flow of electrons that are part of an electric charge moving along a path in a circuit. This differs from a static electric charge, which is a constant non-moving charge rather than a continuous flow. The rate of flow of electric charge is expressed using the ampere (amp or A) and can be measured using an ammeter. A current of 1 ampere means that 1 coulomb of charge passes through a given area every second. Electric charges typically only move from areas of high electric potential to areas of low electric potential. To get charges to flow into a high potential area, you must connect it to an area of higher potential, by introducing a battery or other voltage source.

Direct and Alternating Current

Direct current (DC) is the flow of an electric charge in one direction. Batteries and solar cells typically use direct current. Alternating current (AC) is current that periodically reverses direction. AC is typically used in houses and other buildings. A diode is an electronic device used to conduct electric current in one direction. The process of conduction in one direction is known as rectification. A rectifier is used to convert alternating current to direct current. Diodes are also used to remove modulation from radio signals. An inverter is the opposite of a rectifier in that it converts direct current to alternating current. Electromotive force (emf) is what causes electrons to move when there is potential difference between two points (voltage). Devices that can provide emf include batteries, voltaic cells, thermoelectric devices, solar cells, electrical generators, transformers, and Van de Graaff generators.

Electric Motor

An electric motor converts electric energy into mechanical energy. Energy can be provided by an AC or DC source. The power provided has many practical applications. The basic premise of a motor is that the electric current passing through a wire or coil creates a magnetic field that opposes the poles of a permanent magnet. The repelling forces between one pole of the electromagnet and the opposing pole of the fixed magnet cause the coil to move about ½ a turn. As it approaches the pole of like attraction, the coil would normally stop moving. In a motor, however, the current is reversed at this time, which reverses the poles and again forces rotation. In a DC motor, a switch or commuter can be used to reverse the charge. In an AC motor, the charge alternates on its own. The coil is attached to a shaft that is rotated, which provides the mechanical energy necessary to do work.

Generator

An electrical generator is the opposite of a motor in that it transforms magnetic force into electrical energy. Like a motor, however, it uses an electromagnetic field and a permanent magnet to achieve electromagnetic induction. Generators do not create electricity, but rather convert mechanical energy into electric energy. Smaller gas generators are used as backup or primary power sources of electricity for equipment, homes, and other small-scale applications. Larger generators may use mechanical energy from many different sources, including water, steam, wind, compressed air, or even a hand crank.

Simple Circuit

Movement of electric charge along a path between areas of high electric potential and low electric potential, with a resistor or load device between them, is the definition of a simple circuit. It is a closed conducting path between the high and low potential points, such as the positive and negative terminals on a battery. One example of a circuit is the flow from one terminal of a car battery to the other. The electrolyte solution of water and sulfuric acid provides work in chemical form to start the flow. A frequently used classroom example of circuits involves using a D cell (1.5 V) battery, a small light bulb, and a piece of copper wire to create a circuit to light the bulb.

Review Video: Resistance of Electric Currents
Visit mometrix.com/academy and enter code: 668423

Series and Parallel Circuits

As they relate to electric current, series circuits are circuits in which there is only one path through which electrons can flow. If a load in this type of circuit is removed, disabled, or switched off, the circuit is open and electricity does not flow. A parallel circuit is one in which there is more than one path through which electrons can travel. In a series circuit, the same current flows through all components. In a parallel circuit, on the other hand, the same voltage exists across all parallel paths, though the current may be vastly different among them. An example of a series circuit is a string of old-fashioned Christmas tree lights. If one bulb breaks or comes loose, the entire string will not work.

Ohm's Law

Electric currents experience resistance as they travel through a circuit. Different objects have different levels of resistance. The ohm (Ω) is the measurement unit of electric resistance. The symbol is the Greek letter omega. Ohm's Law, which is expressed as $I = V/R$, states that current flow (I, measured in amps) through an object is equal to the potential difference from one side to the other (V, measured in volts) divided by resistance (R, measured in ohms). An object with a higher resistance will have a lower current flow through it given the same potential difference.

Magnet

A magnet is a piece of metal, such as iron, steel, or magnetite (lodestone) that can affect another substance within its field of force that has like characteristics. Magnets can either attract or repel other substances. Magnets have two poles: north and south. Like poles repel and opposite poles (pairs of north and south) attract. The magnetic field is a set of invisible lines representing the paths of attraction and repulsion. Magnetism can occur naturally, or ferromagnetic materials can be magnetized. Certain matter that is magnetized can retain its magnetic properties indefinitely and become a permanent magnet. Other matter can lose its magnetic properties. For example, an iron nail can be temporarily magnetized by stroking it repeatedly in the same direction using one pole of another magnet. Once magnetized, it can attract or repel other magnetically inclined materials, such as paper clips. Dropping the nail repeatedly will cause it to lose its charge.

Magnetic Fields

The motions of subatomic structures (nuclei and electrons) produce a magnetic field. It is the direction of the spin and orbit that indicates the direction of the field. The strength of a magnetic field is known as the magnetic moment. As electrons spin and orbit a nucleus, they produce a magnetic field. Pairs of electrons that spin and orbit in opposite directions cancel each other out, creating a net magnetic field of zero. Materials that have an unpaired electron are magnetic. Those with a weak attractive force are referred to as paramagnetic materials, while ferromagnetic materials have a strong attractive force. A diamagnetic material has electrons that are paired, and therefore does not typically have a magnetic moment. There are, however, some diamagnetic materials that have a weak magnetic field.

A magnetic field can be formed not only by a magnetic material, but also by electric current flowing through a wire. When a coiled wire is attached to the two ends of a battery, for example, an electromagnet can be formed by inserting a ferromagnetic material such as an iron bar within the coil. When electric current flows through the wire, the bar becomes a magnet. If there is no current, the magnetism is lost. A magnetic domain occurs when the magnetic fields of atoms are grouped and aligned. These groups form what can be thought of as miniature magnets within a material. This is what happens when an object like an iron nail is temporarily magnetized. Prior to magnetization, the organization of atoms and their various polarities are somewhat random with respect to where the north and south poles are pointing. After magnetization, a significant percentage of the poles are lined up in one direction, which is what causes the magnetic force exerted by the material.

WAVES

Waves have energy and can transfer energy when they interact with matter. Although waves transfer energy, they do not transport matter. They are a disturbance of matter that transfers energy from one particle to an adjacent particle. There are many types of waves, including sound, seismic, water, light, micro, and radio waves. The two basic categories of waves are mechanical and electromagnetic. Mechanical waves are those that transmit energy through matter. Electromagnetic waves can transmit energy through a vacuum. A transverse wave provides a good illustration of the features of a wave, which include crests, troughs, amplitude, and wavelength.

Waves are divided into types based on the direction of particle motion in a medium and the direction of wave propagation:

- Longitudinal waves: These are waves that travel in the same direction as the particle movement. They are sometimes called pressure, compressional, or density waves. Longitudinal sound waves are the easiest to produce and have the highest speed. A longitudinal wave consists of compressions and rarefactions, such as those seen by extending and collapsing a Slinky toy.
- Shear or transverse waves: These types of waves move perpendicular to the direction of the particle movement. For example, if the particles in a medium move up and down, a transverse wave will move forward. Transverse waves are possible only in solids and are slower than longitudinal waves.
- Surface (circular) waves: These waves travel at the surface of a material and move in elliptical orbits. They are a little slower than shear waves.
- Plate waves: These waves move in elliptical orbits and only occur in very thin pieces of material.

FREQUENCY, PERIOD, AND SPEED

Frequency is a measure of how often particles in a medium vibrate when a wave passes through the medium with respect to a certain point or node. Usually measured in Hertz (Hz), frequency might refer to cycles per second, vibrations per second, or waves per second. One Hz is equal to one cycle per second.

Period is a measure of how long it takes to complete a cycle. It is the inverse of frequency; where frequency is measured in cycles per second, period can be thought of as seconds per cycle, though it is measured in units of time only.

Speed refers to how fast or slow a wave travels. It is measured in terms of distance divided by time. While frequency is measured in terms of cycles per second, speed might be measured in terms of meters per second.

AMPLITUDE, REST POSITION, CREST, TROUGH, AND WAVELENGTH

Amplitude is the maximum amount of displacement of a particle in a medium from its rest position, and corresponds to the amount of energy carried by the wave. High-energy waves have greater amplitudes; low energy waves have lesser amplitudes. Amplitude is a measure of a wave's strength.

Rest position, also called equilibrium, is the point at which there is neither positive nor negative displacement.

Crest, also called the peak, is the point at which a wave's positive or upward displacement from the rest position is at its maximum.

Trough, also called a valley, is the point at which a wave's negative or downward displacement from the rest position is at its maximum.

A wavelength is one complete wave cycle. It could be measured from crest to crest, trough to trough, rest position to rest position, or any point of a wave to the corresponding point on the next wave.

WAVE INTERACTIONS

Waves can be in phase or out of phase, which is similar to the concept of being in sync or out of sync. For example, if two separate waves originate from the same point and the peaks (crests) and valleys (troughs) are exactly aligned, they are said to be in phase. If the peak of a wave aligns with the valley of another wave, they are out of phase. When waves are in phase their displacement is doubled. If they are out of phase they cancel each other out. If they are somewhere in between being completely in phase and completely out of phase, the wave interaction is a wave that is the sum of the amplitudes of all points along the wave. If waves originate from different points, the amplitude of particle displacement is the combined sum of the particle displacement amplitude of each individual wave.

INTERFERENCE

When waves traveling in the same medium interact, it is known as wave interference. While a single wave generally remains the same in terms of waveform, frequency, amplitude, and wavelength, several waves traveling through particles in a medium take on a more complicated appearance after they interact. The final properties of a wave are dependent on many factors, such as the points of origin of waves and whether they are in phase, out of phase, or somewhere in between. Constructive interference refers to what happens when two crests or two troughs of a wave meet. The resulting amplitude of the crest or trough is doubled. Destructive interference is what happens when the crest of one wave and the trough of another that are the same shape meet. When this occurs, the two waves cancel each other out. An example of destructive interference is when two unlike sound waves reduce the volume of the sound.

DOPPLER EFFECT

The **Doppler effect** refers to the effect the relative motion of the source of the wave and the location of the observer has on waves. The Doppler effect is easily observable in sound waves. What a person hears when a train approaches or a car honking its horn passes by are examples of the Doppler effect. The pitch of the sound is different not because the *emitted frequency* has changed, but because the *received frequency* has changed. The frequency is higher (as is the pitch) as the train approaches, the same as emitted just as it passes, and lower as the train moves away. This is because the wavelength changes.

Sound

Sound is a pressure disturbance that moves through a medium in the form of mechanical waves, which transfer energy from one particle to the next. Sound requires a medium to travel through, such as air, water, or other matter since it is the vibrations that transfer energy to adjacent particles, not the actual movement of particles over a great distance. Sound is transferred through the movement of atomic particles, which can be atoms or molecules. Waves of sound energy move outward in all directions from the source. Sound waves consist of compressions (particles are forced together) and rarefactions (particles move farther apart and their density decreases). A wavelength consists of one compression and one rarefaction. Different sounds have different wavelengths. Sound is a form of kinetic energy.

Review Video: Sound
Visit mometrix.com/academy and enter code: 562378

Electromagnetic Spectrum

The electromagnetic spectrum is defined by frequency (f) and wavelength (λ). Frequency is typically measured in hertz and wavelength is usually measured in meters. Because light travels at a fairly constant speed, frequency is inversely proportional to wavelength, a relationship expressed by the formula $f = c/\lambda$, where c is the speed of light (about 300 million meters per second). Frequency multiplied by wavelength equals the speed of the wave; for electromagnetic waves, this is the speed of light, with some variance for the medium in which it is traveling. Electromagnetic waves include (from largest to smallest wavelength) radio waves, microwaves, infrared radiation (radiant heat), visible light, ultraviolet radiation, x-rays, and gamma rays. The energy of electromagnetic waves is carried in packets that have a magnitude inversely proportional to the wavelength. Radio waves have a range of wavelengths, from about 10^{-3} to 10^{5} meters, while their frequencies range from about 10^{3} to 10^{11} Hz.

Light

Light is the portion of the electromagnetic spectrum that is visible because of its ability to stimulate the retina. It is absorbed and emitted by electrons, atoms, and molecules that move from one energy level to another. Visible light interacts with matter through molecular electron excitation (which occurs in the human retina) and through plasma oscillations (which occur in metals). Visible light is between ultraviolet and infrared light on the spectrum. The wavelengths of visible light cover a range from 380 nm (violet) to 760 nm (red). Different wavelengths correspond to different colors.

When Light Encounters a Solid Object

When light waves encounter an object, they are either reflected, transmitted, or absorbed. If the light is reflected from the surface of the object, the angle at which it contacts the surface will be the same as the angle at which it leaves, on the other side of the perpendicular. If the ray of light is perpendicular to the surface, it will be reflected back in the direction from which it came. When light is transmitted through the object, its direction may be altered upon entering the object. This is known as refraction. When light waves are refracted, or bent, an image can appear distorted. The degree to which the light is refracted depends on the speed at which light travels in the object. Light that is neither reflected nor transmitted will be absorbed by the surface and stored as heat energy. Nearly all instances of light hitting an object will involve a combination of two or even all three of these.

Review Video: Reflection, Transmission, and Absorption of Light
Visit mometrix.com/academy and enter code: 109410

Color

The human brain interprets or perceives visible light, which is emitted from the sun and other stars, as color. For example, when the entire wavelength reaches the retina, the brain perceives the color white. When no part of the wavelength reaches the retina, the brain perceives the color black. The particular color of an object depends upon what is absorbed and what is transmitted or reflected. For example, a leaf consists of chlorophyll molecules, the atoms of which absorb all wavelengths of the visible light spectrum except for green, which is why a leaf appears green. Certain wavelengths of visible light can be absorbed when they interact with matter. Wavelengths that are not absorbed can be transmitted by transparent materials or reflected by opaque materials.

Use of the Properties of Light

The various properties of light have numerous real life applications. For example, polarized sunglasses have lenses that help reduce glare, while non-polarized sunglasses reduce the total amount of light that reaches the eyes. Polarized lenses consist of a chemical film of molecules aligned in parallel. This allows the lenses to block wavelengths of light that are intense, horizontal, and reflected from smooth, flat surfaces. The "fiber" in fiber optics refers to a tube or pipe that channels light. Because of the composition of the fiber, light can be transmitted greater distances before losing the signal. The fiber consists of a core, cladding, and a coating. Fibers are bundled, allowing for the transmission of large amounts of data.

Geometric Optics

Geometric optics uses the concept of rays to determine how light will propagate. Ray diagrams can illustrate the path of light through a lens. Different types of lenses refract light, either convergently or divergently, to form images. After passing through a lens, rays converge at a focal point. Collimated rays are nearly parallel, and can be thought of as having no focal point. There are many types and combinations of lenses. Convergent lenses, also called positive lenses, are thicker in the middle and thinner at the edges. Rays are focused to a point. Divergent lenses, also called negative lenses, are thicker at the ends and thinner in the middle. Rays are spread apart, or diverged. A convex lens is bowed outward, either at one vertical surface or both. A convex lens with two convex surfaces may also be termed biconvex or double convex. A concave lens is bowed inward, while a planar lens is flat.

Important Terms

- *Atom* — The atom is one of the most basic units of matter. An atom consists of a central nucleus surrounded by electrons.
- *Nucleus* — The nucleus of an atom consists of protons and neutrons. It is positively charged, dense, and heavier than the surrounding electrons. The plural form of nucleus is nuclei.
- *Electrons* — These are atomic particles that are negatively charged and orbit the nucleus of an atom.
- *Protons* — Along with neutrons, protons make up the nucleus of an atom. The number of protons in the nucleus determines the atomic number of an element. Carbon atoms, for example, have six protons. The atomic number of carbon is 6. The number of protons also indicates the charge of an atom. The number of protons minus the number of electrons indicates the charge of an atom.

- *Atomic number (proton number)* — The atomic number of an element refers to the number of protons in the nucleus of an atom. It is a unique identifier. It can be represented as Z. Atoms with a neutral charge have an atomic number that is equal to the number of electrons.
- *Neutrons* — Neutrons are the uncharged atomic particles contained within the nucleus. The number of neutrons in a nucleus can be represented as "N."
- *Nucleon* — This refers collectively to both neutrons and protons.
- *Element* — An element is matter with one particular type of atom. It can be identified by its atomic number, or the number of protons in its nucleus. There are approximately 118 elements currently known, 94 of which occur naturally on Earth. Elements from the periodic table include hydrogen, carbon, iron, helium, mercury, and oxygen.
- *Mass* — Mass is a measure of the amount of substance in an object.
- *Weight* — Weight is a measure of the gravitational pull of Earth on an object.
- *Volume* — Volume is a measure of the amount of space occupied. There are many formulas to determine volume. For example, the volume of a cube is the length of one side cubed (a^3) and the volume of a rectangular prism is length times width times height ($l \cdot w \cdot h$). The volume of an irregular shape can be determined by how much water it displaces.
- *Density* — Density is a measure of the amount of mass per unit volume. The formula to find density is mass divided by volume ($D = m/V$). It is expressed in terms of mass per cubic unit (e.g., grams per cubic centimeter $\frac{g}{cm^3}$).
- *Specific gravity* — This is a measure of the ratio of a substance's density compared to the density of water.
- *Elements* — These are substances that consist of only one type of atom.
- *Compounds* — These are substances containing two or more elements. Compounds are formed by chemical reactions and frequently have different properties than the original elements. Compounds are decomposed by a chemical reaction rather than separated by a physical one.
- *Solutions* — These are homogeneous mixtures composed of two or more substances that have become one.
- *Mixtures* — Mixtures contain two or more substances that are combined but have not reacted chemically with each other. Mixtures can be separated using physical methods, while compounds cannot.
- *Molar mass* — This refers to the mass of one mole of a substance (element or compound), usually measured in grams per mole (g/mol). This differs from molecular mass in that molecular mass is the mass of one molecule of a substance relative to the atomic mass unit (amu).
- *Charles's law* — This states that gases expand when they are heated. It is also known as the law of volumes.
- *Boyle's law* — This states that gases contract when pressure is applied to them. It also states that if temperature remains constant, the relationship between absolute pressure and volume is inversely proportional. When one increases, the other decreases. Considered a specialized case of the ideal gas law, Boyle's law is sometimes known as the Boyle-Mariotte law.
- *Ionization energy* — Ionization energy is the energy required for an electron to free itself from the grip of its neutral atom. Ionization energy increases across a row. Groups on the left of the table have fewer valence electrons and noble gases have the maximum number of valence electrons (a filled outer shell). Ionization energy can be measured in kilojoules (kJ) per mole or electron volts (eV) per atom (1 kJ/mol = 0.010364 eV/atom). Elements with low ionization energies are highly reactive because they can easily give up electrons.

- *Electron affinity* — This is a way to measure the change in energy when a negative ion is formed by adding an electron to a neutral atom.
- *Polar bond* — This refers to a covalent type of bond with a separation of charge. One end is negative and the other is positive. The hydrogen-oxygen bond in water is one example of a polar bond.
- *Maxwell-Boltzmann distribution* — This refers to a graph or plot showing the energies or speeds of particles or gas molecules in a system.
- *Calorie* — This is the amount of energy it takes to raise the temperature of a gram of water by one degree Celsius. A kilocalorie refers to the amount of energy it takes to raise the temperature of a kilogram of water by one degree Celsius. A calorie is equal to 4.184 joules.
- *Calorimeter* — This is a measurement device with a thermometer in which chemical or physical processes take place. The resulting change in temperature and the heat capacity can then be determined. Specific heat capacities have already been identified for many materials, and can be viewed in table form. When using a calorimeter and the medium in which the reaction took place (not the reaction itself) gains heat, it would indicate an exothermic reaction. The heat left the reaction and entered the medium, and the difference in heat was what was measured with the calorimeter.
- *BTU* — This stands for British thermal unit. It is a measurement of the amount of energy it takes to raise the temperature of a pound of water by one degree Fahrenheit. A BTU is equal to 252 calories or 1.054 kilojoules (kJ).
- *Endergonic* — This is a chemical reaction in which it takes more energy to instigate the reaction than is produced by it.
- *Exergonic* — This is a chemical reaction in which the net amount of Gibbs free energy is less than zero.
- *Gibbs free energy* — This value is similar to the available energy or maximum work of a closed system.
- *Enthalpy* — This is a measure of heat content in a system. It is usually assumed that the system is closed and the pressure is constant. Enthalpy is represented by the symbol H. The heat of a reaction is the difference between the heat stored in the reactants and in the products. It is represented by ΔH.
- *Circuit* — This refers to the movement of electric charge along a path between areas of high electric potential and areas of low electric potential.
- *Circuit breaker* — A circuit breaker stops the flow of an electric charge through a circuit by creating a break in the path. A fuse also creates a break.
- *Resistance* — This refers to the hindrance to the flow of an electric charge. Resistance is measured in Ohms. Ohms law is $I = V/R$, where "I" is current measured in amps, "V" is potential difference in volts, and "R" is resistance.
- *Resistor* — This refers to a device used in a circuit that opposes the flow of an electric charge.
- *Transistor* — This is a device made of a semiconductive material that can amplify or switch an electric charge.
- *Semiconductor* — This is a material with conductivity between an insulator and a conductor. These materials replaced earlier electric devices such as vacuum tubes.
- *Solid state device* — Used in modern circuits, solid state devices are solid materials in which the charge carriers, or electrons, are contained entirely within the material. Examples include transistors, microprocessors, integrated circuits, light-emitting diodes (LEDs), and liquid-crystal displays (LCDs).

- *Power* — Measured in watts, electric power refers to the rate at which electrical energy is transferred by an electric circuit. It can be calculated using Joule's law — P = V*I, where "P" is power, "V" is the potential difference (in volts) and "I" is current (in amps). Power can be generated, transmitted, and converted into various forms of light.
- *Watt* — A watt is the unit used to measure power. One watt is equal to one joule of energy per second.
- *Transformer* — A transformer is a device that uses induction to transfer current from one circuit to another. Two wound coils act as a pair of inductors. Voltage can be modified to be transferred to another circuit (as in transmission lines) or to a load, such as an electrical device plugged into a socket.
- *Pitch* — Pitch is the quality of sound determined by frequency. For example, a musical note can be tuned to a specific frequency. A, for instance, has a frequency of 440 Hz, which is a higher frequency than middle C. Humans can detect frequencies between about 20 Hz to 20,000 Hz.
- *Loudness* — Loudness is a human's perception of sound intensity.
- *Sound intensity* — Sound intensity is measured as the sound power per unit area, and can be expressed in decibels.
- *Timbre* — This is a human's perception of the type or quality of sound.
- *Oscillation* — This is a measurement, usually of time, against a basic value, equilibrium, or rest point.
- *Thermodynamics* — This refers to a branch of physics that studies the conversion of energy into work and heat. It is especially concerned with variables such as temperature, volume, and pressure.
- *Thermodynamic equilibrium* — This refers to objects that have the same temperature because heat is transferred between them to reach equilibrium.
- *Open, isolated,* and *closed systems* — Open systems are capable of interacting with a surrounding environment and can exchange heat, work (energy), and matter outside their system boundaries. A closed system can exchange heat and work, but not matter. An isolated system cannot exchange heat, work, or matter with its surroundings. Its total energy and mass stay the same.
- *Surrounding environment* — In physics, this term refers to everything outside a thermodynamic system (system). The terms "surroundings" and "environment" are also used. The term "boundary" refers to the division between the system and its surroundings.

Scientific Inquiry

SCIENCE

Science is a method of acquiring and obtaining knowledge. It is the process of gaining reliable information about the real world, including the explanation of phenomena. It is the development of a body of knowledge about observable phenomena, using the best capabilities humans have at their disposal. The process of organizing and classifying knowledge, through objective observation and evaluation, is a major goal of science.

Science can be considered reliable, but it is not infallible. The limits of human knowledge are constantly growing, often making yesterday's science obsolete and simplistic. Science is thus never fixed; it is always subject to change as new information is gained and synthesized with existing knowledge. Ultimately, science is the sum total of knowledge in any period of time, based on the current abilities of man to understand the world of phenomena, verifiable by observable data.

LIMITATIONS OF SCIENCE

There are clear limits on what science can explain. The demand for objectivity both strengthens knowledge we gain from scientific experiments and limits what we can explore. Beyond the realm of scientific inquiry are such questions as "Why does anything exist?" or "What is the meaning of life?" These are subjective questions that do not lend themselves easily to scientific inquiry. These questions, and others like them, come from within, and their conclusions, not validated by science, shape the very fabric of a society. They attempt to give meaning to what may be viewed as chaos. Periodically, science will impact these subjective conclusions with new evidence. For example, the theory of evolution is regarded as blasphemy by many religious fundamentalists. These conflicts may cause great upheavals in society, leaving many to wonder how science and religious belief can be reconciled. Ultimately, observation of the external world must stand as the true test of science.

OVERARCHING CONCEPTS OF SCIENCE

There are several concepts that transcend the branches of science and can be found as integral parts of physics, chemistry, biology, and other areas of study. One of these concepts is the system. A system is an arbitrarily sized group of entities that are taken to be a single unit. Systems may consist of physical bodies or of abstract concepts that intertwine. Systems will often be modeled by either mathematical expressions or physical-scale models, depending on the type of system and the purpose of the scale. In scale models, it is important to keep in mind that scale can have a huge effect on the behavior of a system. This can be seen in models of the solar system. The gravitational effects in a room-sized solar system model will be entirely negligible due to its reduced size. Other phenomena will only be observed on the atomic level. If the state of a system is constant, it is at equilibrium. Equilibrium may be either static or dynamic. A pair of side-by-side pools are in static equilibrium if there is no water being transferred between them. They are in dynamic equilibrium if equal amounts of water are being transferred between the pools in each direction. In the design of physical components, something that may be encountered is the interrelationship between form and function. If one of these two goals takes priority, that one will dictate the other. If the external appearance of a building is considered to be of higher importance than its utility, the functionality of the building may be limited.

CONVERTING FROM DECIMAL NOTATION TO SCIENTIFIC NOTATION

Scientific notation is used because values in science can be very large or very small, which makes them unwieldy. A number in decimal notation is 93,000,000. In scientific notation, it is 9.3×10^7.

The first number, 9.3, is the coefficient. It is always greater than or equal to 1 and less than 10. This number is followed by a multiplication sign. The base is always 10 in scientific notation. If the number is greater than ten, the exponent is positive. If the number is between zero and one, the exponent is negative. The first digit of the number is followed by a decimal point and then the rest of the number. In this case, the number is 9.3. To get that number, the decimal point was moved seven places from the end of the number, 93,000,000. The number of places, seven, is the exponent.

SIGNIFICANT FIGURES AND ESTIMATION

The mathematical concept of significant figures or significant digits is often used to determine the accuracy of measurements or the level of confidence one has in a specific measurement. The significant figures of a measurement include all the digits known with certainty plus one estimated or uncertain digit. There are a number of rules for determining which digits are considered "important" or "interesting." They are: all non-zero digits are significant, zeros between digits are significant, and leading and trailing zeros are not significant unless they appear to the right of the non-zero digits in a decimal. For example, in 0.01230 the significant digits are 1230, and this number would be said to be accurate to the hundred-thousandths place. The zero indicates that the amount has actually been measured as 0. Other zeros are considered place holders, and are not important. A decimal point may be placed after zeros to indicate their importance (in 100. for example).

CONFIRMATION AND VERIFICATION OF DATA

A critical distinction should be made between confirmation and verification of scientific data. Verification establishes once and for all the truth of the statement. Confirmation is the testing of claims to see how true they are. For a claim to be testable, an experiment must be devised to ensure the validity of the results. A claim can only be confirmed when we know the conditions for verification. A claim confirmation is always relative to the testing procedures. Test results must always be objective and observable. Actually, no factual claim can ever be verified because there is always the possibility of new evidence appearing that proves the claim false. A scientific law must also be confirmed by making predictions based on unbiased, observable data.

DATA COLLECTION AND ANALYSIS

In order to take data measurements from their experimental setups, scientists will often use measurement devices wired to a computer running data-acquisition software. This allows them to take numerous readings per second if necessary. Once the data is collected, it will often be organized using a spreadsheet, such as Microsoft Excel. This multipurpose program contains several options for displaying the data in graphs or charts, as well as tools for performing statistical analyses or linear regressions. Linear regression is a technique used to determine whether gathered data fits a particular trend or equation. It attempts to fit a common line or curve equation to the data set. A very important concept to understand when taking data is that of significant figures. Significant figures, or significant digits, indicate how precisely a quantity is known. Each non-zero digit is always significant. A zero is significant if either: 1) it is to the right of both a non-zero digit and the decimal point; or 2) it is between two other significant digits. For instance, 1.0230 has five significant figures while 0.0230 has only three because the trailing zero is the only zero to the right of both a non-zero and the decimal. When multiplying (or dividing), the product (quotient) has as many significant figures as the factor (dividend or divisor) with the fewest. When adding (or subtracting), the sum (difference) should be rounded to the highest final decimal place of the involved terms.

- (3.4 + 56.78 = 60.18 --> 60.2, three significant figures)

Interpretation and Conclusions from Tables, Charts, and Graphs

One of the reasons data are so often plotted on graphs is that this format makes it much easier to see trends and draw conclusions. For instance, on a simple position vs. time graph, the slope of the curve indicates the object's velocity at each point in time. If the curve becomes level, this means the object is not moving. In a simple velocity vs. time graph, the slope of the curve indicates the object's acceleration at each point in time. Additionally, the area contained under the curve indicates the total distance traveled. For instance, if the object is traveling at a constant 5 m/s for 10 s, the velocity vs. time graph will be a straight line at y = 5 between x = 0 and x = 10. The area under this curve is (5 m/s)(10 s) = 50 m. Thus, the object traveled 50 meters. Nearly any type of quantity may be graphed, so it is important to always check the axis labels to ensure that you know what the graph represents and what units are being used.

Data Errors and Error Analysis

No measurements are ever 100% accurate. There is always some amount of error regardless of how careful the observer or how good his equipment. The important thing for the scientist to know is how much error is present in a given measurement. Two commonly misunderstood terms regarding error are accuracy and precision. Accuracy is a measure of how close a measurement is to the true value. Precision is a measure of how close repeated measurements are to one another. Error is usually quantified using a confidence interval and an uncertainty value. For instance, if the quantity is measured as 100 ± 2 on a 95% confidence interval, this means that there is a 95% chance that the actual value falls between 98 and 102. When looking for the uncertainty in a derived quantity such as density, the errors in the constituent quantities, mass and volume in this case, are propagated to the derived quantity. The percent uncertainty in the density, U_ρ/ρ, can be found by the equation:

- $U_\rho/\rho = \text{sqrt}((U_m/m)^2 + (U_V/V)^2)$.

Measuring, Organizing, and Classifying Data

Measuring data is a crucial part of the scientific process. Measurements are most useful if they are quantified—expressed in numbers. Measuring is the process of determining variables such as time, space, and temperature of objects and processes in precise numbers. The metric system is the universal standard of measurement in science. Data must be organized in a practical, useful manner to be valuable. Scientists use graphs, charts, tables, and other organizational tools to make data more useful. Data must then be classified—grouped into organizational schemes for easy access and use. These schemes attempt to organize the maximum amount of useful data in a format that scientists can use. Although these steps may be less glamorous than other areas of science, they are essential.

Presentation of Data

Data collected during a science lab can be organized and presented in any number of ways. While straight narrative is a suitable method for presenting some lab results, it is not a suitable way to present numbers and quantitative measurements. These types of observations can often be better presented with tables and graphs. Data that is presented in tables and organized in rows and columns may also be used to make graphs quite easily. Other methods of presenting data include illustrations, photographs, video, and even audio formats. In a formal report, tables and figures are labeled and referred to by their labels. For example, a picture of a bubbly solution might be labeled Figure 1, Bubbly Solution. It would be referred to in the text in the following way: "The reaction created bubbles 10 mm in size, as shown in Figure 1, Bubbly Solution." Graphs are also labeled as figures. Tables are labeled in a different way. Examples include: Table 1, Results of Statistical Analysis, or Table 2, Data from Lab 2.

Basic Science and Applied Science

Basic science and applied science share many attributes but are generally motivated by different influences:

- Basic science is spurred on by scientific inquiry, the human need to explain the observed physical world. It may have no specific goal, but is mankind's response to questions that arise from human curiosity and interest. It is usually an attempt to explain the laws of nature by using the scientific method.
- Applied science has a specific practical goal or application: It is designed to solve a problem. Industry and government are institutions that use applied science regularly.

Thus, basic and applied science share many qualities, including scientific inquiry and the scientific method. The goals of each can be very different. It should be pointed out that basic science very often provides results that have uses in applied science.

Although basic science may have no stated goal or target, it provides many benefits to society:

- Basic science contributes greatly to human understanding and culture, enriching society in many ways.
- Basic science has been responsible for major breakthroughs that have great social and economic impact.
- Basic science provides derivative solutions that can be used in applied science. For example, basic science was critical to the development of the space program, from which countless valuable applications have been derived.
- Basic science contributes to education and research across the broad spectrum of society.

Laboratory Safety

The following basic rules should be supplemented by standards appropriate to individual laboratories:

- Hazardous areas must be identified and warnings posted regarding risks.
- A hazard containment plan must be in effect and readily available.
- Safe control of airflow must be maintained at all times.
- Safe work practices must be taught to all who work in the lab.
- Proper maintenance of laboratory equipment must be enforced.
- Safe storage of hazardous material must be implemented.
- Procedures for safe disposal of hazardous wastes must be followed at all times.
- An updated emergency procedure manual must be available.
- A complete emergency first aid kit should be accessible at all times.
- Regular education on the basics of lab safety should be implemented.

Scientific Measurement and Unit Systems

The basis of quantitative measurement is the unit system. In order to properly describe how large, how heavy, or how hot something is, it is necessary to have some reference unit. The most commonly used unit system in the world is the SI, short for the Systeme International d'Unites, although the English system is still in popular use in the United States. In SI, there are base units and derived units. Derived units may be stated as some combination of the base units. The SI base units for length, mass, time, temperature, and electric current are meter (m), kilogram (kg), second (s), kelvin (K), and ampere (A), respectively. Some common derived units are newtons ($kg\text{-}m/s^2$) and pascals ($kg/m\text{-}s^2$). Most SI units can be scaled up or down by adding a prefix. To alter a unit by

10^3, 10^6, or 10^9, add a prefix of kilo (k), mega (M), or giga (G). For instance, a kilometer (km) is 10^3 meters. To change the unit by a factor of 10^{-3}, 10^{-6}, or 10^{-9}, add a prefix of milli (m), micro (μ), or nano (n). For instance, a microsecond (μs) is 10^{-6} seconds. It is important to note that the SI base unit kilogram has already employed a prefix to scale up the smaller unit, gram (g). Order of magnitude is a concept that deals with comparison between two values. If one value differs from the other by a factor of 10^n, it may be said that it differs by n orders of magnitude. Other SI base units include the mole and the candela. Some lesser used prefixes include: hecto (h), 10^2; deca (da), 10^1; deci (d), 10^{-1}; and centi (c), 10^{-2}.

Scientific Method

The steps of the scientific method are as follows:

- The scientific method begins with, and absolutely depends upon, the observation of objective, unbiased data. Any prejudice or bias in the observed data nullifies its validity. Thus the basic input from the observations must be rigorously screened to ensure objectivity.
- The development of a theory or hypothesis based on objective data is the next step in the scientific method. These theories or hypotheses pose logical expectations that the experiment may yield.
- Construction of a rigorous and valid experimental method designed to test the theories is the next phase of the scientific method. This experimental method must be carefully constructed to give objective, unbiased conclusions based on the hypotheses posited.
- Careful and statistically correct analysis and evaluation of the experimental results make up the next stage.
- Modification and replication of the experiment must then follow to provide a statistically accurate demonstration of the validity of the hypothesis. Equivalent results must be shown from a number of repetitions of the experiment.

Hypothetico-Deductive Process

The hypothetico-deductive process states that to have an idea and then formulate a hypothesis are essentially creative processes, driven by eons of human experience. Statements about reality are the logical conclusions of observed experience. Such creative propositions are the basis for scientific inquiry. Empirical evidence must then validate these hypotheses. Creative inspiration and scientific validation are interdependent aspects of scientific inquiry. New observations often are the catalyst for creative new theories. Science thus proceeds through creative thinking and scientific validation. There are criticisms of the hypothetico-deductive process: The problem of deduction points out that the original hypothesis may be proved wrong in the future, thus invalidating all subsequent conclusions. The problem of induction, building a theory from generalizations, is that any generalization may be proved wrong by future objective observations. The hypothetico-deductive process, and its problems, is a fascinating subject to philosophers of science.

Hypothesis

It is important to form a hypothesis in order to make a tentative explanation that accounts for an unbiased observation. To be scientific, the hypothesis must be testable through experimentation. Careful construction of the experiment provides that predictions derived from the hypothesis are valid. The hypothesis must be formulated in a manner designed to provide a framework for evaluating the results of an experiment. In many scientific experiments, a hypothesis is posited in negative terms because scientists may accept logically plausible ideas until they are proven false. It is more difficult to prove that a hypothesis is true because its validity must be proven in all possible situations under endless variable conditions. Scientists tend to construct hypotheses for testing by creating experiments that might prove them false. If they succeed in proving it false, the hypothesis must be modified or discarded.

Variables

Testing a hypothesis is the key to both scientific inquiry and the scientific method. While testing, all variables of the experiment must be strictly controlled except the one being studied. Variables, by their definition, are the processes subject to change. Examples of this in a typical experiment would be the degree of heat or light. In an experiment there are three types of variables:

- The variable to be tested. Known as the independent variable.
- Dependent variables. These are dynamic conditions that may change because of the independent variable.
- Controlled variables. These are conditions that are held constant so they do not affect the independent variable.

A well-constructed experiment changes one independent variable at a time, observing the effects it may have on dependent variables. Only one independent variable at a time may be manipulated, so the experiment will yield a clear cause and effect result. If more than one independent variable were applied, the experimenter could not be sure which variable caused the result. This would invalidate the conclusions of the experiment.

Scientific Laws

Scientific principles must meet a high standard to be classified as laws. Scientific laws are identified as follows:

- Scientific laws must be true, not just probable. A highly probable principle may still be proven false.
- Laws are statements of patterns found in nature.
- Laws may have a universal form but be stated conditionally. For example, the statement "All living human beings breathe," may be restated "If a thing is a living human being it must breathe."
- Laws refer to a general, not a particular, class.
- Laws have purely qualitative predicates.
- Laws must have a formal language of expression to be fully understood. Such a language does not exist now.
- Laws may be probabilistic. For example, a law may state "Eight percent of all dogs are terriers."

Criticisms of the Deductive Model

The deductive model of the scientific method has the following criticisms:

- The deductive model fails to make logical distinctions among explanations, predictions, and descriptions of things to be explained.
- The deductive model is restrictive: It excludes most scientific examples.
- The deductive model is too inclusive: It admits data that cannot be explained.
- The deductive model requires an account of cause, law, and probability, which are basically unsound.
- The deductive model leaves out the elements of context, judgment, and understanding.

PREDICTION

These are the two widely accepted definitions of scientific prediction:

- In the language of science, prediction is stating in advance the outcome from testing a theory or hypothesis in a controlled experiment. Based on objective observation of data, scientists move from observation of facts to a general explanation, or hypothesis, which must be confirmed by testing through experimentation.
- Another definition of prediction favored by scientific philosophers is the ability of a hypothesis to lead to deductions of scientific statements that could not be anticipated when the hypothesis was posited. In this sense, prediction means what the scientist can verify from what he or she has deduced from the hypothesis.

MAJOR SCIENTIFIC THEORIES

Some major scientific theories include:

- The once widely accepted received view theory is based on an analysis of theories empirically devised from deductive axiomatic systems. This theory has been widely criticized.
- The model theory states that a model may be constructed to correlate to a real system of relationships, and it can be used to simulate real systems. This allows the model to be manipulated and controlled and be able to predict the dynamics of the real system.
- Mechanistic theories do not attempt to fit phenomena into a set of inferential patterns but focus on the mechanism by which data is produced or realized.

Scientific theories have many different structures that may be applied in various realms of science.

SCIENTIFIC INQUIRY

Scientific inquiry is the impetus and catalyst for all scientific research and experimentation. It grows from questions about the observed world and gives us a template with which to apply the scientific method. Steps in scientific inquiry include the following principles:

1. Determination of the content and scope of the questions to be investigated is the first step. These may range from simple to extremely complex questions to be explored by scientists.
2. The design, strategy, and method of the inquiry are then carefully considered, and a model for the inquiry is constructed.
3. The formulation of theories and models based on the careful observation of objective, unbiased data then follows. This formulation is derived from the scope of the scientific inquiry and the questions to be investigated.
4. Analysis of possible alternative conclusions drawn from the models and results of experimentation follows.
5. Postulating a theory or constructing a scientific statement based on conclusions is the next logical step.
6. Defending the scientific statement against alternative hypotheses is a critical function of scientific inquiry.
7. Defense of the theory or conclusion against critical analysis is the final step in the process.

SKILLS NECESSARY TO THE SCIENTIFIC PROCESS

Perhaps the most important skill in science is that of observation. A scientist must be able to take accurate data from his experimental setup or from nature without allowing bias to alter the results. Another important skill is hypothesizing. A scientist must be able to combine his knowledge of theory and of other experimental results to logically determine what should occur in his own tests. The data-analysis process requires the twin skills of ordering and categorizing. Gathered data must be arranged in such a way that it is readable and readily shows the key results. A skill that may be integrated with the previous two is comparing. A scientist should be able to compare his own results with other published results. He must also be able to infer, or draw logical conclusions, from his results. He must be able to apply his knowledge of theory and results to create logical experimental designs and determine cases of special behavior. Lastly, a scientist must be able to communicate his results and his conclusions. The greatest scientific progress is made when scientists are able to review and test one another's work and offer advice or suggestions.

Labels Given to Scientific Statements

Hypotheses are educated guesses about what is likely to occur, and are made to provide a starting point from which to begin design of the experiment. They may be based on results of previously observed experiments or knowledge of theory, and follow logically forth from these. Assumptions are statements that are taken to be fact without proof for the purpose of performing a given experiment. They may be entirely true, or they may be true only for a given set of conditions under which the experiment will be conducted. Assumptions are necessary to simplify experiments; indeed, many experiments would be impossible without them. Scientific models are mathematical statements that describe a physical behavior. Models are only as good as our knowledge of the actual system. Often models will be discarded when new discoveries are made that show the model to be inaccurate. While a model can never perfectly represent an actual system, they are useful for simplifying a system to allow for better understanding of its behavior. Scientific laws are statements of natural behavior that have stood the test of time and have been found to produce accurate and repeatable results in all testing. A theory is a statement of behavior that consolidates all current observations. Theories are similar to laws in that they describe natural behavior, but are more recently developed and are more susceptible to being proved wrong. Theories may eventually become laws if they stand up to scrutiny and testing.

Experimental Design

Designing relevant experiments that allow for meaningful results is not a simple task. Every stage of the experiment must be carefully planned to ensure that the right data can be safely and accurately taken. Ideally, an experiment should be controlled so that all of the conditions except the ones being manipulated are held constant. This helps to ensure that the results are not skewed by unintended consequences of shifting conditions. A good example of this is a placebo group in a drug trial. All other conditions are the same, but that group is not given the medication. In addition to proper control, it is important that the experiment be designed with data collection in mind. For instance, if the quantity to be measured is temperature, there must be a temperature device such as a thermocouple integrated into the experimental setup. While the data are being collected, they should periodically be checked for obvious errors. If there are data points that are orders of magnitude from the expected value, then it might be a good idea to make sure that no experimental errors are being made, either in data collection or condition control. Once all the data have been gathered, they must be analyzed. The way in which this should be done depends on the type of data and the type of trends observed. It may be useful to fit curves to the data to determine if the trends follow a common mathematical form. It may also be necessary to perform a statistical analysis of the results to determine what effects are significant. Data should be clearly presented.

Effects of Scientific and Technological Improvements

Scientific and technological developments have led to the widespread availability of technologies heretofore unheard of, including cellular phones, satellite-based applications, and a worldwide network of connected computers. Some of the notable recent applications include:

- Health care: Antibiotics, genetic screening for diseases, the sequencing of the human genome. Issues include problems with health care distribution on an increasingly industrialized planet.
- The environment: Computerized models of climate change and pollution monitoring. Issues include increased pollution of the water, air, and soil, and the over-harvesting of natural resources with mechanized equipment.
- Agriculture: Genetic improvements in agricultural practices, including increased output on the same amount of arable land. Issues include unknown environmental effects of hybrid species, cross-pollination with organic species, and pollution caused by synthetic chemical fertilizers.
- Information technology: New Internet-based industries, increased worldwide collaboration, and access to information. Issues include the depletion of natural resources for electronics production.

Since the Industrial Revolution, technological improvements to agricultural production have made agriculture productive on an industrial scale, while advances in medical knowledge have brought about the cures for many diseases. People in many parts of the world live longer and enjoy a higher standard of living than ever before. However, this progress does not come without a price. The effects on the environment of industrialization are almost exclusively negative. Monoculture farming practices resulting from industrialization mean that farming no longer exists as a closed ecosystem; the chemical fertilizers that create record crop yields have changed the nutrient environment, and the waste products of industrial agriculture pollute the water rather than fertilizing the soil. Increased travel creates dangerous carbon dioxide emissions and depletes the earth's limited store of fossil fuels. Water pollution means limited access to potable water, and deforestation has begun to change the makeup of ecosystems and cause the extinction of many species. Through the increased contact made available by improved technology, however, humans are also collaborating on solutions to these new problems.

Recent developments in science and technology have had both positive and negative effects on human society. The issue of sustainable growth is an increasingly important one, as humans realize that the resources they use are not unlimited. Genetic research into diseases, stem cell research, and cloning technology have created great controversies as they have been introduced, and an increasing number of people reject the morality of scientific practices like animal testing in the pursuit of scientific advancement. In addition, an increasingly technology-based world has produced a new social inequality based on access to computers and Internet technology. These issues are beginning to be debated at all levels of human government, from city councils to the United Nations. Does science provide the authoritative answer to all human problems, or do ethics carry weight in scientific debates as well? Ultimately, humans must weigh the competing needs of facilitating scientific pursuits and maintaining an ethical society as they face new technological questions.

Major Energy Issues

Since the Industrial Revolution, energy for industrialized human needs has come from fossil fuels, particularly coal and petroleum, but increased use means that this source of fuel is quickly being depleted, in addition to causing pollution. The search for alternative, safe sources of energy for an increasingly industrialized world population is therefore increasingly important to scientists. An ideal source of energy would be efficient, renewable, and sustainable. Various sources of alternative energy have been proposed, including wind, water, solar, nuclear, geothermal, and biomass, but thus far none have been made practically available on a large scale. Some, such as wind and water, blight the landscape, while the conversion methods for other sources, such as solar and biomass, are still relatively inefficient. The scientific community is still unclear on the best way to harness the power of photosynthesis and biomass for energy needs in a way that would allow a large-scale energy industry to use it. Scientists remain at work studying the long-term solutions to an increasingly urgent problem for humanity.

Controversies Surrounding Nuclear Power

Nuclear fission power, while sustainable, has a host of attendant controversial problems. Among them is the incredibly dangerous transportation and long-term storage of its radioactive waste products, for which there is still no safe long-term solution. Its effects on those environments and creatures that come in contact with nuclear waste are still largely unknown. In addition, nuclear materials can be used in weaponry, and accidents at nuclear power plants like the one at Chernobyl can be devastating for thousands of years. Scientists continue their study of the process of nuclear fusion, hoping that if humans can learn to harness the energy produced by smashing atoms rather than splitting them, the attendant problems of nuclear waste storage will be minimized.

Effects of Increased Production of Consumer Goods

Electric-based, industrial production of manufactured goods has led to an increase in the standard of living for many, especially those in the industrialized world. Consumer goods are produced more cheaply than ever before, since the means of production is not as dependent on the physical abilities of human beings. Scientific advancements have led to a huge number of new synthetic materials from which goods can be made, including plastics and nylon. However, this increased production damages the environment. Waste products are now created of which humans can make no use, a new phenomenon. Trash created from these new products is buried in landfills, where it has no access to the air, water, and sunlight that are a necessary part of biodegradation; trash made from some synthetic materials does not biodegrade at all. While some waste products can be recycled, many byproducts of industrial manufacturing are hazardous, with no safe way to dispose of them. The long-term sustainability of the environment as a result of massively increased consumer production is an issue of increasing urgency for scientists.

Management of Renewable Resources

Natural resources can be divided into two types, renewable and non-renewable. Renewable resources include plants and animals, along with water, air, and soil. A pre-industrial earth was a self-sustaining system, maintaining a natural balance among plants, animals, and non-living elements in which waste products from one natural process were the fuel for another. Modern humans have intervened in this process in a way that upsets the natural balance of life. Humans have introduced non-native species from one part of the world to another, resulting in the devastation of local populations. Industrial-scale buildings can create disasters for local ecosystems, ruining habitats for animal populations. Humans remove an increasing amount of the world's resources for industrial use, too quickly for nature to recover from easily. Renewable resources must be carefully managed to maintain a balanced ecosystem; over-harvesting of forests or over-hunting of animal populations can be devastating. Pollution of the air and water with chemical pollutants has far-reaching effects on the ecosystems of the earth, including the depletion of the ozone layer that protects earth life from ultraviolet rays, as does the removal of forests that produce the earth's oxygen.

Management of non-renewable resources

Non-renewable resources include minerals, which are created naturally over millions of years. The industrialized world extracts minerals for fuel as well as for use in electronic equipment and medicine. Increased human extraction of non-renewable resources has endangered their availability, and over-mining has created other ecological problems, including runoff and water pollution. The use of fossil fuels for energy and transportation causes air pollution and is unsustainable. Fossil fuels cannot be replaced once depleted, and they are being depleted at an increasing rate. The need to find a sustainable alternative to the use of non-renewable fossil fuels is imperative.

Theorists and theories of evolution

The following are five key figures in the development of the theory of evolution and their contributions:

- Cuvier (1744-1829): Cuvier was a French naturalist who used the fossil record (paleontology) to compare the anatomies of extinct species and existing species to make conclusions about extinction. He believed in the catastrophism theory more strongly than the theory of evolution.
- Lamarck (1769-1832): Lamarck was a French naturalist who believed in the idea of evolution and thought it was a natural occurrence influenced by the environment. He studied medicine and botany. Lamarck put forth a theory of evolution by inheritance of acquired characteristics. He theorized that organisms became more complex by moving up a ladder of progress.
- Lyell (1797-1875): Lyell was a British geologist who believed in geographical uniformitarianism, which can be contrasted with catastrophism.
- Charles Robert Darwin (1809-1882): Darwin was an English naturalist known for his belief that evolution occurred by natural selection. He believed that species descend from common ancestors.
- Alfred Russell Wallace (1823-1913): He was a British naturalist who independently developed a theory of evolution by natural selection. He believed in the transmutation of species (that one species develops into another).

Evolution of scientific knowledge

When one examines the history of scientific knowledge, it is clear that it is constantly evolving. The body of facts, models, theories, and laws grows and changes over time. In other words, one scientific discovery leads to the next. Some advances in science and technology have important and long-lasting effects on science and society. Some discoveries were so alien to the accepted beliefs of the time that not only were they rejected as wrong, but were also considered outright blasphemy. Today, however, many beliefs once considered incorrect have become an ingrained part of scientific knowledge, and have also been the basis of new advances. Examples of advances include: Copernicus's heliocentric view of the universe, Newton's laws of motion and planetary orbits, relativity, geologic time scale, plate tectonics, atomic theory, nuclear physics, biological evolution, germ theory, industrial revolution, molecular biology, information and communication, quantum theory, galactic universe, and medical and health technology.

Contributions to field of biology

Leeuwenhoek, Linnaeus, and Darwin

Anton van Leeuwenhoek (d. 1723) used homemade magnifying glasses to become the first person to observe single-celled organisms. He observed bacteria, yeast, plants, and other microscopic organisms. His observations contributed to the field of microbiology. Carl Linnaeus (d. 1778) created a method to classify plants and animals, which became known as the Linnaean taxonomy. This was an important contribution because it offered a way to organize and therefore study large amounts of data. Charles Robert Darwin (d. 1882) is best known for contributing to the survival of the fittest through natural selection theory of evolution by observing different species of birds, specifically finches, in various geographic locations. Although the species Darwin looked at were different, he speculated they had a common ancestor. He reasoned that specific traits persisted because they gave the birds a greater chance of surviving and reproducing. He also discovered fossils, noted stratification, dissected marine animals, and interacted with indigenous peoples. He contributed to the fields of biology, marine biology, anthropology, paleontology, geography, and zoology.

Mendel, McClintock, and Watson and Crick

Gregor Johann Mendel (d. 1884) is famous for experimenting with pea plants to observe the occurrence of inherited traits. He eventually became known as the father of genetics. Barbara McClintock (d. 1992) created the first genetic map for maize and was able to demonstrate basic genetic principles, such as how recombination is an exchange of chromosomal information. She also discovered how transposition flips the switch for traits. Her work contributed to the field of genetics, in particular to areas of study concerned with the structure and function of cells and chromosomes. James Watson and Francis Crick (d. 2004) were co-discoverers of the structure of deoxyribonucleic acid (DNA), which has a double helix shape. DNA contains the code for genetic information. The discovery of the double helix shape was important because it helped to explain how DNA replicates.

Important Terms

- *Mean* — The mean is the sum of a list of numbers divided by the number of numbers.
- *Median* — If there is an even number of values in the set, the median is calculated by taking the average of the two middle values.
- *Standard deviation* — This measures the variability of a data set and determines the amount of confidence one can have in the conclusions.
- *Mode* — This is the value that appears most frequently in a data set.
- *Range* — This is the difference between the highest and lowest numbers, which can be used to determine how spread out data is.
- *Regression analysis* — This is a method of analyzing sets of data and sets of variables that involves studying how the typical value of the dependent variable changes when any one of the independent variables is varied and the other independent variables remain fixed.

Practice Test

Practice Questions

DIRECTIONS: Read each question or incomplete sentence and select the best response.

1. A student is working on a science project and is going through each step of the scientific method. After the student conducts his or her first experiment and records the results of the experimental test, what is the next step?

a. Communicate the results
b. Draw a conclusion
c. Repeat the experiment
d. Create a hypothesis

2. What instrument would be best to use to study the pressure and temperature change of a star?

a. Reflecting telescope
b. Refracting telescope
c. Radio telescope
d. Spectroscope

Use the following information to answer question 3.

> A student is conducting an experiment using a ball that is attached to the end of a string, forming a pendulum. The student pulls the ball back so that it is at an angle to its resting position. As the student releases the ball, it swings forward and backward. The student measures the time it takes the ball to make one complete period. A period is defined as the time it takes the ball to swing forward and back again to its starting position. This is repeated using different string lengths.

3. What would be an appropriate control variable for this experiment?

a. The period
b. The length of the string
c. The mass of the ball
d. The color of the ball

4. Once a hypothesis has been verified and accepted, it becomes a ________.

a. fact
b. law
c. conclusion
d. theory

5. A student has collected data on the width of tree trunks and average precipitation rates for different locations. What type of graph should be used to show the relationship between these two variables?

a. A multi-line graph with the width measurements on the x-axis and precipitation rates on the y-axis.
b. A scatter plot with the width measurements on the y-axis and precipitation rates on the x-axis.
c. A bar graph with the width measurements on the y-axis and precipitation rates on the x-axis.
d. A pie chart with the width of trees shown as a percentage at different precipitation rates.

6. What is one astronomical unit (AU) equivalent to?

a. One parsec
b. One light year
c. The distance between the Earth and Sun
d. The distance across the entire width of the solar system

7. Make the following metric conversion:

5 decimeters = _____ decameters

a. 0.5
b. 0.05
c. 50
d. 500

8. Which of the data sets could be plotted on a pie chart?

a. The total population of the top five largest US cities.
b. The incubation period of a penguin colony as it relates to hours of daylight.
c. The distribution of weight among players of a football team.
d. The percent of vegetation cover and precipitation rates in different national parks.

9. Which of the following processes uses electrical charges to separate substances?

a. Spectrophotometry
b. Chromatography
c. Centrifugation
d. Electrophoresis

10. When using a light microscope, how is the total magnification determined?

a. By multiplying the ocular lens power by the objective being used.
b. By looking at the objective you are using only
c. By looking at the ocular lens power only
d. By multiplying the objective you are using by two.

11. What other planet in the solar system experiences a greenhouse effect similar to that observed on Earth?

a. Mercury
b. Venus
c. Neptune
d. Saturn

12. Which of the following statements comparing the terrestrial planets and the Jovian planets is not true?

a. The terrestrial planets are denser than the Jovian planets.
b. The terrestrial planets are generally warmer than the Jovian planets.
c. The terrestrial planets are smaller than the Jovian planets.
d. The terrestrial planets have a longer orbit than the Jovian planets.

13. The volume of water in a bucket is 2.5 liters. When an object with an irregular shape and a mass of 40 grams is fully submerged in the water, the total volume becomes 4.5 liters. What is the density of the object?

a. 0.1 g/L
b. 2 g/L
c. 20 g/L
d. 80 g/L

14. Which of the following represents a chemical change?

a. Water sublimating
b. An apple turning brown
c. Salt dissolving in water
d. Rock being pulverized

15. The amount of potential energy an object has depends on all of the following except its

a. mass.
b. height above ground.
c. gravitational attraction.
d. temperature.

16. Elements on the periodic table are arranged into groups and periods and ordered according to all of the following EXCEPT:

a. Atomic number
b. Refractive index
c. Reactivity
d. Number of protons

17. The specific heat capacity of ice is half as much as that of liquid water. What is the result of this?

a. It takes half the amount of energy to increase the temperature of a 1 kg sample of ice by 1°C than a 1 kg sample of water.
b. It takes twice the amount of energy to increase the temperature of a 1 kg sample of ice by 1°C than a 1 kg sample of water.
c. It takes a quarter the amount of energy to increase the temperature of a 1 kg sample of ice by 1°C than a 1 kg sample of water.
d. It takes the same amount of energy to increase the temperature of a 1 kg sample of ice and a 1 kg sample of water by 1°C.

18. What happens to the temperature of a substance as it is changing phase from a liquid to a solid?

a. Its temperature increases due to the absorption of latent heat.
b. Its temperature decreases due to the heat of vaporization.
c. Its temperature decreases due to the latent heat of fusion.
d. Its temperature remains the same due to the latent heat of fusion.

19. A long nail is heated at one end. After a few seconds, the other end of the nail becomes equally hot. What type of heat transfer does this represent?

a. Radiation
b. Conduction
c. Convection
d. Entropy

20. Which of the following statements about heat transfer is NOT true?

a. As the energy of a system changes, its thermal energy must change or work must be done.
b. Heat transfer from a warmer object to a cooler object can occur spontaneously.
c. Heat transfer can never occur from a cooler object to a warmer object.
d. If two objects reach the same temperature, energy is no longer available for work.

21. The measure of energy within a system is called _______.

a. temperature
b. heat
c. entropy
d. thermodynamics

22. Which of the following is true of different isotopes of the same element?

a. It has a different number of protons than its element.
b. It has a different number of electrons than its element.
c. It has a different charge as compared to its element.
d. It has a different number of neutrons than other isotopes of the same element.

23. If an atom's outer shell is filled, what must be true?

a. It reacts with other atoms through chemical reactions.
b. It exchanges electrons to form bonds with other atoms.
c. It has 32 electrons in its outer shell.
d. It is a stable atom.

24. Which type of nuclear process features atomic nuclei splitting apart to form smaller nuclei?

a. Fission
b. Fusion
c. Decay
d. Ionization

25. Electrons with greater amounts of energy are found _______ the nucleus than electrons with less energy.

a. closer to
b. farther from
c. more often inside
d. more randomly around

26. The process whereby a radioactive element releases energy slowly over a long period of time to lower its energy and become more stable is best described as ________.

a. combustion
b. fission
c. fusion
d. decay

27. Which of the following is a type of simple machine?

a. A bicycle
b. A pair of scissors
c. A screw
d. A shovel

28. In which of the following scenarios is work not applied to the object?

a. Mario moves a book from the floor to the top shelf.
b. A book drops off the shelf and falls to the floor.
c. Mario pushes a box of books across the room.
d. Mario balances a book on his head.

29. A ball is resting on the front end of a boat. The boat is moving straight forward toward a dock. According to Newton's First law of motion, when the front of the boat hits the dock, how will the ball's motion change with respect to the boat?

a. The ball will remain at rest.
b. The ball will move backward.
c. The ball will move forward.
d. The ball will move sideways.

30. What two things are required for circular motion to occur?

a. Acceleration and centripetal force
b. Acceleration and gravitational force
c. Constant speed and centripetal force
d. Constant speed and gravitational force

31. According to Bernoulli's Principle, where will a gas flowing through a pipe exert the least amount of pressure?

a. Where the pipe is widest
b. Where the pipe is narrowest
c. Where its velocity is lowest
d. Where its kinetic energy is lowest

32. If a glass rod is rubbed with a cloth made of polyester, what will the resulting charge be on each material?

a. The charge on the glass rod is positive and the charge on the cloth is negative.
b. The charge on the glass rod is negative and the charge on the cloth is positive.
c. The charge on the glass rod is neutral and the charge on the cloth is positive.
d. The charge on the glass rod and the cloth both become neutral.

33. According to Ohm's Law, how are voltage and current related in an electrical circuit?

a. Voltage and current are inversely proportional to one another.
b. Voltage and current are directly proportional to one another.
c. Voltage acts to oppose the current along an electrical circuit.
d. Voltage acts to decrease the current along an electrical circuit.

34. A material becomes magnetic when the individual electrons of an atom ___________, allowing their magnetic fields to add together.

a. spin in pairs in opposite directions
b. spin in pairs in the same direction
c. spin unpaired
d. stop spinning

35. In a parallel circuit, there are three paths: A, B and C. Path A has a resistance of 10 ohms, path B a resistance of 5 ohms and part C a resistance of 2 ohms. How do the voltage and current change for each path?

a. Voltage and current are kept the same in each path.
b. Voltage is greatest in path A and current is greatest in path C.
c. Voltage is lowest in path C and current is greatest in path C.
d. Voltage is the same for each path and current is greatest in path C.

36. A rock concert is taking place outdoors. In which of the following conditions will the sound travel the farthest?

a. High temperature and low humidity
b. High temperature and humidity
c. Low temperature and humidity
d. Low temperature and high humidity

37. Which of the following would cause a high angle of reflection of a light wave?

a. A high angle of incidence of the wave
b. A low angle of incidence of the wave
c. A wave that travels through a medium of higher density
d. A wave with a very short wavelength

38. What term is used to describe two waves that are out of phase as they come together to produce a new wave?

a. Incomplete interference
b. Distorted interference
c. Constructive interference
d. Destructive interference

39. What would happen to light waves if they hit a convex lens?

a. They will be refracted and converge.
b. They will be refracted and diverge.
c. They will be reflected and converge.
d. They will be reflected and diverge.

40. If an astronomer observing the stars detects a blue shift, what could he conclude?

a. The star is moving farther away from him.
b. The star is moving closer or toward him.
c. The star is cooling down and becoming smaller.
d. The star is heating up and becoming larger.

41. Salts are made from a combination of what two types of elements?

a. A metal and a nonmetal
b. A nonmetal and an alkaline earth metal
c. A cation from a base and an anion from an acid
d. A metal and a halogen

42. What group of the periodic table makes up the alkaline earth metals?

a. Group 1
b. Group 2
c. Group 13
d. Group 17

43. Which of the following elements is not a noble gas?

a. Neon
b. Argon
c. Astatine
d. Krypton

44. If an atom has a neutral charge, what must be true of the atom?

a. The nucleus contains only neutrons and no protons.
b. The atomic mass is equal to the number of neutrons.
c. The atomic number is equal to the number of neutrons.
d. The atomic number is equal to the number of electrons.

45. Most organic molecules have all of the following properties except

a. high solubility in water.
b. a relatively low melting point.
c. covalent bonds.
d. high flammability.

46. In a single replacement reaction, what products could result from these reactants in the following chemical equation?

$2Al + Fe_2O_3 \rightarrow$

a. $AlO_3 + Fe_2$
b. $2Fe_2 + 2AlO_3$
c. $Al_2O_3 + 2Fe$
d. $2AlFeO_3$

47. What type of compound is formed by the combination of two or more nonmetallic elements with one another?

a. Organic
b. Ionic
c. Covalent
d. Polar

48. Which of the following descriptions of Lewis dot structures is not correct?

a. They show the bonding between atoms of a molecule.
b. They show all the electrons of each atom of a molecule.
c. The total number of electrons is equal to the sum of the number of valence electrons on each atom.
d. They show any lone pairs of electrons that may exist in a molecule that are not bonded to another atom.

49. Which of the following does not describe a carboxyl group correctly?

a. A carbon atom attached to an oxygen atom by a double bond and to a hydroxyl group by a single bond.
b. A carbonyl group bonded to a hydroxyl group.
c. A set of four atoms bonded together and abbreviated as CO_2H.
d. A carbon atom attached to a hydrogen atom by a double bond and to an oxygen atom by a double bond.

50. A gas is held in a closed container and held at constant temperature. What is the effect of increasing the volume of the container by 3 times?

a. The pressure is tripled.
b. The pressure increases by one third.
c. The pressure decreases to one third.
d. The pressure remains constant.

Use the following information to answer questions 51 and 52.

> Four identical liquid samples inside of identical sealed containers initially at room temperature were placed in four isolated environments, each with its own maintained temperature. After each liquid sample is allowed sufficient time to assume the temperature of its environment, the samples changed as follows: In sample A, the liquid vaporized and is now a gas. In sample B, the liquid is boiling. In sample C, the liquid is now a solid. In sample D, the liquid remains a liquid.

51. Which sample's container has the greatest pressure?

a. Sample A
b. Sample B
c. Sample C
d. All containers have equal pressure

52. If the temperature in each environment were increased by 10 degrees Celsius and each sample were allowed time to assume the new temperature, which of the following events is MOST likely to occur?

a. Sample A would become a liquid
b. Sample B would become a gas
c. Sample D would begin to boil
d. None of these are likely to occur

53. Which statement best describes the molecular arrangement of a liquid crystal?

a. The molecular arrangement is random in some directions and regular in others.
b. The molecular arrangement is a regular, repeating pattern in all directions.
c. The molecular arrangement is random in all directions.
d. The molecular arrangement is reduced to one layer with a random pattern.

54. Which of the following is never true of a chemical reaction?

a. Matter is neither gained nor lost.
b. Heat is absorbed or released.
c. The rate of the reaction increases with temperature.
d. There are a different number of atoms for the products and the reactants.

55. Which of the following would increase the reaction rate of a chemical reaction?

a. Low kinetic energy
b. Low temperature
c. High concentration of reactants
d. High activation energy

56. Copper is added to silver nitrate, which reacts to form copper nitrate and silver. What type of reaction has occurred?

a. Compound
b. Decomposition
c. Single Replacement
d. Double Replacement

57. Which statement accurately describes an electrolysis reaction?

a. A reaction that changes the charge of the atoms.
b. A reaction that uses electricity to drive it.
c. A reaction that creates electricity as a by-product.
d. A reaction that lowers the pH of the substances.

58. Examine the following reaction. Which of the answer choices is a possible set of products?

ABC → ____ + ____

a. 2AB + C
b. AB + CD
c. A + BC
d. B + C

59. Which action will help dissolve a gas in a liquid if the gas and liquid are placed in a sealed container?

a. Heat the liquid.
b. Cool the liquid.
c. Shake the container.
d. Increase the pressure on the lid.

60. What type of substance is least likely to be soluble in water?

a. Ionic
b. Polar
c. Hydrophilic
d. Non-polar

61. How does adding a solute to a liquid solvent affect the vapor pressure of the liquid?

a. The vapor pressure increases by an amount proportional to the amount of solute.
b. The vapor pressure increases by an amount proportional to the amount of solvent.
c. The vapor pressure decreases by an amount proportional to the amount of solute.
d. The amount of solute present in a liquid solvent does not have any effect on vapor pressure.

62. Which of the following liquids will have the highest electrical conductivity?

a. Pure water
b. Water plus salt
c. Water plus vinegar
d. Water plus carbonated soda

63. The main function of _______ is to reduce the number of chromosomes to half the number of parent cells?

a. mitosis
b. telophase
c. meiosis I
d. meiosis II

64. This organelle contains digestive enzymes that break down food and unneeded substances. They are also thought to be linked to the aging process. What part of a cell does this describe?

a. Lysosomes
b. Chromatin
c. Plastids
d. Golgi Apparatus

65. Which of the following describes the difference between an anabolism reaction and a catabolism reaction?

a. Anabolism undergoes ionic reactions, while catabolism undergoes covalent reactions.
b. Anabolism undergoes condensation reactions, while catabolism undergoes hydrolysis.
c. Anabolism reactions use water, while catabolism reactions do not.
d. Anabolism reactions release glucose, while catabolism reactions release water.

66. Plant A undergoes C4 photosynthesis. What type of environment would the plant most likely live in?

a. Plant A lives in a very cold environment.
b. Plant A lives in a very hot environment.
c. Plant A lives in a marine environment.
d. Plant A lives in a dark environment that lacks solar energy.

67. Where is the type of RNA that carries and positions amino acids for further assembly located in the cell?

a. Cytoplasm
b. Nucleus
c. Ribosome
d. Mitochondria

68. The following is the anticodon sequence formed during translation. What is the mRNA codon sequence?

A C G U A C G C U

a. T G C A T G C G A
b. U G C T U G C G T
c. U G C A U G C G A
d. U C G A U C G C A

69. A student makes a dihybrid cross involving genes for eye color and hair color. In the P generation, one parent is homozygous for the dominant alleles, brown eyes (B) and blonde hair (S), and the other is homozygous for the recessive alleles, blue eyes (b) and red hair (s). What fraction of offspring would have the genotype BbSs in the F2 generation?

a. 1/16
b. 3/16
c. 4/16
d. 9/16

70. What type of mutation is represented by the following sequence?

1 5 4 3 2 6

a. Breakage
b. Deletion
c. Insertion
d. Inversion

71. Many people have their wisdom teeth removed because they no longer serve a function in humans and may cause problems if left in. What are wisdom teeth an example of?

a. Analogous structure
b. Homologous structure
c. Vestigial structure
d. Paralogous structure

72. Which statement best explains the Biological Species Concept (BSC)?

a. It states that the status of species is based on the ability to pass on the most successful traits to their offspring.
b. It states that the status of species is based on the reproductive isolation of populations.
c. It states that the status of species is based on the ability of populations to mix and produce fertile hybrids.
d. It states that the status of a species is due to the theory of natural selection.

73. What is the result of allopatric speciation?

a. New species due to geographic isolation.
b. New species due to geographic overlap.
c. Hybrid species due to geographic overlap.
d. Loss of diversity of a species due to geographic divergence.

74. How did Jean Baptiste Lamarck's theory of evolution compare to Darwin's theory of natural selection?

a. He expanded Darwin's theory of natural selection by stating that some genes allow for better survival than others.
b. He proposed an alternate theory by stating that favorable traits developed due to environmental conditions and the desire and needs of the organisms.
c. He provided evidence to Darwin's belief that the desires and needs of organisms affected evolution of populations.
d. He opposed Darwin's view that evolution was predetermined and believed that the selection of traits was more random.

75. Which of the following would not be used as evidence for evolution?

a. Fossil record
b. DNA sequences
c. Anatomical structures
d. Reproductive habits

76. In which taxonomic group are organisms most alike?

a. Phylum
b. Family
c. Class
d. Order

77. Which division of plants produces seeds for reproduction?

a. Anthophyta
b. Lycophyta
c. Sphenophyta
d. Pterophyta

78. What do all animals belonging to the Echinodermata phylum have in common?

a. They use multiple appendages for locomotion.
b. They use tube feet for locomotion and feeding.
c. They have an exoskeleton made of chitin.
d. They must shed their outer layer of skin to grow.

79. Where are the reproductive organs of a plant?

a. Style
b. Stigma
c. Flowers
d. Sepals

80. Plants begin to break down the products of photosynthesis through respiration. What is the result of respiration?

a. Water
b. Oxygen and glucose
c. Carbon dioxide and sugar
d. Carbon dioxide and water

81. Which of the following is NOT an advantage angiosperms show over other types of plants?

a. Larger leaves
b. Double fertilization
c. Dormant seeds
d. Lower seed dispersal

82. How do animals of the phylum Mollusca respire?

a. Through gills
b. Through a trachea
c. Through book lungs
d. Through muscle contraction

83. What part of a plant system responds to stimuli by releasing water via transpiration, except during adverse conditions like a drought when it closes up to prevent the plant from dehydration?

a. Pith
b. Stomata
c. Guard cells
d. Sepals

84. Which of the following animal structures is NOT paired to its correct function?

a. Muscle System – controls movement through three types of muscle tissue
b. Nervous System – controls sensory responses by carrying impulses away from and toward the cell body
c. Digestive System – breaks down food for absorption into the blood stream where it is delivered to cells for respiration
d. Circulatory System – exchanges gases with the environment by delivering oxygen to the bloodstream and releasing carbon dioxide

85. If a population reaches a maximum size and ceases to grow due to a limited availability of resources, the population is

a. unstable.
b. shrinking exponentially.
c. at carrying capacity.
d. moving towards extinction.

86. The following represents a simple food chain. What trophic level contains the greatest amount of energy?

tree → caterpillar → frog → snake → hawk → worm

a. Tree
b. Caterpillar
c. Hawk
d. Worm

87. Which of the following sources of fresh water is generally NOT available for human consumption?

a. Rivers
b. Estuaries
c. Aquifers
d. Glaciers

88. Which of the following animals would most likely be found in the taiga?

a. Antelope
b. Snake
c. Moose
d. Polar Bear

89. Which of the following words is not connected to the process of mountain building?

a. Folding
b. Faulting
c. Transform
d. Convergent

90. Which of the following processes is NOT part of the formation of sedimentary rock?

a. Layering
b. Cementation
c. Compaction
d. Heat

91. Which of the following is an example of chemical weathering?

a. Rain freezing on the roadway
b. Ivy growing on the side of a wooden house
c. Vinegar fizzing when poured on a rock
d. A river carrying sediment downstream

92. Which of the following situations would result in the generation of new crust?

a. Two crustal plates converge.
b. Two crustal plates move apart.
c. Two crustal plates slide past one another.
d. A crustal plate is pushed down into the mantle.

93. Which of the following terms describes an intrusion of magma injected between two layers of sedimentary rock, forcing the overlying strata upward to create a dome-like form?

a. Sill
b. Dike
c. Laccolith
d. Caldera

94. Which statement best describes the process of absolute dating?

a. It compares the amount of radioactive material in a rock to the amount that has decayed into another element.
b. It measures the age of a rock by comparing it to fossils found in the same stratigraphic layer as the rock.
c. It measures the amount of daughter elements that have broken down by half.
d. It measures the mass loss of a rock by estimating the amount of material that has eroded due to catastrophic events.

95. Fossils are least likely to be found in

a. sedimentary rock.
b. metamorphic rock.
c. igneous rock.
d. Fossils are commonly found in all types of rock.

96. Which of the following is an example of a trace fossil?

a. A mouse jaw
b. A footprint
c. A shark tooth
d. A cast of a skull

97. A time interval in which particular plants and animals were dominant or present in great abundance is defined as a(n)

a. era.
b. eon.
c. epoch.
d. period.

98. What is the major difference between the two paradigms of Earth's geologic past: catastrophism and uniformitarianism?

a. The first implies that the Earth was shaped by destructive processes, while the second implies it was shaped by constructive processes.
b. The first implies that the Earth has changed shape drastically several times, while the second implies it has not changed much over time.
c. The first implies that the same natural catastrophes occur on Earth today that occurred in the past, while the second implies that catastrophes did not occur in the past like they do today.
d. The first implies that the Earth was shaped by a series of quick, violent events, while the second implies that it changed slowly and incrementally.

99. Which of the following types of ocean currents would be the densest?

a. Warm and high salinity
b. Warm and low salinity
c. Cold and high salinity
d. Cold and low salinity

100. Which of the following does NOT control the movement of ocean currents?

a. Wind
b. Landmasses
c. Earth's rotation
d. Phase of the Moon

101. Compared to fresh water, the ________ point of sea water is ________.

a. freezing; higher
b. freezing; lower
c. triple; the same
d. boiling; lower

102. Which of the following statements best describes the mixed layer of the ocean?

a. It is the layer between the warm, surface layer and the cold, deeper layer below.
b. It is the transition zone where it becomes increasingly cold with depth due to loss of sunlight.
c. It is the surface layer where wave action is present due to interaction with winds at the surface.
d. It is the layer where upwelling and downwelling currents form due to density differences between the warm surface layer and the cold deeper layer.

103. Which of the following describes the physical or non-biological part of the carbon cycle?

a. Phytoplankton use carbon dioxide and other nutrients to produce carbohydrates and oxygen.
b. Cold water dissolves atmospheric carbon dioxide, stores it, and releases it back out to the atmosphere as needed.
c. Carbon dioxide is dissolved in sea water and is broken up to free carbon for use by marine life.
d. Warm, surface water dissolves carbon dioxide where it is converted to nitrogen and phosphorus for use by marine life.

104. What drives weather systems to move west to east in the mid-latitudes?

a. The prevailing westerlies
b. The prevailing easterlies
c. The trade winds
d. The doldrums

105. If land cools off rapidly at night and the ocean water stays relatively warm, what type of wind is created?

a. Sea breeze
b. Land breeze
c. Monsoon
d. Trade wind

106. If the current air temperature is 65°F and the current dew point is 62°F, what is most likely the current relative humidity?

a. 3%
b. 10%
c. 50%
d. 90%

107. On a topographic map, an area where the contour lines are very close together indicates that

a. a stream is present.
b. the slope is very gentle.
c. the slope is very steep.
d. the area surrounds a depression.

108. What is the major driving force that controls Earth's heat budget?

a. Advection
b. Evaporation
c. Solar radiation
d. Tilt of the Earth

Answers and Explanations

1. C: Repeating the experiment validates data. Each separate experiment is called a repetition. It should be possible to replicate the results of experiments or tests. Similar data gathered from many experiments can also be used to quantify the validity of the hypothesis. Repeating the experiments allows for the observation of variation in the results. Variation in data can be caused by a variety of errors or may be evidence against the hypothesis.

2. D: Spectroscope. A spectroscope would be the best instrument to use to study the pressure and temperature change of a star. A spectroscope measures properties of light and wavelengths. It can be used to make spectral lines and measure their subsequent wavelengths and intensities. A reflecting telescope, does not make measurements. It reflects light and uses curved mirrors to form an image. A refracting telescope, also does not make measurements. It bends light using a lens to form the image. A radio telescope is an antenna that collects radio wavelength frequencies. These are typically large concave dishes.

3. C: The mass of the ball is appropriately called a control variable for the experiment. A control or controlled variable is a factor that could be varied, but for testing purposes should remain the same throughout all experiments; otherwise, it could affect the results. In this case, if the mass of the ball was changed, it could also affect the length of the period. The length of the string is meant to be an independent variable, one that is changed during experiments to observe the results upon the dependent variable, which is the variable (or variables) that are affected. In this case, the period would be the dependent variable.

4. D: theory. Once a hypothesis has been verified and accepted, it becomes a theory. A theory is a generally accepted explanation that has been highly developed and tested. A theory can explain data and be expected to predict outcomes of tests. A fact is considered to be an objective and verifiable observation, whereas a scientific theory is a greater body of accepted knowledge, principles, or relationships that might explain a fact. A law is an explanation of events for which the outcome is always the same. A conclusion is more of an opinion and could be based on observation, evidence, fact, laws, or even beliefs.

5. B: Scatter plots are useful for illustrating two sets of numerical data on the two axes and their relationship. In this case, by plotting the width of the tree trunks along the y-axis and the corresponding average precipitation rates along the x-axis, any relationship between the two can be found. Scatter plots are also useful when there are many data points. A multi-line graph is useful for showing sets of data that change over time. A bar graph is a good choice for comparing individual data points. A pie chart is useful for graphically comparing the parts to a whole.

6. C: The distance between the Earth and Sun. One astronomical unit (AU) is equivalent to the distance between the Earth and Sun, 93 million miles (150 million km). Scientists use astronomical units since cosmic distances are so great. Answer A, One parsec (pc), is the parallax of one arcsecond and is about 19 trillion miles (31 trillion km), or about 3.26 light years. It is used to calculate distances by triangulation with the distance from the Earth to the Sun forming the side of a right triangle. Answer B, One light year, is the distance light travels in a vacuum in one year. It is equal to about 10^{13} km or 64,341 AU.

7. B: 0.05. In the metric system, 5 decimeters is equal to 0.05 decameters. A meter is the standard measurement of length. Prefixes are defined in increments of 10 to increase or decrease quantity. The prefix "deci" is equivalent to 10^{-1} or a tenth (0.1). A decimeter would be equal to 0.1 meters. The prefix "deca" is equivalent to 10 or 10^{1}. A decameter would be equal to 10 meters. To convert a smaller unit to a larger one, move the decimal place to the left. Since 10 decimeters make up 1 meter, for 5 decimeters, move the decimal 1 place to the left to find meters, which would be 0.5 meters. Because a decameter is larger than 1 meter (10 meters in 1 decameter), move the decimal another place to the left to change from meters to decameters, which would be 0.05 decameters. An alternate method is to set up conversion factors. This method involves canceling units and is very helpful to learn for other scientific problems.

8. C: The distribution of weight among players of a football team. In this case, a pie chart can illustrate the whole number of players as well as the number (or percentage) of players at given weights. It would be easy to interpret the data that, for example, 75% of the team weigh 250 pounds or more, 20% weigh between 200 and 250 pounds, and a mere 5% weight less than 200 pounds. The other answers would be better served in bar or line charts to compare variables or amounts that do not vary greatly.

9. D: Electrophoresis. Electrophoresis, also known as gel electrophoresis, uses electrical charges to separate substances such as protein, DNA and RNA. Depending upon the electrical charge and size of the molecules, they will travel through a porous gel at different rates when a charge is applied. Spectrophotometry refers to the measurement of visible light, near-ultraviolet, and near-infrared wavelengths. Chromatography refers to a number of techniques that separate mixtures of chemicals based on the differences in the compound's affinity for a stationary phase, usually a porous solid, and a mobile phase, which can be either a liquid or a gas. Centrifugation separates mixtures by spinning to generate centripetal force, which causes heavier particles to separate from lighter particles.

10. A: When using a light microscope, total magnification is determined by multiplying the ocular lens power times the objective being used. The term "ocular lens" refers to the eyepiece, which has one magnification strength, typically 10x. The objective lens also has a magnification strength, often 4x, 10x, 40x or 100x. Using a 10x eyepiece with the 4x objective lens will give a magnification strength of 40x. Using a 10x eyepiece with the 100x objective lens will give a magnification strength of 1,000x. The shorter lens is the lesser magnification; the longer lens is the greater magnification.

11. B: Venus. Venus experiences a greenhouse effect similar to that observed on Earth as its dense atmosphere traps the solar radiation and creates a greenhouse effect. The greenhouse gases, including ozone, carbon dioxide, water vapor, and methane, trap infrared radiation that is reflected back toward the atmosphere. Human activity generates more of the greenhouse gases than necessary. Some practices that increase the amount of greenhouse gases are burning natural gas and oil; farming, which leads to more methane and nitrous oxide; deforestation, which decreases the amount of offset oxygen; and population growth in general, which increases the volume of greenhouse gases. Increased gases mean more infrared radiation is trapped and the overall temperature at the Earth's surface rises.

12. D: The terrestrial planets have a longer orbit than the Jovian planets. This statement is false as the four Jovian planets, Jupiter, Saturn, Uranus and Neptune, are farther away from the sun than the four terrestrial planets, Mercury, Venus, Earth and Mars. The other statements are true as the terrestrial planets are denser, generally warmer, and smaller than the Jovian planets. The four Jovian planets are also known as the gas giants.

13. C: 20 g/L. One way to measure the density of an irregularly shaped object is to submerge it in water and measure the displacement. This is done by taking the mass (40 grams), then finding the volume by measuring how much water it displaces. Fill a graduated cylinder with water and record the amount. Put the object in the water and record the water level. Subtract the difference in water levels to get the amount of water displaced, which is also the volume of the object. In this case, 4.5 liters minus 2.5 liters equals 2 liters. Divide mass by volume (40 grams divided by 2 liters) to get 20 g/L (grams per liter).

14. B: A spoiling apple. A spoiling apple is an example of a chemical change. During a chemical change, one substance is changed into another. Oxidation, a chemical change, occurs when an apple spoils. Sublimation of water refers to the conversion between the solid and the gaseous phases of matter, with no intermediate liquid stage. This is a phase change, not a chemical reaction. Dissolution of salt in water refers to a physical change, since the salt and water can be separated again by evaporating the water, which is a physical change. Pulverized rock is an example of a physical change where the form has changed but not the substance itself.

15. D: temperature. The amount of potential energy an object has depends on mass, height above ground and gravitational attraction, but not temperature. The formula for potential energy is PE = mgh, or potential energy equals mass times gravity times height. Answers A, B, and C are all valid answers as they are all contained in the formula for potential energy. Potential energy is the amount of energy stored in a system particularly because of its position.

16. D: All of the above. Elements on the periodic table are arranged into periods, or rows, according to atomic number, which is the number of protons in the nucleus. The periodic table illustrates the recurrence of properties. Each column, or group, contains elements that share similar properties, such as reactivity.

17. A: It takes half the amount of energy to increase the temperature of a 1 kg sample of ice by 1°C than a 1 kg sample of water. Heat capacity refers to the amount of heat or thermal energy required to raise the temperature of a specific substance a given unit. A substance with a higher heat capacity requires more heat to raise its temperature than a substance with a lower heat capacity. The comparison here is that the specific heat capacity of ice is half as much as that of liquid water, so it takes half the amount of energy to increase the same amount of ice one temperature unit than it would if it were liquid water.

18. D: The temperature of a substance during the time of any phase change remains the same. In this case, the phase change was from liquid to solid, or freezing. Latent heat of fusion, in this case, is energy that is released from the substance as it reforms its solid form. This energy will be released and the liquid will turn to solid before the temperature of the substance will decrease further. If the substance were changing from solid to liquid, the heat of fusion would be the amount of heat required to break apart the attractions between the molecules in the solid form to change to the liquid form. The latent heat of fusion is exactly the same quantity of energy for a substance for either melting or freezing. Depending on the process, this amount of heat would either be absorbed by the substance (melting) or released (freezing).

19. B: Conduction. A long nail or other type of metal, substance, or matter that is heated at one end and then the other end becomes equally hot is an example of conduction. Conduction is energy transfer by neighboring molecules from an area of hotter temperature to cooler temperature. Radiation, or thermal radiation, refers to heat being transferred without the need for a medium by electromagnetic radiation. An example is sunlight heating the earth. Convection refers to heat being transferred by molecules moving from one location in the substance to another creating a heat current, usually in a gas or a liquid. Entropy relates to the second law of thermodynamics and refers to how much heat or energy is no longer available to do work in a system. It can also be stated as the amount of disorder in a system.

20. C: Heat transfer can never occur from a cooler object to a warmer object. While the second law of thermodynamics implies that heat never spontaneously transfers from a cooler object to a warmer object, it is possible for heat to be transferred to a warmer object, given the proper input of work to the system. This is the principle by which a refrigerator operates. Work is done to the system to transfer heat from the objects inside the refrigerator to the air surrounding the refrigerator. All other answer choices are true.

21. B: heat. The measure of energy within a system is called heat. Temperature is a measurement of the average kinetic energy of molecules in a substance. A higher temperature means greater kinetic energy or faster moving molecules. Entropy is the amount of energy that is no longer available for work, related to the second law of thermodynamics. Thermodynamics is the study of the conversion of energy into heat and work in a system.

22. D: It has a different number of neutrons than other isotopes of the same element. Isotopes are variations of an element that have different numbers of neutrons. The various isotopes of an element have the same numbers of protons and electrons. For example, carbon has three naturally occurring isotopes: carbon-12, carbon-13, and carbon-14 (which is radioactive). Isotopes of an element differ in mass number, which is the number of protons and neutrons added together, but have the same atomic number, or number of protons.

23. D: It is a stable atom. If an atom's outer shell is filled, it is a stable atom. The outer shell refers to one of many energy levels, or shells, that electrons occupy around a nucleus. An atom whose outer shell is not filled wants to become stable by filling the outer shell. It fills its outer shell by forming bonds. The atom can do this by gaining electrons or losing electrons in ionic compounds, or if the atom is a part of a molecule, by sharing electrons. If an atom has a full outer shell, such as the noble gases, it does not readily react with other atoms and does not exchange electrons to form bonds. These atoms are known as inert. Therefore, Answers A and B cannot be true. Answer C, It has 32 electrons in its outer shell, is not necessarily true because not all elements have the fourth shell that can hold 32 electrons. Some have fewer shells that hold fewer electrons.

24. A: Fission. Fission is a nuclear process where atomic nuclei split apart to form smaller nuclei. Nuclear fission can release large amounts of energy, emit gamma rays and form daughter products. It is used in nuclear power plants and bombs. Answer B, Fusion, refers to a nuclear process whereby atomic nuclei join to form a heavier nucleus, such as with stars. This can release or absorb energy depending upon the original elements. Answer C, Decay, refers to an atomic nucleus spontaneously losing energy and emitting ionizing particles and radiation. Answer D, Ionization, refers to a process by which atoms obtain a positive or negative charge because the number of electrons does not equal that of protons.

25. B: farther from. Electrons with greater amounts of energy are found farther from the nucleus than electrons with less energy. The principle quantum number describes the level or shell that an electron is in. The lower the number, the closer the electron is to the nucleus and the lower it is in energy.

26. D: decay. The process whereby a radioactive element releases energy slowly over a long period of time to lower its energy and become more stable is best described as decay. The nucleus undergoing decay, known as the parent nuclide, spontaneously releases energy most commonly through the emission of an alpha particle, a beta particle, or a gamma ray. The changed nucleus, called the daughter nuclide, is now more stable than the parent nuclide, although the daughter nuclide may undergo another decay to an even more stable nucleus. A decay chain is a series of decays of a radioactive element into different more stable elements.

27. C: A screw. A screw is a type of simple machine. A screw is an inclined plane wrapped around a shaft. A wedge is also an inclined plane. A compound machine is a machine that employs two or more simple machines. Answer A, a bicycle, is a compound machine, consisting of a combination of the simple machines: wheels, levers, pulleys and wedges (used as stoppers). Answer B, a pair of scissors, is also a compound machine consisting of two wedges (the blades) that pivot on a lever. Answer D, a shovel, is a compound machine consisting of a lever (the handle) and a wedge (the head of the shovel).

28. D: Mario balances a book on his head. In this example, work is not applied to the book because the book is not moving. One definition of work is force acting on an object to cause displacement. In this case, the book was not displaced by the force applied to it. Mario's head applied a vertical force to the book to keep it in the same position.

29. C: The ball will move forward with respect to the boat. Newton's First law of motion states that an object in motion tends to stay in motion until a force acts to change it. The ball is initially at rest with respect to the boat, but the boat is moving forward. When the front of the boat hits the dock, the boat quickly decelerates, but the ball does not. It continues to move forward because the force acting to stop the boat does not significantly affect the ball. With the ball now moving forward faster than the boat, the ball's motion relative to the boat is forward motion.

30. A: Acceleration and centripetal force. Acceleration and centripetal force are required for circular motion to occur. Acceleration is defined as a change in direction of velocity. Centripetal force is force directed toward the center, or inward force. The force of gravity is not required for circular motion, nor is constant speed.

31. B: Where the pipe is narrowest. A fluid, either a gas or a liquid, will flow faster through a narrow section of a pipe than a wider section of pipe. Bernoulli's Principle says that the faster a fluid flows, the less pressure the fluid exerts. Therefore, a fluid will exert a lower amount of pressure in the narrow section of pipe. A fluid moving through the pipe has the same flow throughout the wider and narrow portions. This means that the same volume and mass of fluid must go a specific distance in a certain amount of time. In a narrow portion of pipe, there is less area for the same volume and mass of fluid to flow, so the fluid must move faster to maintain the same flow as in the wider portion of pipe. A fluid moving faster through a narrow portion of pipe will exert less pressure and a fluid moving slower through a wide section of pipe will exert a greater pressure.

32. A: The charge on the glass rod is positive and the charge on the cloth is negative when the glass rod is rubbed with a cloth made of polyester. This is an example of static electricity — the collection of electrically charged particles on the surface of a material. A static charge can be quickly discharged, commonly called a "spark," or discharged more slowly by dissipating to the ground. A static charge occurs because different materials have a capacity for giving up electrons and becoming positive (+), or for attracting electrons and becoming negative (-). The triboelectric series is a list of materials and their propensities for either giving up electrons to become positive or to gain the electrons to become negative. Polyester has a tendency to gain electrons to become negative and glass has a tendency to lose electrons to become positive.

33. B: Voltage and current are directly proportional to one another. Ohm's Law states that voltage and current in an electrical circuit are directly proportional to one another. Ohm's Law can be expressed as V=IR, where V is voltage, I is current and R is resistance. Voltage is also known as electrical potential difference and is the force that moves electrons through a circuit. For a given amount of resistance, an increase in voltage will result in an increase in current. Resistance and current are inversely proportional to each other. For a given voltage, an increase in resistance will result in a decrease in current.

34. C: spin unpaired. In an atom with paired electrons, the opposite spins of each electron in the pair cancel out the magnetic field of each electron. A material becomes magnetic when the individual electrons of an atom spin unpaired thus allowing their magnetic fields to add together. The spin of an unpaired electron generates its own magnetic field. This can be used to make a magnet. When an external magnetic field is applied, these spins are lined up and the combined forces make a magnet.

35. D: In a parallel circuit, the voltage is the same for all three paths. Because the resistance is different on each path but the voltage is the same, Ohm's law dictates that the current will also be different for each path. Ohm's law says that current is inversely related to resistance. Therefore, the current will be greatest in path C as it has the least resistance, 2 ohms.

36. B: High temperature and humidity. Sound travels the farthest with high temperature and humidity. Sound is a mechanical wave. The sound wave travels through matter by causing a molecule to vibrate which then collides with a neighboring molecule causing it to vibrate and so on. A solid whose molecules are closely packed together will transmit the wave faster than a liquid or a gas whose particles are further apart. This is because the solid particles are more rigid and will respond to the disturbance quicker than a liquid or a gas, whose molecules are fluid. For this reason, solids can also propagate a wave further than a liquid or a gas. The principles of how sound travels through a solid can be applied to sound traveling through the air, as in this question. Air that is high in humidity has a higher density than dry air and can propagate the sound wave faster and farther than dry air. Sound waves also travel faster and farther at high temperatures. This is because at higher temperatures molecules have more kinetic energy to transmit the sound wave. At higher temperatures, molecules will also have more collisions which will result in the sound wave traveling farther and faster.

37. A: A high angle of incidence of the wave. A high angle of incidence will cause a high angle of reflection of a light wave. The angle of incidence is the angle of the incoming light and the angle of reflection is the angle of the light after being reflected. They are equal. A low angle of incidence of the wave would cause an equally low angle of reflection. A wave that travels through a medium of higher density would cause an angle of refraction, not reflection. Wavelength is not changed by reflection.

38. D: Destructive interference. Destructive interference describes two waves that are out of phase as they come together to produce a new wave. Out of phase refers to the crest of one and the trough of another arriving together. Interference, when used to discuss wave phenomenon, is the interaction of two or more waves passing the same point, which could be either destructive or constructive. Incomplete interference and distorted interference are not real terms. Constructive interference refers to wave interference that results in higher peaks than the waves singularly because the waves arrive in phase with one another (the crests arrive together).

39. A: They will be refracted and converge. When light waves hit a convex lens, they are refracted and converge. A convex lens curves or bulges with the middle being thicker and the edges thinner. A magnifying glass is an example. Light rays are refracted by different amounts as they pass through the lens. After light rays pass through, they converge at a point called the focus. An object viewed with a magnifying glass looks bigger because the lens bends the rays inwards. Answer B would indicate a concave lens as it would cause the light to be refracted and diverge. Light is not reflected in this case, so neither C nor D would be applicable.

40. B: When an astronomer observing stars detects a blue shift, he can conclude the star is moving closer or toward him. This is an example of the practical application of the Doppler Effect in astronomy as applied to electromagnetic waves. The Doppler Effect explains the change of wavelength caused by motion of the source or the relative difference in velocity between the observer and the source. When observing stars, a red shift or blue shift can be used to measure the speed that stars and galaxies are approaching or receding. Blue light has a higher frequency than red light. A red shift indicates a receding source.

41. C: A cation from a base and an anion from an acid. A salt is a general term for the neutral ionic product of a neutralization reaction between an acid and a base. Often, table salt, or sodium chloride, is mistakenly characterized as "salt", indicating that all salts are this compound. Although it is very common for a salt to be composed of a metal and a nonmetal, this is not always true, as in the case of the salt ammonium chloride. The ammonium ion (NH_4^+) is a polyatomic ion composed of non-metals. Likewise, many salts are composed of an alkali or alkaline earth metal and a halogen, but this is not always the case.

42. B: Group 2. Group 2 makes up the alkaline earth metals on the periodic chart of elements. There are 18 groups, or vertical columns, on the periodic table. In general, Group 2, alkaline earth metals, are characterized by silver colored, soft metals that melt at high temperatures. They also combine well with halogens to form salts and have two electrons in their valence level. Group 1 elements are called the alkali metals or lithium family. Group 13 is the boron family. Group 17 elements are known as the halogens or fluorine family.

43. C: Astatine. Astatine is not a noble gas (Group 18). Astatine is a halogen (Group 17). It is believed to be the rarest naturally occurring element. Its symbol is At and has an atomic number of 85. It is radioactive and has a short half life. Neon, Argon, and Krypton are all noble gases. These gases have low reactivity as their valence levels are filled with 8 electrons, except for helium, whose valence level is filled with 2 electrons.

44. D: The atomic number is equal to the number of electrons. An atom has a neutral charge if its atomic number is equal to its number of electrons. The atomic number (Z) of an element refers to the number of protons in the nucleus. If an atom has fewer or more electrons than its atomic number, then it will be positively or negatively charged, respectively. Cations are positively charged ions; anions are negatively charged ones. Answers A and B both describe a nucleus containing only neutrons with no protons. An element of this nature is referred to as neutronium, but is theoretical only.

45. A: high solubility in water. Most organic molecules are not highly soluble in water. A low melting point, covalent bonds, and high flammability are all characteristics of organic molecules. Organic molecules are those that contain carbon molecules, with a few exceptions. Organic molecules tend to be less soluble in water than inorganic salts. They are good at forming unique structures and there are many organic compounds. Examples of organic compounds include hydrocarbons, carbohydrates, lipids and proteins.

46. C: $Al_2O_3 + 2Fe$. In a single replacement reaction equation, $2Al + Fe_2O_3 \rightarrow Al_2O_3 + 2Fe$. The reactants of the original equation are aluminum and iron (III) oxide (rust). The products are aluminum oxide and elemental iron. Single replacement reactions occur when one uncombined element replaces another. In this reaction, the aluminum replaces the iron. This reaction is an example of a thermite reaction and generates a large amount of heat and light. It can be used in fireworks or welding.

47. C: Covalent. Covalent compounds are usually formed by the combination of two or more nonmetallic elements with one another. In these compounds, atoms share electrons. Ionic compounds are most often formed between a metal and a nonmetal. Organic compounds are covalent compounds that contain carbon and hydrogen atoms. Some of the compounds formed by non-metallic elements are polar, but not all of them.

48. B: They show all the electrons of each atom of a molecule. This is not correct. Lewis dot structures do not show all the electrons of each atom of a molecule. Lewis structures only show the valence electrons, or the outermost electrons, of all of the atoms in the molecule. The other answers are correct as Lewis dot structures show the bonding between atoms of a molecule and the lone pairs on an atom, and that the total number of electrons is equal to the sum of the number of valence electrons on each atom.

49. D: A carbon atom attached to a hydrogen atom by a double bond and to an oxygen atom by a double bond. This is not a correct description of the carboxyl group. Hydrogen can never have more than one bond since it only has a 1s level and can only accommodate two electrons. The other answers are correct, as a carboxyl group does have a carbon atom attached to an oxygen atom by a double bond and to a hydroxyl ($-OH$) group by a single bond and is a set of four atoms bonded together and abbreviated as CO_2H.

50. C: The pressure decreases to one third. A gas in a closed container at constant temperature will decrease in pressure to one third when the volume of the container is tripled. The ideal gas law is $PV = nRT$ where P is pressure, V is volume, n is the moles of the gas, R is the gas constant and T is temperature. A variation to solve for pressure is: $P = nRT/V$. Boyle's Law indicates that pressure and volume are inversely proportional. The pressure cannot be increased because that would imply that pressure and volume are directly proportional.

51. A: Sample A. Sample A is the only one of the four that was heated enough to completely change its phase to gas, so it is exerting the most pressure on its container. Sample B is boiling, but it is still partially liquid, so it is not exerting the most pressure. Sample C is unchanged in phase, and we do not even know if it was heated or cooled. Sample D was cooled to below the freezing temperature, so it is exerting very little if any pressure on its container.

52. B: Sample B would become a gas. Since each sample was given sufficient time to assume the temperature of its environment, we know from the description that sample B was first placed in an environment exactly at its boiling temperature. If this temperature were then increased by 10 degrees Celsius, it would be above the boiling point and sample B would have to vaporize completely in order to assume this temperature. None of the other events are guaranteed to occur. Answer C might occur, but we do not have enough information to determine this. Answer A is not possible as there would need to be a decrease in temperature for the gas to revert to a liquid.

53. A: The molecular arrangement is random in some directions and regular in others. This best describes the molecular arrangement of a liquid crystal. A liquid crystal may seem like a contradiction as it seems to refer to two different states of matter. Liquid crystals have properties of both liquids and solids. The molecules of a liquid crystal are loosely bound allowing them to flow, like a liquid, yet they arrange themselves in a repeating pattern, like the molecules of a solid which are rigidly fixed in a pattern. Liquid crystals can also organize into layers, but with randomness in the layers.

54. D: There may be a different number of atoms for the products and the reactants. This is not true of a chemical reaction. Chemical equations must be balanced on each side of the reaction.

Balancing means the total number of atoms stays the same, but their arrangement within specific reactants and products can change. The law of conservation of matter states that matter can never be created or destroyed. Heat may be absorbed or released in a reaction; these are classified as endothermic and exothermic reactions, respectively. The rate of the reaction increases with temperature for most reactions.

55. C: High concentration. A higher concentration could increase the reaction rate of a chemical reaction. The rate of reaction is affected by concentration, pressure and temperature. A higher concentration would allow for more potential collisions that set off the reaction. Low kinetic energy would lead to a lower rate of reaction, as does a lower temperature (usually). The term activation energy refers to the specific threshold that must be overcome for a reaction to occur. If the activation energy is lowered, for example, by a catalyst or enzyme, then the reaction can occur quicker. This rules out high activation energy.

56. C: Single Replacement. When copper is added to silver nitrate, copper nitrate and silver are formed in a single replacement reaction. In a single replacement reaction, one element replaces another. In this case, copper replaces the silver in the silver nitrate solution, forming copper nitrate and silver. The equation for this is $2AgNO_3 + Cu \rightarrow Cu(NO_3)_2 + 2Ag$. Combustion reactions require oxygen as one of the reactants. Decomposition, refers to a type of reaction by which one reactant is broken down into two or more products. Double replacement refers to a reaction whereby the cations and anions of two elements switch places.

57. B: A reaction that uses electricity to drive it. An electrolysis reaction is a chemical reaction that uses electricity to drive it. Electrolysis reactions take place in an electrolytic cell, where one substance will be oxidized and another will be reduced using electrical energy from a battery or other source. Usually, an electrolytic cell is made up of a battery connected to two metal electrodes which are placed in two separate ionic solutions. A salt bridge connects the two beakers of solution and allows positive or negative ions to flow into the solutions as needed to keep the charge balanced as the reaction takes place. The electrode where oxidation takes place is called the anode, which would be connected to the negative terminal on a battery. The electrode where reduction takes place is called the cathode and is connected to the positive terminal of a battery. These reactions are very important for electroplating metals.

58. C: A + BC. When the reactant ABC is decomposed, it will produce the products A + BC. 2AB + C would not be a balanced equation according to the law of conservation of mass since this would produce 2 A, 2 B and 1 C. Since the original reactant was ABC, this could not be balanced. AB + CD, is incorrect as an element "D" was not an original reactant. This does not follow the law that matter cannot be created nor destroyed. B + C has a similar problem as element "A" drops out of the equation; because "A" was a part of the reactant, it needs to be part of the product.

59. B: Cool the liquid. If a gas and a liquid are placed in a sealed container, cooling the liquid will help dissolve the gas into the liquid. Gases have higher solubility in liquids at lower temperatures. At higher temperatures, the gas molecules will have more kinetic energy and will have enough energy to overcome intermolecular interactions with the liquid solvent and leave the solution. This also explains why heating the liquid is incorrect. Shaking the container is also incorrect as this would give the gas energy to escape. Decreasing the pressure on the lid may or may not significantly affect the pressure inside the vessel depending on the nature of the vessel, but decreasing the pressure inside the vessel would decrease the solubility of the gas in the liquid.

60. D: Non-polar. A non-polar substance is least likely to be soluble in water. A rule of thumb for a substance's solubility is that like dissolves like. Polarity is affected by the types of bonds between atoms and the bonds are affected by the types of atoms. An unequal sharing of electrons leads to polar bonding and polar substances. Water is polar and can dissolve many other polar substances. Hydrophilic molecules are polar and this word means "water-loving". Water also dissolves many ionic substances since they are composed of charged ions and can interact with the polar water molecules. Many organic compounds are non-polar and do not dissolve well in water.

61. C: The vapor pressure decreases by an amount proportional to the amount of solute. Raoult's law states that the vapor pressure of a solution containing a non-volatile solute is equal to the vapor pressure of the volatile solvent multiplied by its mole fraction, which is basically the proportion of the solution that is made up by solvent. In a liquid, some of the surface particles have higher than average energy and can break away to become a gas, or evaporate. The pressure of this gas right above the surface of the liquid is called the vapor pressure. Increasing the amount of solute in a liquid decreases the number of solvent particles at the surface. Because of this, fewer solvent molecules are able to escape, thus lowering the vapor pressure.

62. B: Water plus salt. Water plus salt has the highest electrical conductivity. To conduct electricity, ions must be present to move electrons through the solution. Electrolytes are substances that break apart to become ions. Pure water is actually a very poor conductor, since it is a covalent molecule and not an electrolyte. A very small portion of water molecules may break apart to form H+ ions and OH- but not enough to make it a good conductor. Salt is an electrolyte and completely breaks apart into Na+ ions and Cl- ions upon dissolving. This solution is highly conductive. Sugar is a non-electrolyte because it is a covalent molecule and does not produce ions when it dissolves. Water plus vinegar would conduct electricity but would not be as conductive as the salt solution because vinegar is a weak electrolyte. This means that only a portion of the vinegar molecules break apart into ions. Water plus carbonated soda would not be a good conductor since CO_2 is a covalent molecule and is a non-electrolyte.

63. C: In humans, diploid cells are those that contain 46 chromosomes. There are 23 pairs of chromosomes each made up of one chromosome from the father and one from the mother. In meiosis I, each chromosome replicates itself and lines up, or synapses, with its homologous chromosome, and each of the daughter cells ends up with one copy of each of the chromosomes. The two daughter cells at the end of meiosis I are haploid because they contain half of the chromosomes of the parent cell. In humans, this would be 23 chromosomes. However, each of these chromosomes is made of two sister chromatids. In meiosis II, the sister chromatids in the daughter cells separate and result in the production of the gametes. These are also haploid cells because they contain one copy of half of the genetic material of the parent cell. Four haploid cells result from meiosis. Mitosis refers to the process of cell division where each daughter cell contains exactly the same genetic material as the parent cell. Telophase refers to phases of both mitosis and meiosis, during which chromosomes move toward the opposite ends of the cell.

64. A: Lysosomes. A lysosome is an organelle that is thought to be linked to the aging process and contains digestive enzymes that break down food and unneeded substances. Chromatin is the structure created by DNA and various proteins in the cell nucleus during interphase and condenses to form chromosomes. Plastids are found in plants and algae. They often contain pigments and usually help make chemical compounds for the plant. The Golgi apparatus prepares macromolecules like proteins and lipids for transport.

65. B: Anabolic processes are those that use energy to build larger molecules. In cells, adenosine triphosphate (ATP) is used as a source of energy. A condensation reaction joins two molecules together to make a larger molecule and, in the process, also produces a water molecule. Condensation reactions are important in protein synthesis. Anabolic processes are often reduction reactions. Catabolism breaks down molecules and usually generates energy. Catabolic reactions are often oxidation reactions. Hydrolysis is a catabolic process where water is added to a molecule and then split, resulting in the molecule breaking apart into two different molecules. Hydrolysis is the opposite of condensation.

66. B: Photosynthesis converts carbon dioxide into sugars that plants use. Three types of photosynthesis are C3, C4, and CAM. C3 is used by most plants. C4 first forms a four carbon sugar instead of the three carbon sugar formed by C3. Also, the stomata of C4 plants are faster at absorbing carbon dioxide and do not have to open as long, so less water is lost by transpiration. A C4 plant, such as saltbush, corn, or some grasses, would live in a very hot environment rather than a cold, marine, or dark environment. Plants that use the CAM (Crassulacean Acid Metabolism) type of photosynthesis also use water more efficiently as their stomata are closed during the day and open at night. Desert cacti are examples.

67. A: Cytoplasm. The type of RNA described by the question is transfer RNA (tRNA). The tRNA is found in the cytoplasm and carries and positions amino acids at the ribosome for protein synthesis. There are two other types of RNA. Messenger RNA (mRNA) contains the coding for the amino acid sequence in the protein. The mRNA is first made in the nucleus before traveling through the cytoplasm to a ribosome. Ribosomal RNA (rRNA) is the RNA that is found in the ribosome along with proteins, which allows the mRNA and tRNA to bind for protein synthesis. All three types of RNA originate in the nucleus where they are transcribed from DNA. Mitochondria are organelles that harbor mitochondrial DNA (mtDNA).

68. C: U G C A U G C G A. Translation is the process of the tRNA bringing the correct amino acid to the ribosome according to the sequence of the mRNA. Since translation only involves RNA, the four bases are adenine (A), cytosine (C), guanine (G), and uracil (U). There is no thymine (T) used in RNA. Cytosine (C) and guanine (G) pair and adenine (A) and uracil (U) pair. A codon is the triplet sequence that represents a specific amino acid or a start/stop point. It is on the messenger RNA (mRNA). The anticodon is on tRNA and corresponds to the amino acid used by the ribosome during translation. They are complementary. UGC becomes ACG; AUG becomes UAC; CGA becomes GCU. The original codon sequence is U G C A U G C G A if the anticodon sequence formed during translation is A C G U A C G C U.

69. C: 4/16. The fraction of offspring that have the genotype BbSs is 4/16. A dihybrid cross considers two traits at a time, in this case, eye color and hair color. In the parent (P) generation, a parent with the genotype BBSS would be crossed with a parent with the genotype bbss. The offspring are considered the F1 generation and all would have the genotype BbSs. This question asks about the F2 generation, which is the offspring between a cross of the F1 generation. Therefore, the parent genotypes in this question would be BbSs. To solve, develop a Punnet square of 16 cells. Each parent will produce the following gametes: BS, Bs, bS, bs. Place these across the top and the side. After completing the square, the resulting offspring show that four would have the genotype BbSs.

P → F1

	BS
bs	BbSs

F1 → F2

	BS	**Bs**	**bS**	**bs**
BS	BBSS	BBSs	BbSS	BbSs
Bs	BBSs	BBss	BbSs	Bbss
bS	BbSS	BbSs	bbSS	bbSs
bs	BbSs	Bbss	bbSs	bbss

70. D: Inversion. This type of mutation is represented in the sequence 1 5 4 3 2 6. An inversion error is a type of mutation where an entire sequence of DNA is reversed. In this case, 2 3 4 5 has been reversed to 5 4 3 2. Breakage in a gene can mess up its function entirely or lead to a translocation of genetic information. Deletion occurs when a section of DNA is omitted or lost. Insertion occurs when an extra base pair is added to a DNA sequence. Deletions and insertions can lead to a frameshift effect where entire sequences are thrown off because one nucleotide is wrong. This could result in coding for the wrong amino acid and non-functioning proteins.

71. C: Vestigial structure. Wisdom teeth are an example of a vestigial structure. A vestigial structure is one that still exists in an organism, but through evolution has lost most of its original purpose. Wisdom teeth, or third molars, in humans were useful in grinding down plant matter in larger jaws. Human diet has changed and jaws have become smaller, yet wisdom teeth still develop. Some vestigial organs may gain a new function. An analogous structure is one that exists for the same purpose in two species but in different forms. A homologous structure is one that has the same basic structure but not purpose in two different species. A paralogous structure is a particular type of homologous structure.

72. B: The Biological Species Concept (BSC) states that the status of "species" is based on the natural reproductive isolation of populations. Populations that could potentially interbreed and produce fertile offspring but do not do so in nature are considered different species under the BSC. This species concept does not consider the ability to interbreed under artificial conditions: if two groups do not breed with one another for any reason (in nature), they are reproductively isolated and therefore different species according to the BSC. The isolation may be due to geography, behavior, appearance, or other factors. For example, the Eastern and Western meadowlark look very similar and have overlapping territories, but they have different songs. Individual meadowlarks identify others by their songs and only breed with those with the same song. Because the two populations are reproductively isolated from one another, they are considered different species under the BSC. If individuals with different songs did interbreed and produce fertile offspring, they would be considered the same species.

73. A: New species due to geographic isolation. Allopatric speciation refers to a new species brought about by geographic isolation. Speciation in general refers to the formation of a new species. Geographic isolation can be because of a great physical barrier or insurmountable distance between groups of individuals. The term "hybrid species" has many definitions that do not necessarily relate to geography. Loss of diversity of a species due to geographic divergence is also incorrect as it does not refer to loss of diversity.

74. B: He proposed an alternate theory by stating that favorable traits developed due to environmental conditions and the desire and needs of the organisms. Jean Baptiste Lamarck's theory of acquired characteristics predated Darwin's book about theory of natural selection. Lamarck explained evolution as occurring when individual organisms of a species changed as a response to environmental conditions. Contrast this with Darwinism, which states that individuals with more successful characteristics are more likely to survive to breed and pass on those traits. Since Lamarck died in 1829 and Darwin published *On the Origin of the Species* in 1859 the other answers that Lamarck "expanded," "provided evidence for," or "opposed" Darwin's theories are not likely.

75. D: Reproductive habits. Reproductive habits would not be considered evidence for evolution. Usually how a species reproduces does not support nor add to the body of evidence for the theory of evolution. Reproductive habits might exemplify how any given organism can adapt to changes in its environment as a way to survive. This does not necessarily show evolution. Fossil record is evidence for evolution as it shows evolutionary change of organisms over time. DNA sequences show that organisms that are related evolutionarily also have related gene sequences. Anatomical structures such as having an internal bony structure provide evidence of descent from a common ancestor.

76. B: Family. Organisms that belong to the same taxonomic group of family are most alike. In biological taxonomy, the ranks in descending order are Domain, Kingdom, Phylum, Class, Order, Family, Genus and Species. The ranks become more exclusive and specific as the classification descends. Phylum, class, and order, are all higher than the family group. The higher the rank, the fewer requirements it takes to be a member. Two mnemonics for taxonomy are Dashing Kings Play Cards On Fat Green Snakes or Dear King Philip Cuts Open Five Green Snakes.

77. A: Anthophyta. Anthophyta is a division of plants that produces seeds as part of reproduction. Anthophyta are also known as the group that contains flowering plants. It is the largest and most diverse grouping of plants and includes many food, clothing and medicinal uses for humans. Grains, beans, nuts, fruits, vegetables, spices, tea, coffee, chocolate, cotton, linen and aspirin are all derived from plants from anthophyta. Lycophyta is a small group of plants including club mosses and scale trees. Sphenophyta contains about 30 species including horsetails, foxtails, or scouring rushes. Pterophyta contains non-seed plants like ferns. Lycophyta, sphenophyta, and pterophyta all use spores to reproduce sexually.

78. B: They use tube feet for locomotion and feeding. Animals belonging to the phylum Echinodermata have tube feet for locomotion and feeding. About 7,000 species are extant in this phylum, including starfish and sand dollars. Tube feet are an organ system that provides locomotion, respiration, feeding and sensory functions. Not all echinoderms have appendages. Having an exoskeleton made of chitin is characteristic of arthropods. Not all echinoderms must shed their outer layer of skin to grow.

79. C: Flowers are the reproductive organs of a plant. Flowering plants reproduce by sexual reproduction where the gametes join to form seeds. Pollen is sperm. Pollinators help transfer the sperm to the ovule, the egg. The style is the part of the female reproduction system that transports the sperm between the stigma and the ovary, which are all parts of the pistil. The stigma is the sticky tip of the style on which the pollen lands. Sepals are usually small leaves between or underneath the petals and are not as obvious or as large and colorful as the petals.

80. D: Carbon dioxide and water. Respiration produces carbon dioxide and water. The net equation of respiration is the reverse of the equation for photosynthesis. Respiration is a series of reactions that consume glucose and oxygen to release energy and produce carbon dioxide and water. Oxygen and glucose are the substances that are broken down in respiration.

81. D: Lower seed dispersal is not an advantage that angiosperms show over other types of plants. Gymnosperms, for example, have plentiful amounts of pollen, but it does not always hit its mark. Angiosperms are the most recently evolved plant division and contain at least 260,000 extant species. They are very diverse and occupy many habitats. Many other species in other plant divisions do not have true leaves. Gymnosperms have modified leaves in the form of needles. Double fertilization refers to how one sperm cell fuses with an ovule, forming the zygote. The second sperm forms into a triploid endosperm that provides energy for the embryo.

82. A: Animals of the phylum Mollusca or mollusks, respire (breathe) through gills. Respiration is the process of taking in oxygen and releasing carbon dioxide. Mollusca consists of several classes that include species as diverse as chitons, clams, land and marine snails, and squid. This represents a diverse range of body structures. Many mollusks have a mantle that includes a cavity that is used for both breathing and excretion. Within the mantle are gills (ctenidia). Mollusks do not have tracheas. Some land snails have a respiratory cavity that is often called a lung but is not a true lung. Spiders, which are not mollusks (they are arachnids), have a type of lungs called book lungs. Muscle contraction is not required for the gills to function. Other structures, such as cilia, work to pass water over the gills.

83. B: A stoma (plural: stomata) is the part of a plant system that responds to stimuli by releasing water via transpiration. It can also close during adverse conditions like a drought to prevent the plant from dehydration. Stomata closure can also be triggered by the presence of bacteria. Pith refers to the central, spongy part of the stem in vascular plants. Guard cells flank stomata and regulate the opening. Sepals are modified leaves that protect the flower bud before it opens.

84. D: Circulatory System – exchanges gases with the environment by delivering oxygen to the bloodstream and releasing carbon dioxide, is not paired correctly. It is the respiratory system that exchanges gases with the environment by delivering oxygen to the bloodstream and releasing carbon dioxide. The circulatory system transports nutrients, gases, hormones, and blood to and away from cells. The muscle system controls movement through three types of muscle tissue. The nervous system controls sensory responses by carrying impulses away from and toward the cell body. The digestive system breaks down food for absorption into the blood stream where it is delivered to cells for respiration.

85. C: at carrying capacity. A population that reaches maximum size and ceases to grow due to a limited availability of resources is said to be at carrying capacity. The carrying capacity of a species is influenced by many factors such as the amount of land or water available, food supply, and predators. Unstable and moving towards extinction are not correct as carrying capacity does not necessarily mean it is unstable or becoming extinct. Shrinking exponentially is also incorrect as the question says it has stopped growing, not that it is reducing in size.

86. A: Tree. In the food chain of tree → caterpillar → frog → snake → hawk → worm, the tree is at the trophic level with the greatest amount of energy. Trophic level refers to the position of an organism in a food chain. Energy is lost according to the laws of thermodynamics as one moves up the food chain because it is converted to heat when consumers consume. Primary producers, such as autotrophs, are organisms who are at the base and capture solar energy. Primary consumers are herbivores that feed on the producers. Secondary consumers consume primary consumers and so on. Decomposers get their energy from the consumption of dead plants and animals.

87. B: Glaciers. Fresh water suitable for drinking can be found as surface water and in groundwater, which is obtained through wells. Rivers (surface water) and aquifers (groundwater) are both sources of fresh water that are available to humans. Glaciers and ice caps are indirect sources of fresh water–when they melt, the runoff forms streams and rivers. Water from all of these sources is suitable for drinking with little to no treatment. Estuaries, however, are not sources of fresh water; they are bodies of brackish (moderately salty) water formed where freshwater from a river mixes with salt water from an ocean. This water is not suitable for drinking without treatment such as desalinization.

88. C: Moose. Moose are most likely to be found in the taiga. Biomes are classifications of areas and communities of predominant plant and animal life that live within the area. The six major types of biomes are freshwater, marine, dessert, forest, grassland, and tundra. The taiga or boreal is one of the three major types of forests: tropical, temperate and taiga. They can be divided by latitude and the taiga runs through Canada, northern Europe, and Russia, sandwiched between the tundra and deciduous forests. Taiga is a Russian word meaning swampy, moist forest.

89. C: Transform. Transform is not connected to the process of mountain building. Orogeny, or mountain building, occurs at the Earth's lithosphere or crust. Folding, or deformation, is a process that occurs to make mountains where two portions of the lithosphere collide. One is subducted and the other is pushed upward forming a mountain. This action produces various types of folding. Faulting can be characterized by a brittle deformation where the rock breaks abruptly (compared with folding). Faulting and fault types are associated with earthquakes and relatively rapid deformation. Convergent is a more general term used to describe plates interacting.

90. D: heat. The formation of sedimentary rock does not include heat. Of the three types of rock igneous, sedimentary and metamorphic, heat is essential to two: igneous and metamorphic. Sedimentary rocks are formed by sediments that get deposited and then compacted or cemented together. Sedimentary rocks are classified into detrital, organic or chemical sediments. Layering is correct since sediments can be deposited or otherwise formed in layers. Cementation is also called lithification. Compaction refers to the pressure forming sedimentary rock leading to cementation.

91. C: Vinegar fizzing when poured on a rock is an example of chemical weathering. Mechanical and chemical weathering are processes that break down rocks. Mechanical weathering breaks down rocks physically but does not change their chemical composition. Frost and abrasion are examples. Water, oxygen, carbon dioxide, and living organisms can lead to the chemical weathering of rock. Vinegar is a weak acid and will undergo a chemical reaction, evidenced by fizzing, with the rock. Rain freezing on the roadway is an example of the phase change of water from a liquid to a solid and may lead to physical weathering. Ivy growing on the side of a wooden house is incorrect since the house is not a rock. A river carrying sediment downstream is an example of erosion.

92. B: Two crustal plates move apart. When two crustal plates move apart, magma welling up could result in the formation of new crust. This has been shown to be occurring on the ocean floor where places of the crust are weaker. The crust spreads apart at these trenches, pushing outward and erupting at the ridges. When two crustal plates converge, sublimation occurs as one plate runs under another pushing it up. Two crustal plates sliding past one another is an example of a transform fault, which does not create new crust. A crustal plate being pushed down into the mantle does not form new crust but perhaps recycles the old one.

93. C: Laccolith. A laccolith is formed when an intrusion of magma injected between two layers of sedimentary rock forces the overlying strata upward to create a dome-like form. Eventually, the magma cools, the sedimentary rock wears away and the formation is exposed. Sills and dikes are both examples of sheet intrusions, where magma has inserted itself into other rock. Sills are horizontal and dikes are vertical. A caldera is a crater-like feature that was formed from the collapse of a volcano after erupting.

94. A: The process of absolute dating compares the amount of radioactive material in a rock to the amount that has decayed into another element. Answer B is not usually done. Usually the stratigraphic layer of rock is used to date the fossils, referred to as relative dating. Answer C is incorrect as this would not lead to a correct date since the daughter elements may have a different half-life than the parent material.

95. C: igneous rock. Fossils are least likely to be found in igneous rock. Igneous rock is formed by extreme heat as magma escapes through the Earth's crust and cools. The remains of plants and animals in fossil form are not usually preserved under these conditions. Sedimentary rock is where the abundance of fossils are found. Sedimentary rock is formed more slowly and is very abundant. Since soft mud and silts compress into layers, organisms can also be deposited. Metamorphic rock is rock that has undergone change by heat and pressure. This usually destroys any fossils, but occasionally fossil remains are distorted and can be found in metamorphic rock.

96. B: A footprint. A trace fossil is that which shows evidence of existence but is not an organism itself. A trace fossil can be contrasted with a body fossil, which has been formed from an organism. Other examples of trace fossils include eggs, nests, burrows, borings and coprolites (fossilized feces). A mouse jaw and a shark tooth are examples of body fossils. A cast of a skull is a replica and neither a body nor a trace fossil.

97. A: era. A time interval in which particular plants and animals were dominant or present in great abundance is defined as an era. On the geologic time scale, stratigraphy is used to provide approximate dates of events related to the Earth on a much grander time scale than our lives. Eons are divided into eras. Eras are separated by major events, such as the Cretaceous–Tertiary extinction event, which marked the end of the Mesozoic Era and the beginning of the Cenozoic Era. Eras are divided into periods, epochs and ages.

98. D: The first implies that the Earth was shaped by a series of quick, violent events, while the second implies that it changed slowly and incrementally. Catastrophism is the belief that the Earth was shaped by sudden, short-term catastrophic events. Uniformitarianism, also known as gradualism, is the belief among modern geologists that the forces, processes, and laws that we see in effect today have been in effect for a long period of time, that is, throughout geologic time. It involves the belief that the present is the key to the past, and that these relatively slow processes have shaped the Earth.

99. C: Cold and high salinity. Ocean currents that are cold and have high salinity are the densest. Sea water with a higher salinity is denser that lower salinity sea water. The density of ocean water can also affect currents. Water from denser areas will flow to areas of lower density. Denser ocean water sinks and becomes cooler. As the depth of the water increases, the pressure and density also increase.

100. D: Phase of the Moon. Ocean currents are not controlled by the phase of the moon. The phases of the moon refer to our viewpoint from Earth of the sun's illumination of the moon. Half the moon is illuminated by the sun at any given time. For example, a new moon is one we do not see because the side being lit by the sun is not facing us. The revolution of the moon around the earth affects the ocean tides, providing two highs and two lows at any given point during the day. Wind affects the surface currents of the ocean. Landmasses affect ocean currents as well. Earth's rotation affects the deep currents.

101. B: The freezing point of sea water is lower than that of fresh water as sea water is denser. It is denser because it has more dissolved salts. The freezing point changes with salinity, pressure, and density, but can be as low as -2°C (28.4°F), compared with 0°C (32°F) for fresh water.

102. C: It is the surface layer where wave action is present due to interaction with winds at the surface. The mixed layer of the ocean can be affected mainly by three processes: winds, cooling and an increase in density. The winds at the surface drive surface currents and therefore, mixing. The action of breaking waves imparts a large amount of energy to the surface mixed layer. Surface density can be changed by an increase in salinity, which can be caused both by the addition of brine from sea ice or net evaporation because of temperature and a lack of influx of more water.

103. B: Cold water dissolves atmospheric carbon dioxide, stores it, and releases it back out to the atmosphere as needed. This describes the physical or non-biological part of the carbon cycle. The carbon and nutrient cycles of the ocean are processed in part by the deep currents, mixing, and upwelling that occurs. Carbon dioxide (CO_2) from the atmosphere is dissolved into the ocean at the higher latitudes and distributed to the denser deep water. When upwelling occurs, CO_2 is brought back to the surface and emitted into the tropical air.

104. A: The prevailing westerlies. The prevailing westerlies drive weather systems to move west to east in the mid-latitudes. The direction refers to that which the wind is coming from. The polar easterlies that travel from the northeast occur between 90-60 degrees north latitude. The ones from the southeast are between 90-60 degrees south latitude. The trade winds refer to those occurring near the equator in the tropics moving east. The doldrums are also in the tropics, but refer to an area of low-pressure where frequently the winds are light and unpredictable.

105. B: Land breeze. When land cools off rapidly at night and the ocean water stays relatively warm, it creates a land breeze. Sea breeze, or onshore breeze, occurs when the land heats the air above it. This heated, warmer air is less dense and rises. The cooler air from above the sea and higher sea level pressure creates a wind flow in the direction of the land. Coastal areas often have these cooler breezes. A monsoon is a seasonal wind in southern Asia that blows southwest in one season and northeast in another. The southwest winds in the summer bring heavy rain. The trade winds are the steady easterlies about the equator.

106. D: 90%. If the air temperature is 65°F and the dew point is 62°F, the relative humidity will be closest to 90%. Relative humidity is the ratio of the amount of water vapor contained in the air to the amount it would be possible for the air to contain at that temperature. Absolute humidity is the total moisture capable at a certain temperature. Warm air can hold more water vapor. When the air is at the dew point, it is holding all the water that it possibly can at that temperature (relative humidity of 100%).

107. C: On a topographic map, an area where the contour lines are very close together indicates that the slope is very steep. Lines very far apart would indicate a more gradual change in elevation. Contour lines help represent the actual shape of the Earth's surface features and geographic landmarks like rivers, lakes, and vegetation. Topographic maps also show man-made features such as roads, dams, and major buildings. They are based on aerial photography, and the quadrangle maps are produced in various scales. The 7.5-minute quadrangle is very common and provides a 1:24,000 scale, where 1 inch represents 2,000 feet.

108. C: Solar radiation. Solar radiation is the major driving force that controls Earth's heat budget. The Earth's heat budget, or energy budget, refers to the total heat that moves through the Earth's system. Almost all of the energy is obtained by solar radiation and this heats the air, land and oceans. Insolation is a measure of the incident solar radiation and tells how much energy is absorbed on a given area in a given amount of time. Advection is the transportation of a substance or property, like silt in a river or heat in an atmosphere. Evaporation is a phase change from a liquid to a gas. The tilt of the earth does not affect the heat budget but is responsible for seasons.

How to Overcome Test Anxiety

Just the thought of taking a test is enough to make most people a little nervous. A test is an important event that can have a long-term impact on your future, so it's important to take it seriously and it's natural to feel anxious about performing well. But just because anxiety is normal, that doesn't mean that it's helpful in test taking, or that you should simply accept it as part of your life. Anxiety can have a variety of effects. These effects can be mild, like making you feel slightly nervous, or severe, like blocking your ability to focus or remember even a simple detail.

If you experience test anxiety—whether severe or mild—it's important to know how to beat it. To discover this, first you need to understand what causes test anxiety.

Causes of Test Anxiety

While we often think of anxiety as an uncontrollable emotional state, it can actually be caused by simple, practical things. One of the most common causes of test anxiety is that a person does not feel adequately prepared for their test. This feeling can be the result of many different issues such as poor study habits or lack of organization, but the most common culprit is time management. Starting to study too late, failing to organize your study time to cover all of the material, or being distracted while you study will mean that you're not well prepared for the test. This may lead to cramming the night before, which will cause you to be physically and mentally exhausted for the test. Poor time management also contributes to feelings of stress, fear, and hopelessness as you realize you are not well prepared but don't know what to do about it.

Other times, test anxiety is not related to your preparation for the test but comes from unresolved fear. This may be a past failure on a test, or poor performance on tests in general. It may come from comparing yourself to others who seem to be performing better or from the stress of living up to expectations. Anxiety may be driven by fears of the future—how failure on this test would affect your educational and career goals. These fears are often completely irrational, but they can still negatively impact your test performance.

Elements of Test Anxiety

As mentioned earlier, test anxiety is considered to be an emotional state, but it has physical and mental components as well. Sometimes you may not even realize that you are suffering from test anxiety until you notice the physical symptoms. These can include trembling hands, rapid heartbeat, sweating, nausea, and tense muscles. Extreme anxiety may lead to fainting or vomiting. Obviously, any of these symptoms can have a negative impact on testing. It is important to recognize them as soon as they begin to occur so that you can address the problem before it damages your performance.

The mental components of test anxiety include trouble focusing and inability to remember learned information. During a test, your mind is on high alert, which can help you recall information and stay focused for an extended period of time. However, anxiety interferes with your mind's natural processes, causing you to blank out, even on the questions you know well. The strain of testing during anxiety makes it difficult to stay focused, especially on a test that may take several hours. Extreme anxiety can take a huge mental toll, making it difficult not only to recall test information but even to understand the test questions or pull your thoughts together.

Effects of Test Anxiety

Test anxiety is like a disease—if left untreated, it will get progressively worse. Anxiety leads to poor performance, and this reinforces the feelings of fear and failure, which in turn lead to poor performances on subsequent tests. It can grow from a mild nervousness to a crippling condition. If allowed to progress, test anxiety can have a big impact on your schooling, and consequently on your future.

Test anxiety can spread to other parts of your life. Anxiety on tests can become anxiety in any stressful situation, and blanking on a test can turn into panicking in a job situation. But fortunately, you don't have to let anxiety rule your testing and determine your grades. There are a number of relatively simple steps you can take to move past anxiety and function normally on a test and in the rest of life.

Physical Steps for Beating Test Anxiety

While test anxiety is a serious problem, the good news is that it can be overcome. It doesn't have to control your ability to think and remember information. While it may take time, you can begin taking steps today to beat anxiety.

Just as your first hint that you may be struggling with anxiety comes from the physical symptoms, the first step to treating it is also physical. Rest is crucial for having a clear, strong mind. If you are tired, it is much easier to give in to anxiety. But if you establish good sleep habits, your body and mind will be ready to perform optimally, without the strain of exhaustion. Additionally, sleeping well helps you to retain information better, so you're more likely to recall the answers when you see the test questions.

Getting good sleep means more than going to bed on time. It's important to allow your brain time to relax. Take study breaks from time to time so it doesn't get overworked, and don't study right before bed. Take time to rest your mind before trying to rest your body, or you may find it difficult to fall asleep.

Along with sleep, other aspects of physical health are important in preparing for a test. Good nutrition is vital for good brain function. Sugary foods and drinks may give a burst of energy but this burst is followed by a crash, both physically and emotionally. Instead, fuel your body with protein and vitamin-rich foods.

Also, drink plenty of water. Dehydration can lead to headaches and exhaustion, especially if your brain is already under stress from the rigors of the test. Particularly if your test is a long one, drink water during the breaks. And if possible, take an energy-boosting snack to eat between sections.

Along with sleep and diet, a third important part of physical health is exercise. Maintaining a steady workout schedule is helpful, but even taking 5-minute study breaks to walk can help get your blood pumping faster and clear your head. Exercise also releases endorphins, which contribute to a positive feeling and can help combat test anxiety.

When you nurture your physical health, you are also contributing to your mental health. If your body is healthy, your mind is much more likely to be healthy as well. So take time to rest, nourish your body with healthy food and water, and get moving as much as possible. Taking these physical steps will make you stronger and more able to take the mental steps necessary to overcome test anxiety.

Mental Steps for Beating Test Anxiety

Working on the mental side of test anxiety can be more challenging, but as with the physical side, there are clear steps you can take to overcome it. As mentioned earlier, test anxiety often stems from lack of preparation, so the obvious solution is to prepare for the test. Effective studying may be the most important weapon you have for beating test anxiety, but you can and should employ several other mental tools to combat fear.

First, boost your confidence by reminding yourself of past success—tests or projects that you aced. If you're putting as much effort into preparing for this test as you did for those, there's no reason you should expect to fail here. Work hard to prepare; then trust your preparation.

Second, surround yourself with encouraging people. It can be helpful to find a study group, but be sure that the people you're around will encourage a positive attitude. If you spend time with others who are anxious or cynical, this will only contribute to your own anxiety. Look for others who are motivated to study hard from a desire to succeed, not from a fear of failure.

Third, reward yourself. A test is physically and mentally tiring, even without anxiety, and it can be helpful to have something to look forward to. Plan an activity following the test, regardless of the outcome, such as going to a movie or getting ice cream.

When you are taking the test, if you find yourself beginning to feel anxious, remind yourself that you know the material. Visualize successfully completing the test. Then take a few deep, relaxing breaths and return to it. Work through the questions carefully but with confidence, knowing that you are capable of succeeding.

Developing a healthy mental approach to test taking will also aid in other areas of life. Test anxiety affects more than just the actual test—it can be damaging to your mental health and even contribute to depression. It's important to beat test anxiety before it becomes a problem for more than testing.

Study Strategy

Being prepared for the test is necessary to combat anxiety, but what does being prepared look like? You may study for hours on end and still not feel prepared. What you need is a strategy for test prep. The next few pages outline our recommended steps to help you plan out and conquer the challenge of preparation.

Step 1: Scope Out the Test

Learn everything you can about the format (multiple choice, essay, etc.) and what will be on the test. Gather any study materials, course outlines, or sample exams that may be available. Not only will this help you to prepare, but knowing what to expect can help to alleviate test anxiety.

Step 2: Map Out the Material

Look through the textbook or study guide and make note of how many chapters or sections it has. Then divide these over the time you have. For example, if a book has 15 chapters and you have five days to study, you need to cover three chapters each day. Even better, if you have the time, leave an extra day at the end for overall review after you have gone through the material in depth.

If time is limited, you may need to prioritize the material. Look through it and make note of which sections you think you already have a good grasp on, and which need review. While you are studying, skim quickly through the familiar sections and take more time on the challenging parts.

Write out your plan so you don't get lost as you go. Having a written plan also helps you feel more in control of the study, so anxiety is less likely to arise from feeling overwhelmed at the amount to cover.

Step 3: Gather Your Tools

Decide what study method works best for you. Do you prefer to highlight in the book as you study and then go back over the highlighted portions? Or do you type out notes of the important information? Or is it helpful to make flashcards that you can carry with you? Assemble the pens, index cards, highlighters, post-it notes, and any other materials you may need so you won't be distracted by getting up to find things while you study.

If you're having a hard time retaining the information or organizing your notes, experiment with different methods. For example, try color-coding by subject with colored pens, highlighters, or post-it notes. If you learn better by hearing, try recording yourself reading your notes so you can listen while in the car, working out, or simply sitting at your desk. Ask a friend to quiz you from your flashcards, or try teaching someone the material to solidify it in your mind.

Step 4: Create Your Environment

It's important to avoid distractions while you study. This includes both the obvious distractions like visitors and the subtle distractions like an uncomfortable chair (or a too-comfortable couch that makes you want to fall asleep). Set up the best study environment possible: good lighting and a comfortable work area. If background music helps you focus, you may want to turn it on, but otherwise keep the room quiet. If you are using a computer to take notes, be sure you don't have any other windows open, especially applications like social media, games, or anything else that could distract you. Silence your phone and turn off notifications. Be sure to keep water close by so you stay hydrated while you study (but avoid unhealthy drinks and snacks).

Also, take into account the best time of day to study. Are you freshest first thing in the morning? Try to set aside some time then to work through the material. Is your mind clearer in the afternoon or evening? Schedule your study session then. Another method is to study at the same time of day that you will take the test, so that your brain gets used to working on the material at that time and will be ready to focus at test time.

Step 5: Study!

Once you have done all the study preparation, it's time to settle into the actual studying. Sit down, take a few moments to settle your mind so you can focus, and begin to follow your study plan. Don't give in to distractions or let yourself procrastinate. This is your time to prepare so you'll be ready to fearlessly approach the test. Make the most of the time and stay focused.

Of course, you don't want to burn out. If you study too long you may find that you're not retaining the information very well. Take regular study breaks. For example, taking five minutes out of every hour to walk briskly, breathing deeply and swinging your arms, can help your mind stay fresh.

As you get to the end of each chapter or section, it's a good idea to do a quick review. Remind yourself of what you learned and work on any difficult parts. When you feel that you've mastered the material, move on to the next part. At the end of your study session, briefly skim through your notes again.

But while review is helpful, cramming last minute is NOT. If at all possible, work ahead so that you won't need to fit all your study into the last day. Cramming overloads your brain with more information than it can process and retain, and your tired mind may struggle to recall even previously learned information when it is overwhelmed with last-minute study. Also, the urgent nature of cramming and the stress placed on your brain contribute to anxiety. You'll be more likely to go to the test feeling unprepared and having trouble thinking clearly.

So don't cram, and don't stay up late before the test, even just to review your notes at a leisurely pace. Your brain needs rest more than it needs to go over the information again. In fact, plan to finish your studies by noon or early afternoon the day before the test. Give your brain the rest of the day to relax or focus on other things, and get a good night's sleep. Then you will be fresh for the test and better able to recall what you've studied.

Step 6: Take a Practice Test

Many courses offer sample tests, either online or in the study materials. This is an excellent resource to check whether you have mastered the material, as well as to prepare for the test format and environment.

Check the test format ahead of time: the number of questions, the type (multiple choice, free response, etc.), and the time limit. Then create a plan for working through them. For example, if you have 30 minutes to take a 60-question test, your limit is 30 seconds per question. Spend less time on the questions you know well so that you can take more time on the difficult ones.

If you have time to take several practice tests, take the first one open book, with no time limit. Work through the questions at your own pace and make sure you fully understand them. Gradually work up to taking a test under test conditions: sit at a desk with all study materials put away and set a timer. Pace yourself to make sure you finish the test with time to spare and go back to check your answers if you have time.

After each test, check your answers. On the questions you missed, be sure you understand why you missed them. Did you misread the question (tests can use tricky wording)? Did you forget the information? Or was it something you hadn't learned? Go back and study any shaky areas that the practice tests reveal.

Taking these tests not only helps with your grade, but also aids in combating test anxiety. If you're already used to the test conditions, you're less likely to worry about it, and working through tests until you're scoring well gives you a confidence boost. Go through the practice tests until you feel comfortable, and then you can go into the test knowing that you're ready for it.

Test Tips

On test day, you should be confident, knowing that you've prepared well and are ready to answer the questions. But aside from preparation, there are several test day strategies you can employ to maximize your performance.

First, as stated before, get a good night's sleep the night before the test (and for several nights before that, if possible). Go into the test with a fresh, alert mind rather than staying up late to study.

Try not to change too much about your normal routine on the day of the test. It's important to eat a nutritious breakfast, but if you normally don't eat breakfast at all, consider eating just a protein bar. If you're a coffee drinker, go ahead and have your normal coffee. Just make sure you time it so that the caffeine doesn't wear off right in the middle of your test. Avoid sugary beverages, and drink enough water to stay hydrated but not so much that you need a restroom break 10 minutes into the test. If your test isn't first thing in the morning, consider going for a walk or doing a light workout before the test to get your blood flowing.

Allow yourself enough time to get ready, and leave for the test with plenty of time to spare so you won't have the anxiety of scrambling to arrive in time. Another reason to be early is to select a good seat. It's helpful to sit away from doors and windows, which can be distracting. Find a good seat, get out your supplies, and settle your mind before the test begins.

When the test begins, start by going over the instructions carefully, even if you already know what to expect. Make sure you avoid any careless mistakes by following the directions.

Then begin working through the questions, pacing yourself as you've practiced. If you're not sure on an answer, don't spend too much time on it, and don't let it shake your confidence. Either skip it and come back later, or eliminate as many wrong answers as possible and guess among the remaining ones. Don't dwell on these questions as you continue—put them out of your mind and focus on what lies ahead.

Be sure to read all of the answer choices, even if you're sure the first one is the right answer. Sometimes you'll find a better one if you keep reading. But don't second-guess yourself if you do immediately know the answer. Your gut instinct is usually right. Don't let test anxiety rob you of the information you know.

If you have time at the end of the test (and if the test format allows), go back and review your answers. Be cautious about changing any, since your first instinct tends to be correct, but make sure you didn't misread any of the questions or accidentally mark the wrong answer choice. Look over any you skipped and make an educated guess.

At the end, leave the test feeling confident. You've done your best, so don't waste time worrying about your performance or wishing you could change anything. Instead, celebrate the successful completion of this test. And finally, use this test to learn how to deal with anxiety even better next time.

Review Video: Test Anxiety
Visit mometrix.com/academy and enter code: 100340

Important Qualification

Not all anxiety is created equal. If your test anxiety is causing major issues in your life beyond the classroom or testing center, or if you are experiencing troubling physical symptoms related to your anxiety, it may be a sign of a serious physiological or psychological condition. If this sounds like your situation, we strongly encourage you to seek professional help.

Thank You

We at Mometrix would like to extend our heartfelt thanks to you, our friend and patron, for allowing us to play a part in your journey. It is a privilege to serve people from all walks of life who are unified in their commitment to building the best future they can for themselves.

The preparation you devote to these important testing milestones may be the most valuable educational opportunity you have for making a real difference in your life. We encourage you to put your heart into it—that feeling of succeeding, overcoming, and yes, conquering will be well worth the hours you've invested.

We want to hear your story, your struggles and your successes, and if you see any opportunities for us to improve our materials so we can help others even more effectively in the future, please share that with us as well. **The team at Mometrix would be absolutely thrilled to hear from you!** So please, send us an email (support@mometrix.com) and let's stay in touch.

If you'd like some additional help, check out these other resources we offer for your exam:

http://MometrixFlashcards.com/MCA

Online Resources

Due to our efforts to try to keep this book to a manageable length, we've created a link that will give you access to all of your online resources:

mometrix.com/resources719/ssmcaghssci

It's Your Moment, Let's Celebrate It!

Share your story @mometrixtestpreparation